I0815135

# Writing for the Public Good

*Government and Politics in the South*

UNIVERSITY PRESS OF FLORIDA

Florida A&M University, Tallahassee
Florida Atlantic University, Boca Raton
Florida Gulf Coast University, Ft. Myers
Florida International University, Miami
Florida State University, Tallahassee
New College of Florida, Sarasota
University of Central Florida, Orlando
University of Florida, Gainesville
University of North Florida, Jacksonville
University of South Florida, Tampa
University of West Florida, Pensacola

# Writing for the Public Good

## Essays from David R. Colburn and Senator Bob Graham

Edited by Steven Noll

University Press of Florida
Gainesville · Tallahassee · Tampa · Boca Raton
Pensacola · Orlando · Miami · Jacksonville · Ft. Myers · Sarasota

Published in the United States of America

27 26 25 24 23 22  6 5 4 3 2 1

Library of Congress Control Number: 2021950051
ISBN 978-0-8130-6917-3

The University Press of Florida is the scholarly publishing agency for the State University System of Florida, comprising Florida A&M University, Florida Atlantic University, Florida Gulf Coast University, Florida International University, Florida State University, New College of Florida, University of Central Florida, University of Florida, University of North Florida, University of South Florida, and University of West Florida.

University Press of Florida
2046 NE Waldo Road
Suite 2100
Gainesville, FL 32609
http://upress.ufl.edu

# Contents

## PART IV. FOREIGN POLICY

# Acknowledgments

It is with a great deal of pride and appreciation that many articles by David Colburn and Senator Bob Graham have been published in this book. Several people deserve thanks, but none more than Dr. Steve Noll. He graciously and without hesitation agreed to take on the project at the time of David Colburn's death. We thank him for ensuring that these articles will be forever available. The articles represent the civic devotion of Senator Graham and David Colburn, a devotion that was evident in both of their long careers. We send a special thank you also to the former director of the University Press of Florida, Meredith Babb, for her wise advice and friendship over the years.

The Graham Family
The Colburn Family

# Introduction

In 2018, Alexander Coppock, assistant professor of political science at Yale, published an article in the *Quarterly Journal of Political Science* titled "The Long-Lasting Effects of Newspaper Op-Eds on Public Opinion." In the piece, Coppock asked, "Are people persuaded by op-eds?" His answer was a resounding YES. He concluded that "op-ed pieces have a lasting effect on people's views regardless of their political affiliation or their initial stance on an issue. People read an argument and were persuaded by it. It's that simple."[1] But what exactly is an op-ed piece? According to a 2019 online *Forbes* posting, an op-ed is a newspaper or online article designed "to prompt cultural, political and intellectual discourse among readers."[2] The op-ed pieces authored by David Colburn and Bob Graham in this volume certainly verify the conclusions reached by Coppock and *Forbes*. Written over a period of approximately thirty years, these articles represent the work of two of Florida's most important public intellectuals.

Though the idea of an op-ed page in the newspaper has been around since the 1920s with the *New York World*, it only became an official, fully functioning part of a paper in 1970. In the September 21, 1970, *New York Times*, John Oakes, the influential editor of the *Times* editorial page, announced the inauguration of a "new page opposite the Editorial Page." Oakes saw that "as the world has grown smaller, the nation more powerful, the problems besetting man infinitely more complex, the pressure more intense, the health of this democracy has increasingly depended on deeper public understanding of difficult issues." In order to effect that, the new op-ed page would "afford greater opportunity for exploration of issues and presentation of new insights and new ideas by writers and thinkers."[3] That idea caught hold and has been a staple of newspapers around the country ever since. In 2017, *Times* reporter Remy Turin, in an article entitled "The Op-Ed Pages, Explained," quoted then-*Times* opinion editor James Bennet. "'The goal is to supply readers with a steady stream of big ideas and provocative arguments, and to entertain them,' Bennet said. 'It should be an exciting experience and often a challenging one.'"[4] Originally conceived by Oakes to provide a forum for a wide range of differing opinions on major topics of the day, the editor quickly found that his inspiration would not be so easy to implement. Editors found that non-journalists, particularly academics, either had trouble writing for a public audience or had little incentive to do so. Iconoclastic MIT professor Noam Chomsky could not complete a piece solicited for the *Times* op-ed page. "I am afraid that I will have to abandon the project, reluctantly," he wrote. "For some reason, I find it enormously more difficult to write 700 words than 7000—a typical professorial defect, I suppose."[5] While Chomsky never finished his piece, other, less-activist academics refrained from participating in the public forum entirely. "Many academics frown on public pontificating as a frivolous distraction from real research," reported Will McCants, a Middle East specialist at the Brookings Institution. "This attitude affects tenure decisions. If the sine qua non for academic success is peer-reviewed publications, then academics who 'waste their time' writing for the masses will be penalized."[6]

Oakes's idea about the rationale for op-eds was to provide a forum for the dissemination of differing informed opinions. But Oakes also meant it to expand the conversation even further. As an editorial writer for the Emory University student newspaper explained in 2014, "Opinions shape ideology, and ideology shapes action."[7] Nothing can describe better the motivation for Bob Graham and David Colburn to write op-ed pieces than that statement. Colburn and Graham wrote their op-ed articles not simply to get their names in the paper or to broadcast their knowledge to others. They wrote their commentaries to motivate fellow citizens to do something positive—to engage in decisive action to enact change. Their pieces were designed to make people think and then challenge their own assumptions about their existing beliefs and preconceived notions. These op-eds afforded Graham and Colburn the "opportunity not just to express [themselves] but to inform, challenge, provoke, and, yes, persuade readers to see things as [they] do."[8] They viewed their job in writing these myriad articles as that of a vanishing species in American society—the public intellectual. Public intellectuals provide an important benefit to their wider audience by performing "a service in laying the intellectual groundwork for collective action and the cultivation of our mutual sympathies."[9] In their collected op-eds, Colburn and Graham did not simply address the specifics of a particular hot-button issue such as race relations or divisive politics. They moved past that to examine "the big questions of human life," while not forgetting the details of the issue they were discussing.[10] Their articles examined both the forest and the trees, as they provided readers with specific solutions to particular problems as well as broad ideas that spoke to the heart of civic responsibility and public service. The importance of these works lies in not only their placing contemporary issues in historical perspective, but also, and perhaps more importantly, the implicit (and sometimes quite explicit) calls to action Colburn and Graham were issuing. They wanted people to read their work, think about it, discuss it with relatives, colleagues, and friends—and then DO something based on what they read. For them, readers needed to become active responders rather than passive recipients.

Bob Graham was born for public service. As the son of Ernest "Cap" Graham, a Florida state senator and gubernatorial candidate, and the half-brother of Phil Graham, a Washington powerbroker and publisher of the *Washington Post*, Graham seemed destined to make his mark in the public sphere. Following in Phil's footsteps (twenty-one years later) at the University of Florida and then at Harvard Law School, Bob Graham took the political path and ran for a seat in the Florida House of Representatives at the tender age of 29. It was a transitional time in the political arena, both nationwide and in Florida. The civil rights movement, the divisive issue of the Vietnam War, and the beginnings of environmental activism created an atmosphere that allowed for a new generation of politicians to challenge the existing power structure centered in rural north Florida. The demise of an overtly malapportioned legislature combined with the beginnings of a two-party state after ninety years of conservative Democratic Bourbon rule allowed a new breed of more liberal politician to be elected, especially from south Florida.[11] Graham won that race easily and was reelected to the seat in 1968. Two years later, he switched over to run for the Florida Senate and won that election as well. He saw that victory as a salute to his father; he announced that "the fact that my dad had been in the Senate—that was a goal I had set, that I would like to follow in his footsteps."[12] The matters Graham worked on during his time in the Florida House and Senate presaged many of the subjects of his op-eds written later in his political and post-political career. Focusing on environmental concerns and education, Graham received the Allen Morris Award for the Most Valuable Legislator.

Building on his legislative success, Graham tossed his hat in the ring for the 1978 Democratic gubernatorial primary. This was a stacked field of well-known and well-financed candidates, and Graham appeared headed for defeat. Instead, he upset the crowded field of Democrats, won a state-mandated primary runoff, and defeated Republican Jack Eckerd to become Florida's governor at the relatively young age of 42. David Colburn credited his victory to "the most effective media campaign Florida had seen in the twentieth century."[13] That campaign centered on Graham's use of workdays as a strategy to connect with everyday people. Graham traveled around the state, stepping into a variety of jobs, working next to ordinary Floridians in their places of employment. "Days like these—scooping horse manure at the Ocala Breeders auction hall, attending to patients at the Macclenny state mental hospital, rolling cigars in Tampa and busing tables in Little Havana—left lasting impressions on Graham."[14] Those impressions carried through his two terms as governor, his three terms as a U.S. senator, and into his time as a political pundit and op-ed writer.

As governor, Graham emphasized many of the issues he would later spotlight in his op-ed pieces. Centering on education, the environment, and the economy, Graham crafted a governorship that "pushed for changes in the very way that Floridians look at their state."[15] Yet issues beyond his control also shaped both his tenure in Tallahassee and his understanding of large societal problems. The 1979–1980 Arthur McDuffie case, which foreshadowed the myriad of police brutality incidents that roiled the nation leading up to and in the wake of the 2020 murder of George Floyd, certainly forced Graham to examine the idea of systemic American racism. Similarly, the Mariel boatlift in the spring and summer of 1980, in which over 100,000 Cuban refugees flooded south Florida ports, shaped Graham's views on immigration, foreign policy, and the relationship between Washington and Tallahassee. All these would become major themes in Graham's later newspaper writing.

After a landslide second-term victory in 1982, Bob Graham rode a wave of electoral popularity to become a U.S. senator in 1986. He served three terms in the Senate, "leaving that body in 2005 as one of its most respected members."[16] During his Senate tenure, Graham continued to advocate for those same issues that had motivated him as governor—chief among them education, the environment, and immigration reform. His concern for environmental problems led President Obama to name him co-chair of the commission to investigate the disastrous 2010 Deepwater Horizon oil spill in the Gulf of Mexico. As chairman of the Senate Intelligence Committee, Graham expanded his interests into concerns over foreign policy and international terrorism. When he left the Senate on his own terms after the November 2004 election, the ideas and beliefs nurtured through almost forty years of public service continued with his push as a private citizen for improved citizen involvement and civics education. In 2006, Graham established the Bob Graham Center for Public Service on the campus of his alma mater—the University of Florida. Its mission to produce "informed and active participants in our democracy—equipped with the skills needed to shape policy for the betterment of their families and communities" tied in directly with Graham's op-ed writing in Florida and national newspapers.[17] Graham's persistent voice provided a platform for a nuanced treatment of important state and national issues at a time when serious discussion began to be overtaken by hyperbolic rhetoric and partisan polemics. While obviously leaning to the left in his political punditry, Graham made it clear that he spoke to a larger audience—that group of civically engaged individuals of both political persuasions.

David Colburn's journey to becoming a newspaper commentator was very different from Bob Graham's. Born into a working-class Catholic family in Providence, Rhode Island in the middle of World War II, Colburn attended hometown Providence College where he received both his BA and MA in history. After joining ROTC at Providence, he was sent to Vietnam in 1966, where he served honorably and returned stateside as a captain. After leaving the army, Colburn used the G.I. Bill to enter the PhD program in history at the University of North Carolina Chapel Hill. Graduating in 1971 with a dissertation on the early career of New York political kingpin Al Smith, he entered a tight job market with few job prospects. Completing a one-year teaching job at East Carolina University, Colburn fortuitously latched on to a position with the University of Florida's University College (UC), basically teaching large sections of introductory courses with little opportunity to do outside research. In 1978, with the merger of UC and the College of Arts & Sciences, Colburn migrated to the history department proper, where he remained for the rest of his UF career.

Once entrenched in a program that combined teaching and research,

Colburn flourished in both areas. Students flocked to his courses on political history, especially his History of the American Presidency class. And he began to write a series of books on Florida that would reshape the landscape of the state's historical record. Beginning with *Racial Change and Community Crisis: St. Augustine, Florida, 1877–1980,* published in 1985, Colburn "helped bring to light many of the uncovered racial stories of Florida."[18] This book started Colburn's career turn toward concerns about Florida's troubled racial past. In 1994, he, along with Vanderbilt professor (and Colburn's former student) Jane Landers, edited *The African American Heritage of Florida,* which won the Rembert W. Patrick Book Prize for best book in Florida history and a special commendation from the Association of State and Local History. "Groveland: Florida's Little Scottsboro," his article in that volume, cowritten with Steven Lawson, became the basis for Gilbert King's magisterial *Devil in the Grove,* which won the Pulitzer Prize in 2013. At that same time, he was appointed to the three-member state team that issued the 1993 Rosewood Report. This report supplied the research and analysis that allowed the state of Florida to recognize its role in the 1923 Rosewood massacre and provide $2.1 million in compensation to survivors and their descendants.

Colburn's research and writing also focused on Florida politics. Starting with his 1980 *Florida's Gubernatorial Politics in the 20th Century* (cowritten with UF political scientist Richard Scher) and progressing to his 2007 *From Yellow Dog Democrats to Red State Republicans: Florida and Its Politics since 1940,* he consistently examined the trends and problems that marked the political landscape of the Sunshine State. Gary Mormino, the leading historian of modern Florida, called the latter book Colburn's "best work. He was one of the first writers to utilize the term 'bellwether state,' recognizing the Sunshine State's significance and symbolism."[19] In these works, Colburn moved past the simplistic clichéd racist description of the shift toward Republican ascendancy by providing a more nuanced explanation that tied racial concerns to economic and demographics ones.

As he moved up the administrative ladder at the University of Florida, Colburn continued with his prolific research agenda. Just as importantly, however, he moved more and more into the public sphere, providing guidance and leadership to both the Florida Historical Society and the Florida Humanities Council (now rebranded as simply Florida Humanities). Working through these organizations, Colburn reached beyond the campus walls to provide historical insight into contemporary issues—something he would continue as he became a regular contributor to newspapers around the state. "His commitment to the humanities at the state and national level was unprecedented," said Steve Seibert, former Executive Director of the Florida Humanities Council. "No one has done more to support the humanities, in deed and in cause."[20]

Ending his administrative career as UF's provost, Colburn could easily have opted for a well-deserved retirement. Instead, he took a path that connected him with Bob Graham in their mutual desire to improve the lives of Floridians through civics education and community awareness. As founder and director of UF's Reubin O'D. Askew Institute on Politics and Society, Colburn worked with Florida communities to help them plan and prepare for a post-recession economy, and addressed a wide range of challenges facing the state, from aging to family concerns, health care, ethnicity, race and the environment.[21] In 2013, the Institute merged with the Bob Graham Center for Public Service, with Colburn as its director. Graham and Colburn became an inseparable team, using both the Center and their voice in state newspapers to opine about pressing state issues and to beat the drum for improved statewide civics education for Floridians of all ages. Their combined work at the Graham Center became the germ for this edited collection as they strove to provide an accessible forum for their best newspaper writing. Tragically, David Colburn died in September 2019, before he and Bob Graham could finish the book.

In April 2020, Dr. Joanne Meyerowitz, the Arthur Unobskey Professor of History and American Studies at Yale, was set to give her Presidential Address to the 2020 Annual Meeting of the Organization of American Historians in Washington D.C. when the meeting was cancelled because of the COVID-19 pandemic. Her speech, though never delivered, became the lead article in the September 2020 issue of the *Journal of American History.* Entitled "180 Op-Eds: Or How to Make the Present Historical," it examined both the relevance and power of the op-ed, a category of writing she called "short-form history."[22] Written for a "broad nonhistorical readership," op-eds rely on "carefully chosen shards of evidence, on the art of persuasion, and on the reader's trust in the author's expertise." Bob Graham and David Colburn are among the few op-ed writers who possess the rare combination of authorial expertise and readership trust that Meyerowitz so admired. Their knowledge of both the American political process and the historical antecedents of contemporary hot-button issues makes their op-eds valuable, informative, and remarkably readable.

Meyerowitz ends her essay by making a bold statement about the value of op-eds. The best of them, she proclaims, "open the space to imagine a different future."[23] Colburn and Graham did that consistently with their articles, as they spoke not only about current issues and problems but also about how they could help shape the future in a more positive direction. As David Colburn wrote in a May 3, 2005 *Orlando Sentinel* op-ed (one not chosen for this volume), "We have indeed made progress. It seems to me fitting . . . that we can celebrate our humanity and our diversity . . . I know: we still have hate-mongers among us, and we still have racial progress to make. But our nation and our state have renounced hate as its future."[24]

The op-eds in this volume span an important time in contemporary American history. Stretching from the George W. Bush administration through that of Donald Trump, they examine a nation coming to grips with the end of the Cold War and the rise of Muslim radicalism. The writings touch on those issues that roiled America in general and Florida in particular during the first two decades of the 21st century—racial injustice, climate change, and the increasing presence of right-wing extremism. They inform, engage, maybe anger, but most of all they force readers to think. To think about where we are as a nation, as a state, as a people—and where we might be going in the future. This is especially important in periods of crisis, such as the Great Recession of the first decade of the 21st century and the racial unrest that marked 2020 during the COVID pandemic. During perilous times, the words of Colburn and Graham seem to have special meaning. In May 2020, Bob Graham penned an op-ed (again, not chosen for this volume) for the *Tampa Bay Times* entitled "Halt Wetlands Permitting Changes until Public Can Comment in Person." While the title indicates the piece will be simply an esoteric examination of arcane bureaucratic procedure, Graham ends the op-ed by speaking to broader themes of civic engagement and a future built around citizen activism. "As a former U.S. senator, Florida governor and member of both houses of the Florida Legislature," he wrote, "I recognize public engagement as an essential part of our democratic process. One of the biggest roadblocks to participatory democracy is the perception that everyday Americans cannot influence government policy, and that only the privileged and special interests can command the levers of power or change bureaucracies." He concluded by asserting that "now more than ever, we need leaders who are willing to commit to the right decisions that protect the environment, the public and our democracy."[25]

The pieces chosen for this volume are only a representative sample of the dozens (maybe hundreds) that these two men wrote during their long and illustrious careers in politics and academia. Many of the earlier pieces selected for this volume are written by David Colburn, while Bob Graham's writings make up more of the later pieces, coinciding with his departure from the U.S. Senate in 2005. Though these articles deal with a variety of contemporary issues, they all focus on one thing—the importance of an informed, involved, and diverse citizenry. In 2017, Bob Graham bemoaned the death of civics education in Florida. "Two generations of Americans and Floridians have finished their high school education with little or no instruction in what it means to be a citizen in a democracy," he wrote. "They have never learned the centrality of civility and reasoned compromise in a democracy or the rights, responsibilities and skills necessary to be an effective citizen."[26] David Colburn also expressed concern about government policies that functioned to what he viewed as the detriment of America's population and economy. A decade earlier than Graham, he presciently wrote that "new U.S. immigration policies are making it very difficult for American universities to recruit the best international students." These "students contribute an estimated $13 billion to the American economy annually."[27]

In August 2018, Northwestern University history professor Geraldo Cadava wrote that "writing op-eds and seeing them through to publication takes time and emotional energy, and there are only so many hours in a day to fill with tasks that compete for our attention."[28] That certainly was the case for Bob Graham and David Colburn, who both had full schedules all day, every day. They did not have to take the time to write op-eds on a wide variety of public-interest topics. Just as important, once newspapers published their writing, they did not even know whether those op-eds made any difference. As Cadava explains, "How do I know if anyone listens? I guess I don't. Expressing ideas that I hope will have an impact is a bit like advertising. Companies spend billions to make commercials that they hope will sell whatever they're selling. They won't know if an advertisement they produced led a particular individual to buy their product, yet they keep doing it."[29] And Graham and Colburn kept writing op-eds as well—month after month, year after year. Why? Because for them, the writing of op-eds mattered, as those articles provided "historical depth and complexity to the world in which we currently live."[30] If, as Cadava argues, "a good op-ed always has tension," the work of Graham and Colburn fits that bill exactly. Their writing informs, elucidates, and challenges. The pieces in this book are the best of that work. They speak to our collective past, our problematic present, and a future filled with both hope and concern. As David Colburn wrote in 1996, "the way [Florida] harmonizes this diversity, builds a sense of community and governs itself in the 21st century, is what stimulates so much interest in the state. For as Florida goes in the 21st century, so, many political observers believe, will the nation."[31]

These op-ed pieces remain valuable and significant as print journalism continues to decline. In 2020, the University of North Carolina's Hussman School of Journalism and Media reported that "in the fifteen years leading up to 2020, more than one-fourth of the country's newspapers disappeared, leaving residents in thousands of communities—inner-city neighborhoods, suburban towns and rural villages—living in vast news deserts."[32] With the demise of papers such as the *Tampa Tribune,* which ceased publication in 2016, we see a diminished presence of op-ed pieces such as the ones collected in this volume. Their place has been taken by online blogs and Twitter posts, usually more timely but often less thoughtful and objective than the pieces by Graham and Colburn. In fact, in an April 2021 article titled "Why the *New York Times* Is Officially Retiring the Term 'Op-Ed,'" author Kathleen Kingsbury announced that the paper would henceforth use the term "Guest Essays" instead. She concluded that the change was necessary since this is a time when "the geography of the public square is being contested" as never before. And yet the work of Colburn and Graham fits as comfortably under the new rubric as the old one. When Kingsbury declares that the *Times* wants "spaces where voices can be heard and respected, where ideas can linger a while, [and] be given serious consideration," she is talking as much about the "op-ed" pieces in this book as about the "guest essays" that will populate newspapers in the future.[33] As Americans get their news and commentary increasingly from the Internet, it is important to remember that the work of these "old-school" writers still has resonance in an increasingly divided society.

This book is organized into four large sections—Florida, Diversity, Public Policy, and Foreign Policy. Within these divisions are twelve topical segments containing articles by both authors. These parts characterize the broad scope of interest Colburn and Graham showed in a wide variety of topics—from race relations to state and national politics, from environmental concerns to education, from foreign affairs to natural and human-made disasters. The pieces were chosen by the authors and the editor as representative of the best of their writing. The contemporaneous nature of the op-eds is striking—articles written ten, twenty, and even thirty years ago speak to hot-button issues that resonate in today's news. Taken together, this collective body of work by two giants in their respective fields is a fitting coda to their public lives. At a time when learned tempered discourse is in short supply, we can turn to the writings of David Colburn and Bob Graham to show us the way to a better future.

## Editor's Note

The transcriptions in this volume are as originally published, with only very light editorial intervention. Some infelicities in grammar or punctuation are therefore evident.

## Notes

1. Alexander Coppock, Emily Ekins, and David Kirby, "The Long-lasting Effects of Newspaper Op-Eds on Public Opinion," *Quarterly Journal of Political Science* 13, no. 1 (2018): 59–87, 64.

2. https://www.forbes.com/sites/forbesagencycouncil/2019/09/18/is-the-op-ed-dead/#248e1a077084

3. "Op. Ed. Page," *New York Times*, September 21, 1970, 42.

4. Remy Tumin, "The Op-Ed Pages, Explained," *New York Times*, December 3, 2017, A2.

5. Quoted in Michael Socolow, "A Portable Public Sphere: The Creation of the *New York Times* Op-Ed Page," *Journalism and Mass Communication Quarterly* 87, no. 2 (Summer 2010): 281–296, 285.

6. Quoted in Nicholas Kristof, "Professors, We Need You," *New York Times*, February 15, 2014, SR11.

7. "The Importance of Opinions," Editorial, *The Emory Wheel*, January 27, 2014, https://emorywheel.com/the-importance-of-opinions/.

8. John Hood, "Columns Can Change Political Views," *Carolina Journal*, January 30, 2019, https://www.carolinajournal.com/opinion-article/columns-can-change-political-views/.

9. Preston Stovall, "On the Role of the Public Intellectual in the United States," *Heterodox: The Blog*, November 28, 2016, https://heterodoxacademy.org/on-the-role-of-the-public-intellectual-in-the-united-states/.

10. Gideon Strauss, "What Public Intellectuals Need, and Why We Need Public Intellectuals," *Comment*, March 1, 2005, https://www.cardus.ca/comment/article/what-public-intellectuals-need-and-why-we-need-public-intellectuals/.

11. For more on this transition, see David Colburn, *From Yellow Dog Democrats to Red State Republicans: Florida and Its Politics since 1940* (Gainesville, Florida: University Press of Florida, 2007).

12. Quoted in Steven Noll, "Daniel Robert 'Bob' Graham," in *The Governors of Florida*, edited by R. Boyd Murphree and Robert Taylor (Gainesville, Florida: University Press of Florida, 2020), 564–583, 568.

13. Quoted in Noll, "Daniel Robert 'Bob' Graham," 568.

14. Mark Silva and Tamara Lytle, "The Making of Bob Graham," *Orlando Sentinel*, April 20, 2003, https://www.orlandosentinel.com/news/os-xpm-2003-04-20-0304190009-story.html.

15. Noll, "Daniel Robert 'Bob' Graham," 573.

16. Ibid., 580.

17. Bob Graham, quoted in "Graham Center Celebrates 10 years of Strengthening Civic Engagement at UF," March 2, 2016, https://news.hr.ufl.edu/spotlight/graham-center-celebrates-10-years/.

18. Cynthia Barnett, "David Colburn Obituary written for the Graham Center." In author's possession, 2.

19. Gary Mormino, "End Notes," *Florida Historical Quarterly* 98, no. 2 (Fall 2019): 171.

20. Steven Seibert, e-mail to author, October 11, 2020.

21. Barnett, "David Colburn," 3.

22. Joanne Meyerowitz, "180 Op-Eds: Or How to Make the Present Historical," *Journal of American History* 107, no. 2 (September 2020): 323–335, 325.

23. Ibid., 325, 335.

24. David Colburn, "No Tears for J. B. Stoner, Rock Star of Racism," *Orlando Sentinel*, May 3, 2005, https://www.orlandosentinel.com/news/os-xpm-2005-05-03-0505030044-story.html.

25. Bob Graham, "Halt Wetlands Permitting Changes Until Public Can Comment in Person," *Tampa Bay Times*, May 2, 2020, https://www.tampabay.com/opinion/2020/05/02/halt-wetlands-permitting-changes-until-public-can-comment-in-person-column/.

26. Bob Graham, "Civics Isn't Optional," *Tampa Bay Times*, June 18, 2017, P2.

27. David Colburn, "America, Take Back the College Home Front," *Orlando Sentinel*, February 3, 2005, https://www.orlandosentinel.com/news/os-xpm-2005-02-03-0502030030-story.html.

28. Geraldo Cadava, "When, Why, and How I Write Op-Eds," *The American Historian*, August 2016, https://www.oah.org/tah/issues/2016/august/when-why-and-how-i-write-op-eds/.

29. Ibid.

30. Meyerowitz, "180 Op-Eds," 327.

31. David Colburn, "Florida: State of Mind, Reality, U.S. Future," *Orlando Sentinel*, October 6, 1996, G3.

32. Penelope Muse Abernathy, "The News Landscape in 2020: Transformed and Diminished," https://www.usnewsdeserts.com/reports/news-deserts-and-ghost-newspapers-will-local-news-survive/the-news-landscape-in-2020-transformed-and-diminished/.

33. Kathleen Kingsbury, "Why The *New York Times* Is Retiring the Term 'Op-Ed,'" *New York Times*, April 26, 2021, https://www.nytimes.com/2021/04/26/opinion/nyt-opinion-oped-redesign.html.

# FLORIDA

# 1

# Historical Perspectives

It has always seemed that Florida doesn't have a history; that the state really started with Disney World in 1971, or maybe with the population explosion in the 1950s after World War II—or, taking a big stretch, that it began with Henry Flagler's railroad reaching Miami in 1896. But regardless, Floridians tend to look more to the future than the past, since so many of them have little connection to the state itself. Only 36 percent of Florida residents were born in the Sunshine State, making Florida the state with the second-lowest rate of in-state born residents in the United States (trailing only Nevada). That is why this collection of op-ed pieces leads off the collection—because these articles set the stage both for the groups of articles that make up the rest of the book, and also, more importantly, for an examination of how modern Florida got to be where it is today. These pieces examine the rather incredible transition of Florida in the last 80 years from poor rural backwater to a state that currently has the third-largest population in the country. Yet, as Colburn and Graham pointedly explain, many of the vexing problems that plagued that rather unimportant state in 1940 remain today and seem just as intractable. The authors presciently examine issues of race and class, of the battle between economic development and protection of Florida's fragile and unique environment, and of the broad demographic shifts that have transformed the state but not necessarily its political system. Graham and Colburn write about these concerns in all their op-eds, as they recognize the state's long and rather convoluted trajectory to get to where we are today. They also acknowledge that Florida's past, as hidden or irrelevant as it is to most contemporary Floridians, is key to understanding both the state's present problems and its future possibilities. All the sections of this book deal with Florida's history in some form or another. This section analyzes it overtly and recognizes its importance. As David Colburn wrote in 1993, it is imperative that we "acknowledge our state's past and those who have preceded us, [and] . . . recognize both their achievements and their failures. Each is essential in helping us to mature as a people and as a state."

## 'Cincinnati Factor' vs. Florida Identity

**There is no shared heritage in Florida and little appreciation of the complexities of state life**

David Colburn

*Orlando Sentinel,* May 2, 1993

When I asked my barber recently what he thought about events in South Florida and the violence against foreign tourists, he remarked, with a measure of seriousness, that he thought South Florida was a foreign country.

He, of course, is not alone in his view of South Florida, and particularly Dade County. The statewide vote against bilingual education three years ago reflected concerns among many Floridians that the state was in danger of being changed forever by the influx of foreigners.

Is this balkanization of Florida a recent development and does it really threaten the future of the state? Moreover, are Floridians becoming so different that there are no underlying values that unite them?

Although Florida is generally considered to be a Southern or perhaps a Sunbelt state, it has been unique for much of the past 50 years. Political scientist V.O. Key Jr. called it "The Different State" in 1949, because its politics were so fragmented that it lacked a political structure. From 1890 until the late 1960s, Florida had, in effect, a single political party—the Democratic Party. Getting elected meant one had to run as a Democrat, but the individuals within the party had such widely disparate views that there was no such thing as party unity or a party platform.

As many as 14 candidates ran in the Democratic primary election for governor in 1936, and 10 ran as recently as 1960—nearly all of whom represented separate cities or regions of the state. Politicians had no statewide agenda and no statewide constituency. They were chiefly concerned with "getting and holding office." It was the historic counterpart of modern-day Italian politics. Political chaos governed and the needs of an expanding Florida went largely unaddressed.

Politically, then, Florida's balkanization was a historical phenomenon. It has not been rooted in the recent migration but extends back to the early 20th century.

The state's physical geography has added another significant impediment to unity. It is such a long peninsula that the distance from Key West to Pensacola is approximately the same as the distance from Pensacola to Chicago. Floridians are so far removed from one another that they have little understanding or appreciation of their respective needs. Pensacolans, for example, share little in common with Tampans other than that they live within the same border.

Adding to these factors and dramatically exacerbating the state's internal divisions is the massive wave of in-migration from the north and from the Caribbean and Central America.

Since the end of World War II, no fewer than 1 million people have entered Florida each decade. Today, more than 1,000 people enter the state every day (adding roughly 3.5 million new residents in the 1990s, assuming no one moves away), and the recession has not dampened their enthusiasm for Florida. To put this in some sort of perspective, Florida surpasses the population of Rhode Island every three years, and in the past 25 years more people have come to Florida than in the previous 400 years.

Sociologists and criminologists believe that most of the social problems and the violence in Florida today are due to the rootless nature of our society and the absence of a shared sense of community. These people, understandably, have little or no sense of what it means to be a Floridian.

Sen. Bob Graham refers to these new residents as "the Cincinnati factor." These folks move to Florida but return to Cincinnati annually to visit relatives and friends; they may even send their sons and daughters to college in Ohio; they vote only to oppose new taxes; and when they die, they have their remains shipped to Cincinnati for burial. Florida is little more than a brief way stop in their life cycle.

Today's political environment has worsened these social divisions. In the competition between the Republican and Democratic parties for control of the Legislature and the governorship, the needs of all Floridians have received secondary attention. Political leaders in the Legislature have concentrated on getting and holding office and on addressing local needs to ensure their re-election.

Without statewide leadership, Floridians have succumbed to the social and geographic pressures that isolate them. Few people in the state believe they share a common heritage and similar needs.

The elderly lobby for their own interests and generally ignore the needs of children, and urban residents believe that the problems confronting state farmers and citrus growers are not their concern. Resident of Tampa and St. Petersburg resent Miami getting a professional baseball team. There is no shared identity in Florida and little appreciation of the complexities of state life.

So my barber has reason to be concerned. The Florida that he has known is changing, but the new reality is different only in complexion and language from the old Florida. Uniting this divergent and continually evolving population to meet the problems that confront the state and to move forward into the 21st century is the real challenge facing Floridians.

Can we address these problems and possibilities if we do not know who we are and if we share little in common?

Or will we find ourselves following the California model and proposing a new border between the northern and southern sections of the state?

## The Future Is Now for Florida's Past

**State's 150th anniversary time to revisit racial success**

David Colburn

*Orlando Sentinel*, August 29, 1993

As school bells rang this past week, heralding a new year for the children of Florida, they reminded us of the fundamental importance of education for the future of our society.

Education, of course, also informs us about our past and reminds us who we are as a people. Few times during the year are more appropriate than now to remind ourselves about Florida's unique history—and this may be even more appropriate with the state's 150th anniversary less than two years away.

Did you know, for example, that Florida has the oldest community within the present boundaries of the United States? Most now recognize that St. Augustine, founded in 1565, is much older than Jamestown (1607) and Plymouth (1620), although a few history textbooks still struggle to get the facts straight. But did you know that St. Augustine is also the oldest multi-racial community in the United States, where whites, Hispanics and blacks once interacted with one another one a regular basis?

And did you know that Florida had the oldest black community in the United States—Fort Mose, which is just north of St. Augustine? Or that Florida appears to have had the largest number of free black communities in the South during the Colonial period?

Did you know, too, that Florida will celebrate its 150th year of statehood on May 3, 1995?

This is not a quiz nor is it intended to embarrass anyone. Indeed, historians have come to appreciate the uniqueness of Florida's heritage only in the past two decades. Most people think of Florida as a very modern state, a post-World War II phenomenon.

But its legacy as a state and our heritage as a people are much fuller and more remarkable than most would believe.

With 1995 fast approaching, we have an opportunity to revisit Florida's past and to remind ourselves that people of diverse cultures and of different colors did reside and interact together in a positive and constructive manner. For a brief period at least, Florida offered a model of humanity for the rest of the North American continent.

Spaniards and Africans were among the first non-native peoples to set foot in Florida, when black conquistador Juan Garrido and interpreter Juan Gonzalez de Leon arrived with Spanish explorer Ponce de Leon in 1513. Both groups of people were prominent in the early stages of the Spanish settlement of St. Augustine in 1565. They also established and developed Gracia Real de Santa Teresa de Mose in 1738.

The multiracial cast of Florida did not disappear after the transference of the area from Spain to Great Britain in 1763. African-Americans and Native Americans continued to play an important role in the racial developments of the region throughout the British and second Spanish periods and up to Florida's statehood in 1845. Unlike most other sections of the South during the 18th and first half of the 19th centuries, Florida had a diverse population and a number of free black communities, including the Mose site and African-American and Maroon villages that stretched from St. Augustine to Gainesville and Tallahassee.

The early history of Florida also makes evident that African-American and African slaves from the British areas to the north perceived Florida as a haven for freedom. They fled to the region in substantial numbers and faced enormous obstacles in getting here. Even after Florida was ceded to Britain, the Native Americans of the region offered refuge from slavery and an obstacle to the aims of whites to expand plantation slavery in the new territory.

There is much more to Florida's history than has been described in this brief commentary, and most of its racial practices after 1800 were not designed to elicit pride. But for a brief historical moment during the Spanish period, racial patterns in Florida suggested an alternative to the customary direction of American race relations.

There are few occasions during which a state and its people can pause to reflect upon its past. Florida has an important anniversary in 1995, and an opportunity to revisit its heritage.

Sens. Bob Graham and Connie Mack have asked the Library of Congress, the National Archives, the Smithsonian and the U.S. Postal Service to use this occasion to make the public aware of Florida's past through exhibits and special programs.

The state, however, has lagged behind, concerned about costs and about public criticism of the Columbus 500th-year celebration in 1992. It would be so unfortunate if Florida ignored its own past because of mistakes made in 1992. Florida's past is at least as significant as that of Jamestown and Plymouth and its historic diversity has greater meaning for today's society than the conformity of New England.

Yes, Florida probably can make money by celebrating its past, much like Virginia and the states in New England have done. What is more important, however, is that we take a moment to acknowledge our state's past and those who have preceded us, that we recognize both their achievements and their failures. Each is essential in helping us to mature as a people and as a state.

## World War II Forever Transformed Florida

David Colburn

*Orlando Sentinel*, July 11, 2005

On Aug. 14, 1945, 60 years ago Sunday, Japan accepted the Allied surrender terms, effectively ending World War II. Formal surrender papers were signed aboard the USS Missouri in Tokyo Bay on Sept. 2.

Spontaneous celebrations erupted throughout much of the world. After all, war had defined peoples' lives for six years, and for some it was even longer. Americans had not known peace since December 1941.

The war had been devastating by any measure. Nearly 20 million soldiers died on both sides, and the war cost in excess of a trillion dollars. Estimates of civilian casualties ran as high as 49 million, and entire cities lay in ruin in many parts of the world.

Sixty years later, many Americans who participated in the war overseas and on the home front are reaching the end of their lives.

Will we, who have benefited so much from their sacrifices, remember their heroic commitment to restore peace, end fascism and build a better world?

I hope so, because in many ways they are not just our parents, grandparents and great grandparents. Indeed, they have been the builders of a new world, and it is in their shadows that we walk today.

So pause for a moment this weekend and think about their sacrifices and the changes they made possible for our state, nation and the world.

During the war years, nearly 2.2 million trainees, support personnel and families came to Florida, a number larger than the entire population of the state in 1940. And literally overnight, the Great Depression ended.

In the process, they discovered Florida and changed it forever. They wrote home to parents and friends commenting on the beauty of the state and their interest in settling in Florida when the war was over. Dan Moody from Virginia captured the sentiments of most when he wrote his mother from the Hotel Blackstone on Miami Beach: "This is the most beautiful place I have ever seen. . . . I really think when the war is over, I'll move down here."

Moody and others were true to their word. Nearly 900,000 people, or approximately 180,000 per year, moved into the state from 1945 to 1950.

Thus began the massive migration into Florida that would mark the post-war years and with it the economic transformation of the state.

The war required Americans to move throughout the country for training and around the world to defeat our enemies—Germany, Italy and Japan. In the process, it ended American regionalism by introducing Americans to other parts of the nation and to one another. It also made Americans aware of their place in the world and, at home, it began the process of ending segregation.

In the wake of the war, it built the strongest economy and the strongest military the world has ever seen. It did so not for personal or national gain but to enable the United States to preserve peace at home and abroad.

They led efforts to establish the United Nations and offered New York as its home so that nations would negotiate their differences rather than fight over them. And they launched the Marshall Plan to rebuild Western Europe, supported the creation of the European Community and oversaw the reconstruction of Japan.

They pursued all these initiatives because they hoped to protect us from the horrors of war. In the end, of course, they could not accomplish this goal.

We need to remind ourselves periodically of the sacrifices, dedication and accomplishments of this generation. We owe them a great deal, and we owe it to them to see if we can achieve the peace they so wanted for us and the world.

## Sen. Bob Graham Saw South Florida Grow from Farmland to Metropolis

Bob Graham

*Miami Herald*, May 3, 2009

I don't think there could have been a better place for a child to grow up than Miami in the 1940s and '50s. The Depression and World War II were over and the post-war boom was in full swing.

My father, Ernest R. Graham, an engineer, was forced to become a dairy farmer in 1932, after hurricanes, floods and the failure of his employer, the Pennsylvania Sugar Co.

Soon thereafter he lost his first wife to cancer. My mother, Hilda Simmons, was a teacher who left her Panhandle home of DeFuniak Springs because the Depression-strapped school system couldn't pay its faculty.

She met my dad on a bus to Jacksonville, where she hoped to find a job. She found romance. They married with the understanding that Hilda would raise Ernie's three children.

Ten months later, I was born. Shortly after my birth at University Hospital, I was taken to a two-story, coral rock house in the northwest Dade County village of Pennsuco (near Hialeah).

Growing up on the farm was a very formative experience. I learned discipline and responsibility through my summer jobs and after-school chores raising 4-H Club Holstein and Angus heifers. My love of the environment grew from the Everglades.

For nine years, I rode a school bus to Hialeah Elementary and Junior High School (now South Hialeah Elementary). Built in the 1920s as a school for Seminole Indian children, by the war years it was home to children of working-class families and single moms whose husbands had gone to war.

If you wanted a living experience in democracy, few places would equal Hialeah.

There was only one interruption in my nine years at Hialeah. In 1947, two back-to-back hurricanes ripped through South Florida. Our home was under two feet of water and badly damaged.

My parents sent me to live with my paternal grandmother in dad's hometown, Croswell, Mich., while the house was being repaired. I was in sixth grade and received my first exposure to partisan politics.

The Republican candidate for president in 1948 was Tom Dewey, a Michigan native who was popular in conservative Croswell. Our class voted: Dewey, 26, Harry Truman 1 (mine). That vote has endured as one of my proudest political moments.

When I returned to Pennsuco, I was more aware South Florida's Southern lineage. During the boom years of the 1920s, new residents from throughout the eastern United States flocked to Miami. During the Depression, Northerners found better opportunities and left. This was not true for Southerners, who for almost 30 years dominated the culture, economics and politics of Miami.

In 1959, Adele Khoury and I were married. She grew up in Miami. We met as University of Florida students. When we returned to South Florida in 1962, it was a community undergoing unprecedented change.

The first of the Social Security retirees had found Miami and were fundamentally reshaping much of the eastern portion of the county.

At the same time, refugees from Cuba's communist state had begun to settle here and were legitimizing Miami as an international city.

The calm, relaxed, parochial Miami of our youth had transformed into the dynamic, sometimes confounding, always exciting and passionate city of today.

## Why Won't Floridians Learn from Their Own History?

**It is much easier to be ignorant and clueless when you don't know what happened in Florida prior to 1995**

David Colburn

*Gainesville Sun*, February 21, 2010

Florida became a metaphor for the boom-and-bust years, and no state experienced the highs and lows more acutely than Florida.

Investors, developers and real estate hucksters were confident that their speculation in Florida land and housing would bring them a quick fortune.

Signs of decline appeared early when the national press warned about widespread fraud and speculation in Florida.

As migration slowed to a halt and investors pulled back, construction ceased and banks began to foreclose on homes and businesses.

The financial system teetered toward bankruptcy and 220 Florida banks collapsed.

The state as well as many cities and counties had thrown caution to the wind to capitalize on the growth during this period. They granted permits to developers without consideration of their financial risk or their impact on the environment.

And many cities and counties ended up deeply in debt by constructing roads and tourist facilities in the belief that if they built them the investors would come.

This reads eerily like the Great Recession of 2008–10, but these events unfolded between 1926 and 1929 as Florida's economy collapsed and the nation entered the Great Depression.

One can find a similar story for Florida in 1981–83, when nearly all construction cranes disappeared from the landscape.

And again in the recession of 1991–92 as speculation in housing and commercial real estate collapsed.

So what is it about Floridians that keeps us repeating history?

The simple answer is that we don't know our own history.

Only 33 percent of Floridians were born in this state—one the smallest percentages in the nation. By contrast, 81 percent of Pennsylvanians were born in that state. In addition, 17 percent of Florida's population was born in another country and another 17 percent are over 65-years [*sic*] of age and spend approximately half their time in another state. Also, 20.6 percent of our population are Hispanics, and most are "Birds of Passage," who travel frequently to their native country and continue to identify with its history.

Altogether 10.5 million people relocated to Florida in the 35 years between 1970 and 2005, and these non-natives remain largely unaware of the state's history.

This historical amnesia makes it possible for someone in the real estate industry to make the senseless claim at a recent state economic summit that all will be fine in Florida if "the government just gets out of the way in this recession."

And no one challenged this assertion, because they too are unaware that the actions of realtors, land speculators, developers, and bankers drove Florida into the Great Depression and to the severe recessions of 1981–83 and 1991–92.

Nor are they aware that the policies of the federal government during the Great Depression saved Florida and Floridians from abject poverty and bankruptcy, and that the actions of the federal government in both 1981–83 and again in 1991–92 rescued Florida from much deeper recessions.

Historical ignorance is no excuse for stupidity, but it is much easier to be ignorant and, consequently, clueless when you don't know what happened in Florida prior to 1995.

Right now, Florida's political leaders are wrestling with a state budget that has been devastated by this Great Recession, and they are basing their decisions on certain assumptions.

If those ideas are rooted in the same historical ignorance expressed by the real estate agent, then the path taken by legislators is likely to repeat the mistakes of the past.

As we look to the future to construct a healthier and more diverse economy for Florida, we need to be mindful of a speculative past that has frequently placed us in harm's way.

## Reflections on Florida's Past

David Colburn

*Gainesville Sun*, December 23, 2016

As we say goodbye to 2016 and welcome in 2017, this may be a good time to reflect on Florida's spectacular transformation in recent decades.

The Florida we know today sits at the epicenter of the nation and it has become a state of mind. Northerners and Midwesterners, especially this time of year, conjure up images of sitting on the beach, playing golf or just taking a stroll outside. Hundreds of thousands relocate briefly each winter, convinced that a visit to the Sunshine State is the only way to survive another arctic blast back home.

Florida has the largest number of retirees of any state with 19.4 percent. Retirees have embraced the image of Florida as an environment where the aging process is not so daunting. It may not be the fountain of youth but it is close.

Along with California, Florida has also attracted one of the most diverse populations in the United States. The state's Hispanic population now constitutes 24.5 percent of the total and its African American population has increased to 16.4 percent.

The state's booming millennial population has created its own state of mind for Florida in which good paying jobs coincide with a beautiful environment and stunning beaches. The long days at work can be offset by relaxing weekends basking in the surf.

It is this mindset and obsession about Florida that has driven the population boom for the past seven decades. An average of nearly 3 million people per decade have moved into the state since 1945, driving the population from 1.9 million to 20.3 million.

The rapidity of this change together with the state's diversity has resulted in a population that is quite disparate—only 30.3 percent of Floridians, for example, were born here, while 50 percent were born in another state, and 19.7 percent in another country.

The mobility of people, both in and out of Florida, has created a state that constantly seems in search of an identity.

It is also a place that is literally unrecognizable when compared to its image prior to World War II. When the nation entered the war in 1941, Florida had one of the smallest populations in the nation and was also one of the poorest states. Its political leaders struggled unsuccessfully to free the state from the Depression. But despite efforts to recruit northern business and tourists, Florida remained largely a rural, agricultural and frontier-like place and its people remained impoverished.

Confounding efforts to modernize the state, Florida's political, social and cultural mores mirrored the racial divide of the South. As in other southern states, the Democratic Party dominated Florida politics, controlling all political offices and diligently defending segregation.

The racial divide was so firmly embraced by whites that black residents dared not test it. When some tried as in Ocoee in November 1920 and Rosewood in January 1923, heavily armed white mobs destroyed both towns and wantonly murdered black residents. Throughout this prewar era, Florida also had one of the highest lynching rates in the nation, even as lynching was denounced nationally and even in sections of the South.

The Florida of today bears little resemblance to that of 1945. Where once the state was largely ignored and few sought to reside there, it has become a place that is embraced by people from all parts of the world and especially those from this hemisphere.

Its diversity is no longer seen as a liability to its future, but an essential part of it. Blacks and Puerto Ricans from the Caribbean flock to Florida much like Cubans did in the 1970s and 1980s, and for many of the same reasons.

This new Florida offers people from all backgrounds hope, a new beginning, greater longevity and a more promising future.

The state is not, however, without its challenges as white retirees question the state's continuing diversity, as north Florida shies away from the cultural transformation of south Florida, and as some whites still balk at the integration of the workplace and neighborhoods. Its leaders need to be mindful of the pitfalls of the past and the divisions that can occur—North Carolina is but one recent example of the latter.

So here's wishing that Florida continues to embrace the future in 2017 and to include all its people in that embrace.

## Florida: A State in Search of Itself

David Colburn

*Tampa Bay Times*, July 5, 2018

Often characterized as "a state in search of itself," Florida's transformation actually began at the end of WWII, when wave upon wave of migration and immigration washed over the state. While Florida was fundamentally altered in many ways, it remained remarkably unchanged in one major aspect—its politics and, particularly, voting.

Before 1945, Florida has the smallest population in the South with about 2.3 million people and a one-party political system that mirrored the rest of the region. Race still defined southern politics and various obstacles from poll taxes, to voter tests that were nearly impossible to pass, to blatant threats and violence were used to undermine black voting. Even black veterans returning from the war found obstacles everywhere despite their sacrifices.

Voting restrictions were also established to limit the influence of white Republicans. The disparity between the parties was so profound throughout this era that LeRoy Collins, who was elected governor in 1954 and again in 1956, spent a mere $174 to defeat his Republican opponent.

Former Gov. Bob Graham, a native Floridian and a resident of Miami Lakes, was among several who noticed the consequences of migration, particularly senior migration, on its politics. The initial wave of seniors were New Deal Democrats and they joined with native Democrats to ensure that Florida remained Democratic. Known as "condo commandos," they turned out friends and neighbors much like the political machines of the northeast. In the process, they elected moderate Democrats who, together with national leaders, opened the voting booths to black voters.

For most of this period, the Republican Party remained little more than a third party until the early 1980s and it did not take control of state politics until the last decade of the 20th century. Party leaders, however, were confident throughout this period that the migration of Midwesterners and Cubans, who embraced low taxes, small government and the anti-Castro politics of the Reagan administration, would eventually take political control. When they were joined by a new group of seniors and Democrats who flipped to the Republican Party, they seized the majority in 1994.

Despite a severe recession in 2008, the state's population steamrolled past 20 million people in 2018. What had been a small, biracial, rural and agricultural state had morphed into the largest state on the East Coast with a population that was remarkably diverse and overwhelmingly urban. Even with these developments, Florida maintained its one-party politics but that party had now become Republican.

To secure their success, Republicans, much like Democrats before them, redrew legislative voting lines in the early 1990s and again in 2000 to make in extremely difficult for Democrats to secure a legislative majority in the foreseeable future.

Despite the population explosion of the past 50 years, Florida still finds itself saddled with a one-party political state that effectively excludes over 40 percent or more of the population from the political table.

You might ask why Floridians haven't insisted on districts that are equitably drawn; why haven't its leaders supported efforts to make voting easy and accessible; and why haven't we made registration readily available in public spaces? Few voters would take issue with these reforms, many of which have been adopted elsewhere. But in Florida, reforms of this nature potentially threaten one party's control over the other.

So while the population explosion has affected almost every other aspect of life in modern Florida, it has yet to throw off a political culture that is rooted in the 19th century. And thus it remains "a state in search of itself" and in search of a democracy that embraces the voices of all people.

# 2

# Gubernatorial Leadership

For much of Florida's existence, the position of governor was weak and ineffectual. That had less to do with the caliber of the men (and they have all been men!) who filled the position than the way the state constitution defined the parameters of the job. Until the implementation of the current constitution in 1968, the governor's position was, in the words of Chesterfield Smith, chairperson of the Florida Constitutional Revision Commission, a "hydra-headed monster without any centralized control or direction." The previous constitution, passed in 1885 in the midst of the Jim Crow Redemption period, seriously restricted the power of the governor. It limited him to one four-year term, abolished the office of lieutenant governor, and provided significantly more power to cabinet officers, who could be elected to multiple consecutive terms. In spite of these restrictions, some governors proved themselves capable leaders under trying circumstances. In particular, Colburn singles out the experience of LeRoy Collins in the mid-1950s, when the governor's moderate stance on civil rights, though by no means renouncing segregation, proved a model for the South and led his biographer Martin Dyckman to proclaim Collins "Floridian of his Century." In 1968, Florida voters ratified a new Constitution, one that still governs the state today. This frame of government brought Florida's state government into the modern era by, among other things, greatly expanding the power and scope of the executive branch. The governor could now run for reelection after one four-year term, the office of lieutenant governor was reestablished after a hiatus of one hundred years, and the power of cabinet officials was significantly diminished while that of the governor was increased. The effect of this change upon

Florida politics was immediate and long-lasting. For the next fifty years, influential two-term governors of both political persuasions held office and helped shape Florida into a modern state. The remainder of the essays in this section analyze the policies and legacies of these administrations, focusing on both governors' political leadership and the personal attributes that allowed them to lead Florida in profound and important ways. The essays also address the larger issues that faced the state during the administrations of these chief executives. Though these issues, like race, demographics, education, economic policy, and the environment, will be addressed separately in later sections, they also relate to the leadership strategies of the governors discussed. While broad social and economic trends have certainly changed and influenced Florida drastically since World War II, one cannot underestimate the impact of individual governors on the lives of ordinary Floridians.

## Cooperation in Tallahassee? Chiles More Likely to Get a Tussle

David Colburn

*Orlando Sentinel,* March 10, 1991

Lawton Chiles strode into the Governor's Mansion as the most experienced and one of the most popular politicians in Florida history. From all indications, he will need every bit of that experience and popularity in dealing with the state's pressing economic, social and educational problems in this legislative session.

In his State of the State address to the Legislature and "fireside" chat with the citizens of Florida, the governor set the tone for the upcoming session by urging legislators and voters to join with him in restoring public trust in government through the right-sizing of government and through political campaigning and ethics reform. In mapping his agenda for the state, Chiles emphasized the particular importance of gubernatorial and legislative cooperation.

Historically, few legislatures have provided a stiffer challenge to gubernatorial leadership than the Florida's. Many legislators, for example, are politically ambitious and view the halls of the legislature as an opportunity to build a statewide reputation, much like Chiles and MacKay did and often at the expense of the governor.

Since 1972, legislators have also had one of the largest and most professional staff systems in the nation. This fifth estate of government (the press typically being referred to as the fourth) has profoundly altered the relationship between the governor's office and legislative leaders.

Staff members work year-round gathering information, conducting investigations, drafting legislation and revising budgets. They have enabled the Legislature to function independently of the governor's office to a remarkable degree, because legislators are no longer totally dependent on the governor and his staff for information.

To govern in the face of this legislative challenge requires considerable political acumen as former Govs. Bob Graham and Bob Martinez learned with varying degrees of success. The fact that Chiles and the legislative leadership are Democrats in no way guarantees a cooperative relationship, because party loyalty is so fragile and personal ambitions are often present.

Despite his extensive background in politics, Chiles has never governed, nor has Lt. Gov. Buddy MacKay. The challenge of managing an agenda, setting policy and implementing programs for the entire state are new to both men and their staffs.

So far, Chiles and MacKay have moved smoothly into their new roles, but the Chiles' staff, which has the crucial responsibility of interacting with legislative leaders on a daily basis, has not done so well, evincing some of the same shortcomings that made Martinez's staff so unpopular.

Adding to this challenge is an economic recession that is as severe as any Florida has faced since the Arab oil boycott of 1973.

Chiles' approach to this crisis is to right-size state government by cutting expenditures. It is an approach that seems incongruous for a government that ranks near the bottom in funding for nearly all social and educational programs.

But Chiles is determined to avoid new tax initiatives until he has demonstrated that state government is accountable to the public, and new taxes are not only essential but worthwhile.

He is also anxious to avoid the political catastrophe that befell New Jersey Gov. James Florio after he instituted a series of major tax reforms in his first term.

Although legislative leaders have indicated their initial support for the governor's proposals, they and their staffs will test all his skills and those of his aides before the session is over. If Chiles can successfully manage his budget and ethics and political campaign reform through this tangled web of political and legislative infighting and restore public confidence in government in the process, he may well begin building a gubernatorial record the likes of which has not been seen in Tallahassee since the days of LeRoy Collins and Reubin Askew.

For now, however, he must meet the challenge of governing in a state where legislative perogatives [*sic*] are jealousy [*sic*] guarded and where public suspicion of all politicians is widespread.

## Florida's Beacon in Storm

**Collins a fighter for equal justice**

David Colburn

*Orlando Sentinel*, March 14, 1991

LeRoy Collins was a remarkable man and governor. And he leaves behind a personal and political legacy that will leave his fellow citizens of Florida forever in his debt.

It was Collins who modernized the state of Florida in the postwar era, and it was Collins who reminded Floridians and Southerners of their best instincts when they confronted the racial traditions of the past during the tumultuous 1950s.

Florida has not been blessed with great gubernatorial leadership, but when it mattered most, it had LeRoy Collins. A man of great integrity who fought for equal justice and exhibited empathy for the downtrodden throughout his career, he guided Florida through the troubled waters of the 1950s and the dismantling of segregation.

His governorship spanned the critical years from 1955 to 1961, when white Floridians tried desperately to hold on to the racial traditions of the past in the wake of the Brown decision of 1954 and when black Floridians reached out anxiously for promise of freedom and opportunity.

This was an era of demagogues in which governors like Orval Faubus of Arkansas, Ross Barnett of Mississippi and George Wallace of Alabama spurned the Constitution, sneered at the president of the United States and captured the nation's headlines.

But LeRoy Collins refused to succumb to racist appeals even if it threatened his political future (and it would in the 1968 senatorial campaign), and he refused to allow the people of Florida to succumb to such base instincts. As he told his audiences in the 1956 gubernatorial primary: "If you want a governor who will get the white people to hate the Negroes and incite Negroes to hate the white people, then you don't want LeRoy Collins to be your governor."

The rural porkchoppers, who dominated both houses of the Legislature, and even many of the urban legislators challenged him at every step. They passed legislation nullifying the Supreme Court's decision, threatening to close any public school that was desegregated, creating a private school system to avoid desegregation, and making it a criminal offense to teach in an integrated school.

In the midst of this confrontation, Collins held firm like a lighthouse beacon in a swirling storm and refused to endorse any of these measures.

At the height of the Little Rock school crisis, with emotions running high, LeRoy Collins gave the opening address at the Southern Governor's Conference in which he called on the South to resist wrapping itself in a "Confederate blanket" and repudiating change, or it would bury itself politically for decades. Ours is a nation of laws, he told his audience, "It does not sanction violence, defiance and disorder. Above all, it abhors hate."

Near the end of his governorship, he set about to educate Floridians about his sense of ethics and justice. He spoke about the incongruity and injustice of allowing blacks to shop at a store but of not permitting them to sit down at a lunch counter for a drink or a sandwich. And he persuaded Miami to begin the process of desegregating its public school system voluntarily.

His fight for equality went well beyond the battle over desegregation. He led the effort to provide fair representation for all Floridians by reapportioning the Legislature. The porkchoppers defeated him at every turn until the U.S. Supreme Court endorsed the Collins position in the Swann vs. Adams case of 1967. Collins also created the Community College system to provide educational and economic opportunity for Florida's youth who could not afford the expense of a university education.

He was not without his mistakes, and he always regretted blocking Virgil Hawkins's admission to the College of Law at the University of Florida.

Still, in my "field of dreams," LeRoy Collins stands as one of this country's great political heroes who had the moral courage to rise above the expediency of his time and to do the right thing. It would be worth traveling to the Governor's Mansion to see him once again.

## Chiles' Legacy: Beyond the He-Coon

David Colburn

*Orlando Sentinel*, December 11, 1998

Walkin' Lawton, the self-proclaimed "He-Coon" from Lakeland, soon will retire his coonskin cap from state politics. He leaves behind a remarkable record of public service, representing Floridians for 40 years as state representative, state senator, U.S. senator, and governor. His imminent departure from political office has analysts and reporters scurrying to evaluate his legacy. It is a substantial one by any measure.

As a political campaigner, Chiles is unrivaled. Not only unbeaten as a candidate, Chiles has been a pioneer in developing innovative strategies to mobilize voter support.

In 1970, he walked more than 1,000 miles across Florida to draw attention to his candidacy for the U.S. Senate.

In his gubernatorial campaign in 1990, he rejected special-interest money and limited contributions to $100 per individual. More than 75,000 Floridians contributed to his campaign in 1990 in what still stands as a record for individual contributions to a state campaign.

And when all seemed in danger in his 1994 gubernatorial re-election contest against Jeb Bush, Chiles pulled out his coonskin cap to remind Floridians that he was one of them and not just an outsider from a prominent family.

His campaign innovations have resonated with Florida voters at several levels and done much to enhance his reputation as a candidate of the "common man and woman."

As party leader, Chiles was among a small group of progressives who led the effort to revitalize the Democratic Party in Florida in the late 1960s, when it appeared that Republicans were about to seize control of the state. Following the example of LeRoy Collins, who was their mentor,

Chiles, Reubin Askew and Bob Graham breathed life into a party that has been dominated by the narrow, self-interests of North Florida legislators, the so-called porkchoppers.

Chiles' success as party leader during that period, however, has been offset by the disarray in the Democratic Party during his governorship. In the 1998 general election, in particular, it was a party of individuals with little discipline or sense of loyalty. The irony, of course, is that Chiles took few steps to prevent the Democratic bloodletting.

In his role as chief executive, Child has enjoyed more success. He has taken on a host of major issues to improve the quality of life in Florida. From his campaign on behalf of children to welfare reform, the lawsuit against Big Tobacco, reviving the Everglades and building new public schools, Chiles has not shied away from major, and often controversial, initiatives.

Although he has not always been the most effective administrator nor given as much time to the job as he might, he has generally surrounded himself with superior people, most notably Lt. Gov. Buddy MacKay, who have managed state affairs quite well.

In legislative relations, Chiles has had a turbulent eight years, in which he confronted a rising Republican majority in the Legislature. His first four years as governor were particularly tumultuous, when the state seemed to bounce from economic crisis to hurricane disaster to tourist slayings, and Republicans added insult to injury by rejecting his tax reform package. His second term has been much less controversial, with both parties toning down the rhetoric and focusing on the needs of the state. The realization that they had to deal with one another for four years, no doubt, had some impact, but so did a booming economy that improved the civic and political culture.

In the legislative arena, Chiles deserves particular praise for his campaign to build "a constituency for children" through the Healthy Start program, state health insurance for children, promotion of adoption programs and improved educational standards in schools. The status of children in Florida is perhaps the Achilles' heel confronting the state and threatening its future. Florida now ranks among the bottom 10 states in a host of categories that deal with children.

Chiles' retirement represents the passing of an era in Florida politics. The age of progressive Democratic leadership is nearing its end. What the party will offer as a replacement is unclear.

Whether or not Floridians have agreed with Chiles' position on the issues, they have to agree that he has governed with integrity and often with vision. The rest of his legacy will eventually be judged in the context of history.

For now, however, as he sheds his coonskin cap, Floridians owe him thanks for a job well done.

## Bush Leaves Powerful Imprint on Florida

David Colburn

*Orlando Sentinel*, December 10, 2006

Jeb Bush enters his final month in office as perhaps the most influential governor in state history. First introduced to Floridians in the 1994 election, Bush enjoyed almost instant stardom. After all, his father was a former president, and his brother was campaigning to be governor of Texas. Jeb narrowly lost that race to incumbent Gov. Lawton Chiles but came back four years later to thrash Buddy MacKay.

From the outset, Bush energized Republicans as no candidate in Florida had previously. And his conservative, anti-tax, small government, pro-business message resonated beyond Republicans, attracting conservative Democrats and many new voters.

At his inaugural in January 1999, Bush issued a clarion call for a conservative political revolution: "While our government has grown larger, so, too, has the crushing weight of taxes, regulations and mandates on Florida's families and entrepreneurs. As we address these great challenges into the next century, we need not only ask 'What's new?' we should more often ask, 'What's best?'"

Like other neoconservatives, Bush asserted that the private sector offered the best solutions to the challenges facing Floridians: "The best and brightest ideas do not come from the state capital, but from the untapped human capital that resides in our diverse communities."

Over the next eight years, Bush systematically pared government programs, assigning their responsibilities to private agencies—children's services is a case in point—or eliminating them altogether.

Assisting him in overhauling state government was a Republican-dominated Legislature. In 1999, Republicans held majorities in both houses, and party leaders gave Bush credit for the GOP's rise to power. Not since Democrat Reubin Askew assumed office in 1970 had a governor enjoyed such broad support among members of his own party.

But Bush was able to eclipse Askew's influence when voters adopted a constitutional amendment limiting Florida senators and representatives to eight years in office. More popularly known as "Eight is Enough," this amendment forced out of office more than half the experienced members of the Florida House and Senate in 2000. With so many newly elected representatives and senators, the governor commanded legislative influence that had no parallel in Florida history.

Bush's leadership benefited additionally from the decision of voters to consolidate the state Cabinet positions from 6 to 3. Since its inclusion in the Constitution of 1885, the Cabinet had been a thorn in the governor's ability to exercise his executive authority. No more.

Beyond such political and structural developments, Bush enjoyed eight years of prosperity during which he was able to reduce taxes without disrupting state services. Bush boasted that his conservative revolution had led to a $5 billion plus surplus in state revenue and an unemployment rate of 3 percent. Economists, however, credited population growth, home buyers and tourism for the robust economy.

Although Bush's politics were frequently to the right of many Floridians, he managed to mask the differences and presented his policies as if they reflected mainstream thinking. For example, most Floridians embraced public-school reform and accountability measures despite vocal opposition from educators and teachers unions.

But Floridians remained wary of his support for public-school vouchers, the taxpayer-financed scholarships for families to send their children to private schools. Following a legal challenge, the Florida Supreme Court threw out a key element of Bush's voucher plan and lawmakers refused to resurrect it. Voters also insisted on class-size limits in public schools despite resistance from the governor.

His deft handling of the hurricane disasters of 2004 and 2005, however, gave the governor a unique opportunity to shed his policy-oriented image and humanize his relationship with voters. Floridians appreciated Bush's compassion during these events and came to regard him in a new light.

For all his achievements in school reform, privatizing government, economic growth and diversification, tax reform and hurricane relief, Bush has occasionally been tripped up. Much of this can be attributed to his ideology and partisanship, his support for big business at the expense of the public interest, his inclination to punish his enemies, and his commitment to his brother's presidency.

Bush's intervention in the life-and-death struggle of Terri Schiavo and his efforts to evict state Sen. Alex Villalobos of Miami for opposing efforts to weaken the class-size amendment struck supporters and opponents as dictatorial and politically dangerous. Even state Senate Republicans opposed Bush in the Schiavo matters, and voters in Miami opted to re-elect Villalobos.

Reservations also persist in some quarters about the future consequences of Bush's elimination of state agencies and his fiscal policies for the state. While his political future remains unclear (speculation persists that he may be vice president on the 2008 Republican national ticket), he leaves behind a formidable legacy. He redefined state politics and the Republican Party, steering both sharply to the right, while persuading a new generation of Floridians to embrace his conservative political agenda.

Bush did much of this by the force of his own personality and his personal direction.

Florida has not seen his like previously—and the state is not likely to see it again anytime soon.

# 3

# State Politics

In 1949, political scientist V. O. Key, then teaching at Yale, penned his influential opus *Southern Politics in State and Nation.* What is most striking about Key's insight is how contemporary it seems over seventy years later. "Florida's peculiar social structure underlies a political structure of extraordinary complexity," he wrote in a chapter entitled "Florida: every man for himself." "It would be more accurate to say that Florida has no political organization in the conventional sense of the term. . . . In its politics it is almost literally every candidate for himself." Graham and Colburn follow Key's lead and describe a governmental system that reflects a state with no coherent political center. They analyze a Florida political structure that is both geographically distant and demographically diverse. It is approximately the same distance from Key West to Pensacola as it is from Jacksonville to Pittsburgh. Florida politicians have to balance the needs of the nation's second-largest elderly population (both by percentage and by raw numbers) with those of over four million immigrants, 75 percent of whom come from Latin America. The authors analyze the fluid power dynamics within Florida politics over the past seventy years, as the Sunshine State has moved, in the evocative phrasing of David Colburn, "from Yellow Dogs Democrats to Red State Republicans." They tie the larger social and demographic changes within the state to shifting political trends, such as the demise of the rural conservative north Florida Pork Chop Gang, who basically ran Florida through the 1960s. Florida's changing political winds both reflected and shaped wider national trends, and Colburn and Graham discuss that relationship in their pieces in this section. Florida has become a "bellwether" state, one in which state political matters effect national political concerns in profound ways. But Colburn and Graham also examine the mundane aspects of Florida political procedure, ones known quite well to a political insider like Bob Graham. The Byzantine nature of the legislative process, the sausage-making means of reapportionment and redistricting, and the hot-button concerns surrounding citizenship and voting rights are stories that could be ripped directly from today's headlines. Graham and Colburn analyze them all, with careful consideration for contextualizing these issues with historical insight. Most importantly, the authors recognize how the very meaning of "politics" has changed over the past seventy years in both Florida and the nation. The political sphere is no longer controlled completely by elite white men, and these essays both reflect that important change and recognize how far we still have to go to have a political process reflective of all Florida's people.

## In Tallahassee, Is It the Season for Wise Men—or for Folly?

David Colburn

*Orlando Sentinel*, December 13, 1991

'Tis the season to receive a pink slip.

According to the most recent figures, national unemployment remained steady at 6.8 percent, but only because nearly 300,000 workers were removed from the list altogether. Florida's unemployment stood at 8 percent in September, and, although preliminary figures for October suggest that it has fallen to 7.2 percent, few have much confidence in these numbers or in the future.

With both government and industry reducing expenditures and laying off workers, the near term offers little hope for a jolly Christmas.

Adding to the somber mood that has cast a gray pall over the holidays, many state governments are implementing steps to reduce spending for education, children and family care in response to the recession. Tax watch groups urge them on, mindlessly accusing government of reckless spending and excessive fat.

And yet it is hard to conceive that investment in families and children is foolish or wrongheaded. Even conservative economists acknowledge that investment in the health, well-being and education of children and families in this country benefits all areas of human as well as economic activity, from business to science to engineering and the environment.

Ironically, the two societies that the United States defeated in World War II and then helped rebuild—West Germany and Japan—seem to understand the value of citizen investment more fully than we do.

Both these societies have diverted some of the enormous economic profits into the public sector to ensure that the family, children and workers are protected. They regard such investment as significantly more vital to the economic future of their nations than additional housing developments and new roads, for example.

According to a recent article in Newsweek magazine, Germany has the best high schools and teacher training programs in the world, and Japan has the best science programs.

Where does American education rank in such studies?

Newsweek and others place this country near the bottom in almost all educational categories when compared with other industrialized nations—except in graduate education, where it continues to lead the world. It may come as a surprise to many that one of the leading investors in U.S. graduate programs is the Japanese. The Center for Public Integrity reported recently that they have poured more than $175 million into U.S. colleges and universities since 1986 in an effort, according to one observer, to buy "the American mind."

Earlier this week, the Carnegie Foundation reported that more than 42 percent of the children entering kindergarten are less prepared to learn than they were five year ago, and most lack basic reading skills that are essential to success in school. The foundation identified poor health care, inattentive or overworked parents, scarce child-care and pre-school opportunities, unsafe neighborhoods, mindless television and isolation from adults as the principal factors in this new educational dilemma.

Florida's commitment to and investment in children and families remain fair at best and poor at worst. Gov. Lawton Chiles' proposed austerity budget threatens even this modest standing, by reducing per-student spending in Florida to its lowest level since 1988. Our investment in preschool children and families also ranks among the lowest per capita in the nation. And in contrast to the Japanese, Florida's political leaders seem to think graduate education is frivolous.

At the same time, we find ourselves forced to construct one of the largest prison systems in the country. As the Proverbs remind us, you eventually reap what you sow.

The human infrastructure is, of course, where Florida's political leaders face a particular challenge as they seek to address this year's budget deficit in the special session. The governor has challenged them to think about the ramifications of their decisions, but few seem able to look beyond the fall elections of 1992 and the possibility of higher public office through reapportionment.

The recession has severely tested their political will, and most seem paralyzed.

Will they rise to the occasion and begin the process of providing Florida and its citizens with a promising future? Or will they stand idly by, fearful of losing political office? Is it the season for wise men or for folly?

## Custom of Porkchop Politics Thwarts What's Best for Florida

David Colburn

*Orlando Sentinel*, March 1, 1992

Floridians might be thinking that, with the problems confronting the state's sagging economy and the threat to public services posed by the "reality budget," their legislative leaders would be spending most of their time seeking solutions to these difficult matters. Think again.

Legislative leaders on both sides of the aisle are, in fact, engaged in good old-fashioned politics. The Winter Olympics may have ended in France, but the reapportionment games are in full swing in Tallahassee.

Confronted with substantial population shifts that have occurred in Florida since the 1980 census, legislators are busily redrawing legislative and congressional district lines. At the same time, they are also looking for ways to secure their own political future, protect their party's interests, and perhaps provide themselves with an opportunity for higher office.

It is this aspect of the political process that voters find maddening. Instead of focusing their full attention on the state's serious economic and social needs, Senate and House leaders are protecting their own backsides and trying to feather their political nests. So much for the public interest.

Florida Democrats have spent more time and energy on reapportionment during this session than at any time in recent memory, because their party's preeminence in state politics is being seriously challenged for the first time since Reconstruction. Democrats are studying ways to hold off the Republican threat to Democratic majorities in the state Senate and in Congress by using redistricting to preserve their leadership.

The gerrymandering efforts of Democrats resemble the actions of rural legislators, led by the likes of Charley Johns from Starke, in the post-World War II era.

These so-called porkchoppers from North Florida and the Panhandle repeatedly stymied reapportionment efforts by governors and South Florida voters in order to maintain a stranglehold on the Legislature. In 1960, the porkchoppers represented only 12.3 percent of the voters in the state Senate and only 14.7 percent of the state in the House, but they controlled a majority of seats in both bodies.

They repeatedly subverted the will of the majority, because they wanted to maintain their political influence in the state, to preserve North Florida's way of life, to control state funds, and, in the 1950s, to prevent racial reform. Personally and ideologically, they distrusted the people who had settled in South Florida.

Today, state Democrats, led by Senate Majority Leader Gwen Margolis and Speaker of the House T.K. Wetherell, find themselves in a situation similar to that of the porkchoppers. If they do not gerrymander reapportionment, some experts say, they face the likely prospect that the Republicans will capture political control of the state Senate, and perhaps the House and the congressional delegations in the near future. But if they do gerrymander districts to preserve Democratic Party leadership and facilitate their ambitions, they will certainly pass the way of the porkchoppers.

Republicans are no less innocent, even if less prominent, in this process. They are eagerly looking for any angle that will strengthen the party, embarrass the Democrats, and help themselves.

Instead of concentrating their energies and attention on reapportionment, leaders of the two parties might consider addressing the state's pressing economic and social needs. They may be surprised to find in the process that voters will reward them for doing the job for which they were originally elected.

So, will it be a continuation of the porkchop politics of the past, or will legislative leaders step forward to address the needs of the state and the well-being of its citizens?

Stay tuned—we should know in two weeks.

## Legislature Back in Session? Hide your Family, Possessions

David Colburn

*Orlando Sentinel*, March 29, 1992

"Hide the women, children and pets, the Florida Legislature is back in session." So went the adage whenever the state's political leaders convened in Tallahassee.

Before 1945, Florida voters had little confidence in their political representatives when they gathered in regular session, let alone when they reconvened in special session. Floridians felt that too many things could happen when politicians met, and most of them were bad. Although the adage disappeared into the history books in the postwar era, this general view has enjoyed a recent renaissance among voters.

Floridians today are more cynical about politicians and politics than at any time in recent Florida history. And who can blame them?

After a 60-day regular session, the Legislature adjourned in mid-March without resolving the most pressing issues that originally brought its members to Tallahassee. Early last week, legislative leaders convened the first of three special sessions, at $40,000 per day, to address congressional reapportionment. The second session will involve state legislative reapportionment, and the third will focus on the state budget.

The two parties have paralyzed the state with their political machinations over reapportionment (at latest count, there were 190 possible redistricting plans) and with their partisan struggles to secure control of the state Senate. Democrats have sought to preserve their supremacy in state politics through reapportionment, while Republicans have sought to use the tax issue and the recession to capture control of the Senate. In the meantime, the citizens of the state and their children watch from the sidelines in stunned disbelief as Florida falls to 43rd among states in health care for children and 50th in spending per child for education. They would shudder to know that prison officials are releasing convicted felons on a regular basis to make room for more hardened criminals because of overcrowding and the inability of the state to provide prison guards for its new prisons.

The old expression "Thank God for Mississippi" no longer applies, because Florida now ranks below Mississippi in these important statistical categories. Given this trend, it may well rank below Mississippi and every other state in education, health care, technology and perhaps economic development in the not-too-distant future.

All this despite the fact that the state now ranks 19th nationally in per capita income.

The absence of responsible political leadership and commitment to the public good has seldom been so apparent. Political leadership has, in fact, become little more than an oxymoron in this age when politicians refuse to act until they have seen the latest public opinion poll. About the only initiative legislators seem willing to undertake is to recognize various celebrities, such as race car driver Richard Petty, and to pose for pictures beside them. In one of the most memorable state Cabinet meetings in recent history, officials took turns on March 17 alternately throwing their hands in the air and lampooning their own political parties. Secretary of State Jim Smith, a Republican, put it most bluntly when, in reference to the political posturing over the budget in the Senate, he said, "Florida isn't what I hoped it would be. I'm ashamed of us."

Floridians are rightly troubled by the severity of the recession and by the failure of the political process in Tallahassee and Washington, D.C., to address their needs and the future needs of the nation. The unwillingness of politicians at the state and federal levels to set aside their partisan differences to find solutions to the economic crisis confounds and embitters voters and diminishes their faith in the democratic process.

Seldom has the process seemed so inept and so politicized, and seldom have public needs gone more unmet. The public has a right to expect more but appears to have little hope of getting it from the present group in Tallahassee.

As they used to say 40 years ago, protect your family and personal possessions, because the Legislature is back in session. Or, in the words of the baseball player and amateur philosopher Yogi Berra, "It's deja vu all over again."

## Tax Tussle

**What's best for Florida? GOP strategy may ultimately prove successful, but it offers little leadership to Florida and few answers to the state's pressing economic problems.**

David Colburn

*Orlando Sentinel*, July 7, 1993

Gov. Lawton Chiles' offer of an olive branch to the Republican minority in the Legislature in his State of the State speech on Tuesday found few takers. Republicans appear intent on standing as the opposition for the remainder of Chiles' gubernatorial term and using the time before the 1994 elections to lay the political foundation for capturing the governorship and perhaps the Legislature.

What party leaders seem to have lost sight of in pursuing this political strategy are the needs of the state of Florida and its citizens.

Part of the Republican strategy relies on portraying the governor and his Democratic allies in the Legislature as a bunch of taxaholics and spendthrifts. If you read the comments of Republicans after Chiles' address, you will find nearly all of them berating his proposed tax reforms and spending programs. It is a ploy that Republicans have used effectively against Democrats throughout the 1980s at the state and national level.

Florida Democrats, however, are not exactly your liberal, card-carrying Democrats from Massachusetts or Michigan. Most state Democrats are as conservative on fiscal and tax matters as their Republican counterparts, but they have been crippled by the generally perceived liberal spending policies of congressional Democrats in Washington. During the past decade, state Republicans have made substantial gains at all levels in Florida by running against policies of the national Democratic Party, and apparently they intend to continue to do so.

Many state Democrats thought they could derail Republican gains in Florida when they elected Chiles as governor in 1990. But no one anticipated a major recession occurring on Chiles' watch. Nor did they believe that the politically experienced Chiles would have so much difficulty working with legislative leaders in the state Senate. Chiles' efforts at cajoling Democrats and Republicans alike into supporting his programs in the two previous legislative sessions backfired completely. But Republicans, while publicly supportive of measures to address these issues, indicated that they are unwilling to embrace new tax initiatives to pay for them.

Although the Republican political strategy may ultimately prove successful, it offers little in the way of leadership to the people of Florida and few answers to the pressing economic problems still confronting the state. Floridians, for example, may prefer lower taxes, but they also want and need better jobs and greater economic opportunities.

Unfortunately, Florida's sun-and-surf appeal has proved to be less than effective in recruiting new business and industry. Corporate leaders seem content to vacation in Florida, but then they take their businesses elsewhere. According to various reports in The Wall Street Journal and Fortune magazine, most business executives are critical of Florida because it lacks a strong educational and social infrastructure that would enhance their work force. The Republican strategy ignores this continuing problem.

In a related vein, Floridians, like Americans elsewhere, demonstrated in in the recent presidential election that they reject Republican notions of trickle-down economics. Floridians do not like taxes, but what House Republican leader Sandra Mortham does not seem to realize is that voters do not appreciate corporations and other citizens who do not pay their fair share. Former Gov. Reubin Askew discovered during his effort to mobilize support for a corporate tax in the early 1970s that there is a strong populist streak among Floridians that can become quite exercised about issues of fairness and equity.

The political lines have been drawn early this year in anticipation of the general election in 1994, and the consequences for the citizens of Florida appear ominous.

Somehow during the three months since the presidential election, the public interest in moving beyond traditional politics has been lost on Republican strategists. By emphasizing the tax issue at the expense of issues such as health care, hurricane relief, criminal justice and economic development, Republicans run the risk of jeopardizing the needs of the state. It appears that this is a risk they are willing to take if it will lead to political victory in 1994.

## Florida Democrats Get Perishable Gift

**David Colburn**

*Orlando Sentinel*, November 7, 1996

Bill Clinton's victory in Florida on Tuesday not only ensured him the presidential election, but it may have stopped the hemorrhaging of the state Democratic Party.

For the past decade, the political trend has been nearly all bad for Florida Democrats. With the exception of the re-elections of Lawton Chiles as governor in 1994 and Bob Graham as U.S. senator in 1992, Democrats have witnessed the gradual withering away of their once-substantial majorities in state politics. The congressional delegation is now solidly Republican. Republicans control the state Senate and won control of the Florida House of Representatives Tuesday. More striking, registered Republican voters are rapidly overtaking registered Democrats.

The magnitude of the Republican victories in 1994 convinced many that the party would govern for a generation to come.

But a generation can be a very short time in politics. Republican leaders at the national level severely misjudged voter sentiments in 1994. Led by Newt Gingrich, congressional Republicans assumed they had carte blanche to dismantle much of the government.

Then Clinton and his party took a page out of the Republican handbook, focusing their counterattack on the national Republican Party and Gingrich. Calling his "Contract With America" extreme and dangerous for the country, Democrats launched a blistering offensive.

In the process, Clinton initiated efforts to shift the Democratic Party to the right. As a former leader of the moderate Democratic Leadership Conference, Clinton had long felt that the party's liberal establishment and its policies were out of touch with voters and had particularly hurt the party in his native South. He was further encouraged by the likes of Chiles and Graham, who worried that the loss of middle-income voters posed a long-term threat to the party in states such as Florida. Together they fashioned a more-conservative approach to government that, in combination with a healthy economy, enabled them to set the parameters of the political debate in this election.

Florida Republicans, many of whom embraced the Republican revolution, suddenly were faced with defending Republican congressional policies against attacks by state Democrats.

Aided by Clinton's victory and his moderate approach to governing, state Democrats have a rare opportunity to convince voters that the party represents the political mainstream. The alienation of women and senior citizens from the national Republican Party, in particular, has state Democrats smiling.

Seniors are especially important because they are one of the few voting blocs that take part in off-year elections and in local races.

Clinton's victory in Florida was only the second for a Democratic presidential candidate in two decades and only the third in nearly 50 years. The significance of his victory may well go beyond that, however. State Democrats have been presented with a unique opportunity to revive their sagging fortunes and to reconstruct a political majority. Clinton and the national party have done their part, and the rest is now in the hands of state Democratic leaders.

## The Rise of Two-Party Politics

David Colburn

*Gainesville Sun*, July 27, 1997

State and national reforms—especially the removal of race from around the neck of state politics—gradually blew a fresh breeze across Florida.

Without race-based politics and without a rural, North Florida-dominated legislature, the state began to address important issues that had been largely ignored in the battle over segregation.

In the process it changed political loyalties that had gone unchallenged during the 20th century.

The most immediate consequence of these developments involved constitutional revision.

The new governor, Claude Kirk, who served from 1967–91 and was the state's first Republican governor in the 20th century, strongly endorsed constitutional revision. Kirk felt that the Republican Party would enhance its reputation as the party of modernization and democratic reform by championing revision of the 1885 Constitution.

Moreover, most of his electoral support came from Central and South Florida, where opposition to the constitution of 1885 was strongest.

The 1968 Constitution represented a substantial revision, but did not appreciably alter the role of the governor in state politics. It retained the state's unique cabinet system, reflecting voter and legislative suspicion of executive leadership.

This failure to reform the executive office, along with the Legislative Reorganization Act of 1969, led gradually to the Legislature's domination of state politics.

Florida's demographics continued to change dramatically throughout the '60s and '70s. Nearly 500 people migrated per day. What had once been a frontier-like state was no more.

### Florida grows up

Florida rapidly became the largest and most urban state in the region, and its demographic features began to resemble more closely the Sun Belt states of Texas, Arizona and California than its southern neighbors.

A critical component of Florida's population expansion in the post-1960 era was the infusion of retired people and Cubans. Florida's senior citizens constituted more than 18 percent of the population by 1990, the largest segment in the country. They made heavy demands on the state's social and medical services, while simultaneously pressuring state politicians to limit new tax initiatives and other revenue measures that might adversely affect their fixed incomes.

Cuban Americans, who fled communist Cuba in 1959, made a rapid and remarkably successful adjustment to American life and quickly became a political force.

Because of their opposition to Fidel Castro and communism, Cuban Americans focused their attention primarily on foreign affairs.

But they have also been strong advocates of an unfettered American capitalism.

This new ethnic dynamic has, in turn, marginalized the racial concerns that dominated Florida politics for much of the 19th and 20th centuries.

### The GOP gains

The Republican party, which had been making slow but steady gains in the post-war period, benefited considerably from the growth in the number of senior citizens and Cuban Americans. Additionally, a latent Republicanism in national elections gradually began to make itself felt in state politics.

From 1948 on, Floridians voted for Republican presidential candidates in every election but 1964, 1976 and 1996, when they cast their ballots for native southerners Lyndon B. Johnson, Jimmy Carter and Bill Clinton.

Much of this animus to Democratic presidential candidates reflected voter anger with the party's support of desegregation and social reform in the 1950s and 1960s, and voter reaction against the social welfare state in the era after 1960.

The first stirrings of the Republican revival in Florida began with the stunning victory of Claude Kirk in the gubernatorial election of 1966 and Republican Edward Gurney's defeat of LeRoy Collins for the U.S. Senate seat two years later. These elections were early signs of a change in state politics, but they did not mark the beginning of a political revolution in Florida. Kirk's election and Gurney's senatorial success had more to do with voter reaction to the policies of President Johnson, the social revolution of the 1960s, and perceptions that Kirk and Gurney were more likely to preserve traditional social and political values.

The challenge to Democratic supremacy in Florida commenced seriously in 1980, and was led by Ronald Reagan. President Reagan's personal style and his domestic and foreign policy agenda enjoyed widespread support in Florida.

In particular, his denunciation of the social welfare state and federal bureaucracy combined with a military defense effort that sought to bring down the Soviet Union resonated with the conservative views of Floridians.

His enormous popularity in the state sparked a dramatic expansion in Republican voter registration. Reagan helped shift the fault line in state politics further north in Florida, allowing Republicans to gradually secure a political majority.

As evidence of this broadening support, Republicans were able to challenge Democratic candidates at all levels of government by the mid-1980s.

On the eve of the 21st century, Republicans now control both the state Senate and House, command 13 of 21 congressional seats, and one of two U.S. Senate seats.

Will the political momentum in favor of Republicans continue into the 21st century? The obvious answer would appear to be yes, but immigration could alter that political scenario.

The vote of Puerto Rican Floridians in the 1996 presidential race, for example, almost swung Central Florida into the Democratic column for what would have been the first time since 1948, when the region voted for Democratic presidential candidate Harry Truman.

Monday: Florida challenges in the next century.

## Trust Florida's Voters

**Amendment 3 shuts down people's power to fix problems. Vote no.**

Bob Graham

*St. Petersburg Times*, October 15, 2006

My daughter Suzanne taught kindergarten in Florida public schools, and she had 38 students in her class—too many. As good a teacher as she is, she could only be a babysitter for 38 5-year-olds.

Five years ago, less than 20 percent of young children in Florida had an opportunity for a quality pre-kindergarten experience. Hundreds of thousands of families were finding it more and more difficult to live in Florida with a minimum wage of $5.50 an hour. The state university system was becoming wastefully politicized.

The politicians in Tallahassee were deaf, dumb and blind to these problems. The Legislature, which was responsible for many of these ills, didn't seem to care. But you, the people of Florida, did. It was you who took the very difficult challenge to place remedies for these problems on the statewide ballot. Today, thanks to the hard work of thousands of volunteers, these problems have been remedied. Citizens passed constitutional amendments to reduce class size, provide universal pre-kindergarten, raise wages and ensure independence for our state universities.

Now, an amendment on the November ballot threatens to take away your fundamental right to a government by and for the people. A group of big businesses is pushing this very bad constitutional amendment—Amendment 3—to shut down the people's will.

This is not a partisan issue; both candidates for Florida governor oppose Amendment 3. On the surface, it seems fairly benign. The title (written by lobbyists) says the measure will require broader public support for constitutional amendments. But don't let yourself be fooled by the slick title. The subtext is about one thing: power.

Florida's constitutional amendments have always been approved by simple majority. Whichever side gets more than 50 percent wins. Amendment 3 requires an un-democratic supermajority of 60 percent to pass any future constitutional amendment. If a simple majority is good enough for politicians to get elected to office, it should be good enough for citizen initiatives. Our current Constitution, the one we've had since 1968, passed by 55 percent.

If Amendment 3 is allowed to pass, Florida would be a guinea pig—the only state in the nation to require such a big hurdle for citizen initiatives. It's not fair.

I am part of a historic coalition of groups from the middle, left and right called Trust the Voters (www.trustthevoters.org). We are putting aside our political differences to make sure we don't lose our rights through Amendment 3.

Florida is already one of the toughest states in the country to qualify a ballot initiative. Groups need to collect more valid signatures—over 600,000—to place a measure on the ballot than any other state, including California, with twice our population! Of the 50 measures that circulated in Florida last year, only one qualified for the ballot this November.

The 60 percent requirement would be a bath of cold water for anyone even thinking about starting a citizen's petition. People who would otherwise volunteer or contribute also would be discouraged.

The corporations backing Amendment 3 know that they have enormous influence in the halls of the Legislature. That's why they are spending big bucks to stop citizens from providing the needed checks and balances on Tallahassee. Maybe they are afraid that their stranglehold on the Legislature would be broken again for such improvements as fairer property taxes, lower insurance rates, or better schools for our children. I don't know the motives—ask those who have already contributed over $2 million just what they expect to get for their money. I was in public office a long time, and I say, trust the voters.

I urge you to vote no on Amendment 3 and hold on to your rights to address problems that the Legislature won't.

## How to Avoid Florida's Fiscal Hurricane

Bob Graham

*Miami Herald*, September 30, 2007

When Hurricane Humberto slammed into Texas two weeks ago, I was reminded that we Floridians know something about violent tropical weather. It is always dangerous and often unpredictable. But when we do see it coming, we can take steps to limit the damage. Thank goodness, because a new hurricane is headed toward us—not from the Atlantic Ocean or Gulf of Mexico but from Tallahassee.

Due to a shortfall in state government revenues, the Florida Legislature will meet in special session next week to cut the state budget by more than $1 billion. These cuts may be only the first response to a protracted crisis. Thanks to slower-than-expected rates in population and economic growth, revenues may not rebound for as long as three years.

The timing couldn't be worse. Florida desperately needs to make investments in several long-term priorities, such as:

** Universities: In the mid-1980s, Florida state universities were closing in on being in the upper quarter of all U.S. public universities for both financial support and student performance. Today, Florida ranks next-to-last among states in funding per public-university student ($11,700 vs. the $13,100 national average) and has the highest student-to-professor ratio (31 to 1) in the nation.

** K-12 schools: Two decades ago, through general revenues, the state provided 65 percent of the funds for public elementary and secondary schools in Florida. Now, due to repeated shifts of those costs to local property taxpayers, the state contributes only 50 percent of education funding. But thanks to new legislative restrictions on property taxes, Tallahassee legislators can no longer pass the buck. They have to find more money for public education at a time when we are already implementing a $20 billion-plus constitutional amendment to reduce class size.

** Uninsured children: Nationally, just more than 11.7 percent of children have no health-insurance coverage. Florida far exceeds the national average, with 16.8 percent of our children—one in six—going uninsured. Our state is the third-worst in America at ensuring that children have assured access to healthcare. But if Florida invested $100 million in 2007 to help our uncovered children receive reliable care, including preventive measures such as immunizations, we would attract more than $200 million in federal funds.

** Preservation: Through the Florida Forever initiative, our state purchases environmentally sensitive lands and protects them from development, including those lands needed for Everglades restoration. While Florida Forever has identified more than $11 billion in critical land-acquisition projects, the program has only $45 million left to spend and is due to expire in three years.

With vital needs escalating but revenues falling, legislators should take several steps in the special session to protect Florida from the fierce winds of future economic storms.

** First, make use of the old adage "When you're in a hole, stop digging." Earlier this year, the Legislature put a proposed constitutional amendment to slash local property taxes on the January 2008 ballot. That may look good on the surface, but consider the fine print. Under that amendment, Florida public schools would lose $7 billion over the next five years. Earlier this week, teachers and students won a reprieve when a Florida circuit court struck the amendment from the ballot. Rather than spending more taxpayer dollars to appeal the decision, or using valuable time in the October special session to revise the amendment, the Legislature should defer it to a better fiscal climate or at least develop a credible plan to hold public schools harmless from its impacts.

** Second, jump start long-term economic growth. During the five year period from 1985 to 1990, Florida's average per capita income was 100.3 percent of the national average. By the 2000 to 2005 period, our average was only 96.4 percent. Had we not experienced that 4 percent drop, Florida families would have earned, on average, almost $4,000.00 more each year. The governor and the Legislature should commit to policies designed to return Florida families to an above-national-average per capita income—and the best way to do that is to provide our public schools and universities with the financial support they need to reach new heights of national excellence.

** Third, carefully evaluate past revenue reductions. Many of the tax breaks enacted over the last decade were justified as necessary to stimulate economic growth. Those particular cuts cost the state $2.5 billion last year alone. Given the current state of Florida's economy and the slide in relative per capita income, the Legislature should repeal any tax cuts that do not more than pay their way in verifiable economic growth.

History says that Florida will eventually snap out of its current doldrums. But what happens until that revival will determine the future of our state.

If the governor and Legislature make the tough but correct choices now, Florida will emerge from this challenge stronger and as a national leader in educational excellence, transportation, healthcare and environmental preservation.

But if our leaders do nothing but swing a meat ax at key priorities, they will soon fall prey to snake-oil salesmen who promise "easy and painless" solutions like casino gambling. The second we succumb to those intoxicating promises, Florida's character will be forever altered—our future determined by the chance turn of the roulette wheel rather than the character and capabilities of our people. When that happens, our children and grandchildren will find themselves in the middle of the perfect and permanent economic storm.

## Don't Tax You, Don't Tax Me

**The national attitude, especially in Florida, seems to be: Why should we sacrifice when others can do it for us?**

David Colburn

*Gainesville Sun*, July 7, 2008

The currency of the nation had become a standing joke during the war years. The government and those not involved in the prosecution of the war had a deep aversion to paying taxes to support the conflict, and the national government refused to prosecute war profiteers. Meanwhile, soldiers lacked proper medical care and military equipment to protect themselves. Only those soldiers directly involved in the war and their families appeared willing to make the necessary sacrifices to defend the nation.

I know—this reads like another editorial on Iraq and the war against terrorism. Guess again.

What I just described took place during the American Revolution. In the winter of 1780, Washington's army and the new nation were on the verge of defeat by British forces. And still Americans and their political representatives refused to pay the necessary taxes and provide the financial support so that the colonial troops would have rifles, clothing and shoes.

From the nation's very inception, Americans have been wary of a strong central government and taxes.

Although the situation in 2008 is not nearly as dire as 1780, when the very existence of the nation was at stake, there is considerable cause for concern today. The United States currently finds itself with a $9.3 trillion debt; a deteriorating national economy plagued by housing, banking and oil crises; military operations in Iraq and Afghanistan that have cost the nation an estimated $875.5 billion since 2001 (according to the Congressional Research Service); and the loss and injury to thousands of young men and women whose lives and families have been permanently altered.

But President Bush refuses to raise taxes, make significant cuts in domestic spending, or ask the rest of us to contribute in any substantial way to the nation's financial and military challenges. And we sit passively and say little.

Have we learned nothing from the American Revolution? Perhaps not. The attitude of Americans and particularly those of us in Florida seems to be: Why should we sacrifice when others can do it for us and why pay when we can charge it to future generations? We demand better schools for our children, guaranteed Social Security and Medicare payments, a healthy environment, police and fire protection, and economic opportunity as if they were birthrights.

The fact is that the United States became a great nation not because it placed its obligations on a credit card, but because Americans recognized that success required commitment and occasionally sacrifice. As with much of our history, it seems we have forgotten this.

Floridians will have before them at the ballot box in November Amendment 5, which promises us another free ride. We can reduce our property taxes and have "some" of the reductions in state funding offset by increased sales taxes. The sales-tax mentality in Florida has been driven by the old saying, "Don't tax you, don't tax me, tax the man behind the tree." The person behind the tree is the tourist. So this amendment proposes to have someone else, namely the tourists, pay for our schools, transportation, police and fire protection, health care, etc. If we say yes to this amendment, we are, in fact, hiding behind the tree and once again shirking our responsibilities, much as those who refused to support the Continental Army in the nation's struggle for independence.

So what does our citizenship mean? Do we not have an obligation to one another, to the needs of the young and old, and to our veterans?

Challenges have frequently brought out the best in Americans. Will we rise to meet them again?

## Take Politics Out of Florida's Judiciary

### Bob Graham and Talbot "Sandy" D'Alemberte

*St. Petersburg Times*, December 24, 2008

By the early 1970s, patronage politics had severely undermined confidence in Florida's judiciary. After he became governor in 1971, Reubin Askew issued an executive order to limit political influence on judicial selections and establish merit as the basis on which Florida filled vacancies at every level of the court system.

Thirty-seven years later, Gov. Charlie Crist has a unique opportunity to recommit us to the path of choosing judges fairly and based on merit.

Askew established nine-member Judicial Nominating Commissions for the Florida Supreme Court, the five appellate districts and each judicial circuit. When it came time to fill judicial vacancies, these JNCs would take applications, interview candidates and submit a list of nominees for gubernatorial consideration. The governor would then select one of those nominees for service on the bench.

The reform was designed to bring discipline to the selection process and to provide a check on the governor's raw power of appointment.

Recently, news reports and editorials about the JNCs have caused great public concern that the process, originally designed to secure the selection of the best-qualified judges regardless of their politics, has become partisan. These reports and editorials raise legal issues that must be addressed as soon as possible.

The legal controversy relates to questions about the power of Florida's governor to ask that a JNC, once it has submitted finalists, to reconsider and add names to the list. Crist recently asked both the Florida Supreme Court JNC and the 5th District Court of Appeal JNC to take that step. The former agreed and the latter refused. Both decisions have drawn criticism.

Crist, who soon must fill vacancies on the Florida Supreme Court and the 5th District Court of Appeal, has within his power the means to resolve both the legal and the political questions. We make two suggestions.

First, to solve the issue of whether the governor can ask a JNC for additional names, he should ask the Florida Supreme Court for an advisory opinion.

Second, we suggest that the governor enter an executive order to restructure his appointment power and thereby diminish the public concern about partisan politics within Florida's judiciary. This step should be accompanied with a request that all JNC members resign, thus allowing a fresh start for the selection process.

Askew's 1971 executive order established a balanced approach to judicial selection. For each JNC, the governor would select three attorneys. The Florida Bar would select three others. These six members would then select three nonlawyer members from the general public.

Following his action, the Florida Legislature proposed a constitutional change that incorporated Askew's nominating process but did not include the balanced JNC membership. Instead, it allowed the Legislature to regulate JNC composition.

The JNC process worked well for more than three decades and our judiciary has become highly regarded throughout Florida and across the nation. For 30 years, both Democratic and Republican governors erased the taint of partisanship with their commitment to appointing the best judges regardless of party.

Unfortunately, changes made to the system earlier this decade threaten to undo the progress of the last 37 years. In 2001, the Legislature gave the governor authority to select every JNC member—a scenario that dangerously resembles the infamous patronage committees that existed before Askew's reforms.

Crist can restore a balanced JNC process simply by issuing an executive order setting up the rules for selection of JNC members. He could use the original order entered by Askew as a model.

Both of these proposed steps would permit quick resolution of the current controversy. If Crist seeks an advisory opinion from the Florida Supreme Court, the court can address the legal issues without the need for adversary litigation that some have threatened. The advisory process would also permit anyone, even members of the affected JNCs, to submit their thoughts to the court.

The second suggestion also can be accomplished rapidly. A new executive order would demonstrate the governor's commitment to quality judicial selection and help to re-establish the positive culture that has defined the Florida judiciary since 1972.

When Askew reformed the judicial selection process in the 1970s, it cemented his legacy as a leader who valued progress and integrity over politics. In taking similar steps, Crist can confirm his own reputation as someone who looks past partisan politics when it comes to important matters affecting Florida's citizens.

---

Talbot "Sandy" D'Alemberte was former president of the American Bar Association, former president of Florida State University, and a former state legislator.

## Drawing New Lines: Erasing Politicians' Self-Interest in Redistricting Process

**Bob Graham and Bob Milligan**

*South Florida Sun-Sentinel*, February 27, 2010

As two Floridians who have been working on both sides of the partisan aisle to improve Florida government, we are thrilled that voters will have the opportunity to vote this Nov. 2 on two constitutional amendments to stop what amounts to a legalized conflict of interest in our state. One newspaper called it "Florida's dirty little secret." It comes up every ten years when legislators are charged with the awesome responsibility of redrawing their own district boundaries as well as those of the congressional districts.

As the law stands now, there is nothing to prevent those legislators from drawing the lines to tailor districts to ensure their own re-election and victories for their parties. And there is nothing to stop them from drawing districts just to run their political opponents out of office. It is just like allowing the fox to guard the henhouse. Not a good idea!

This is a topic on which Republican, Democratic and Independent leaders agree.

U.S. Sen. John Mc Cain has urged Americans to "stop politicians in both parties from drawing rigged districts they can never lose." President Barack Obama has said, "We now have a system where, too often, our representatives are selecting their voters, as opposed to the voters selecting the representatives. That is a situation that I think the American people should not accept." And Independent New York Mayor Michael Bloomberg thinks, "Both parties have redistricted themselves such that they don't have to worry about a challenge across the aisle . . . so the conservatives are less willing to move to the middle, and the liberals are less willing to move to the middle . . . and we've got to understand that we're all in this together."

Florida voters have shown they will not accept this very unfair situation. They have signed more than 1.6 million petitions to get two constitutional amendments on the November ballot. These amendments, which will appear as Amendments 5 and 6, will establish clear and strong standards for the Florida Legislature to follow when they draw district lines. With voter approval in November, Amendments 5 and 6 will establish state constitutional rules to:

Prohibit the highly political practice of designing districts to favor an incumbent or a political party;

Require that the districts be as compact as possible. Where it makes sense, they will have to follow existing city, county or geographical boundaries; and

Make it impossible for legislators to draw districts to diminish the ability of minority voters to elect representatives.

Under our current system, elections are essentially rigged before the ballots are even printed. Districts are assigned to a particular party, and voters who will be favorable to that party are allocated accordingly. Or even worse, districts are designed to favor a particular incumbent. When this happens, the citizens lose.

Florida has fewer competitive legislative elections than almost any state in the union. Every two years 140 legislative seats are up for election. In the last ten years, only 10 incumbent representatives and only one incumbent senator have been defeated. And seats almost never change hands from one party to another. The one exception was in 2008. This lack of turnover is due to the way the districts are drawn.

Moreover, districts in Florida look like a crazy quilt of lines. Some meander from coast to coast. An example is state Senate District 27, which starts in Boynton Beach and travels more than 100 miles to Ft. Myers. Others, like state House District 29, snake through the state for hundreds of miles. That district contains areas that have nothing in common, like orange groves, cattle ranches, nature preserves, a manufactured-home retirement community, subdivisions and Kennedy Space Center suburbs in multiple cities and counties.

Meanwhile, small towns and counties are divided into multiple districts. The city of Winter Park, population just under 30,000, has four different members of Congress representing slivers of the community. Throughout the state, neighbors on the same street often vote for representatives from different districts. Most people do not even know who their representatives are—and it is impossible for the representatives to know their constituents when the districts are drawn so that they make no sense.

All of this happens as a result of the district line drawing done by those in office for the sole purpose of preserving political power. Florida's legislators are choosing their voters instead of voters choosing their representatives. And when this happens, the voters don't have a real choice. But, now with Amendments 5 and 6, voters have a chance to tell the legislators that they are ready for a change!

It is not surprising that the two amendments have the support of groups like the League of Women Voters, the Florida League of Cities, Florida League of Mayors, Legislative Black Caucus, Florida NAACP, Florida Black Caucus of Local Elected Officials, and Democracia Ahora. Newspaper editorial boards across the state unanimously support these important changes. That is because, as this newspaper elegantly said, "The amendments make sense."

Thousands of Floridians—Republicans, Democrats and Independents—are working for passage of these FairDistricts amendments 5 and 6.

So are we.

And we hope you will too. After all, as Mayor Bloomberg said, "We're all in this together." Please visit http://www.FairDistrictsFlorida.org to learn more and sign up to help.

---

Bob Milligan is a Republican who served as Florida's comptroller general.

## Getting to the Bottom of It

Bob Graham

Miami Herald, September 19, 2010

The mortgage market meltdown has left millions of people in this country financially devastated and has thrown the country into an economic slide unseen since the Great Depression.

Look no further than the latest unemployment estimates (9.6 percent nationally, 11.6 percent in Florida).

The meltdown was facilitated by looser lending standards on the front end, such as no requirement of verification of income, as well as on the back end, with innovative financial instruments, such as collateralized debt obligations, that were sold to investors around the world. From 2003 to 2006 the volume of higher-risk mortgages made to borrowers more than doubled.

The housing bubble was aided by predatory and fraudulent activity—be it subtle inducement for the borrower to lie about his or her salary (according to the Federal National Mortgage Association, more people misrepresented incomes or ability to repay in Florida than in any other state) or the outright manipulation of appraisal values to overstate the value of the home being purchased or refinanced. Between 2007 and 2008, reported incidents of mortgage fraud in the state of Florida more than doubled.

We have felt the effects. The sharp decline of property values in Florida has hurt families, neighborhoods and local government budgets, and Florida remains one of the hardest-hit states in the country when it comes to delinquent mortgage payments.

What people in Florida want to know now is how the crisis developed, and more important, how they're going to recover their lost homes, jobs or savings.

The Financial Crisis Inquiry Commission, of which I am one member of 10, is coming to Miami on Tuesday to examine the effect of the mortgage crisis on the state of Florida. Congress created the Commission last year to take an in-depth look at the factors that caused or contributed to the near-collapse of our financial and economic systems. The Commission serves as an agent for the American people to provide an unvarnished account of what happened.

Thus far, the Commission has held more than a dozen days of hearings with witnesses under oath, conducted hundreds of interviews and collected millions of documents—many of which had never been made public.

Our public hearings have focused on topics such as housing, derivatives, excess risk and whether anything is truly "too big to fail." We have heard from senior executives at major financial institutions about how practices at their organizations contributed to the crisis. We have heard from government bodies including the U.S. Treasury, the Federal Reserve, the Department of Justice, the Securities and Exchange Commission and the Office of the Comptroller of the Currency about how those institutions could have helped prevent the crisis.

The Commission's hearing on Tuesday at Florida International University's Modesto A. Maidique Campus will focus on mortgage fraud and predatory lending. It will be an opportunity for us to hear from experts in fraudulent and predatory lending, from people working on awareness and prevention of such practices, from fellow citizens who suffered from fraudulent practices, and from law-enforcement officials responsible for protecting consumers.

Florida is one of three states—along with California and Nevada—that the Commission is visiting to hear from people on the ground.

Our final report is due to the Congress, President Obama, and most important, the American people on Dec. 15. The Commission's work is important and can have lasting effects on the future of our financial system. But first, we must understand what happened before real reform can take place.

On Tuesday we hope to deepen the Commission's understanding and that of the general public. You are invited to join us. Details on the hearing can be found at www.FCIC.gov.

## Florida–the Sad State of Our State

**The Legislature has a responsibility to Floridians not to turn back decades of progressivism that made the Sunshine State a home, not a commodity**

Bob Graham

*St. Petersburg Times*, April 1, 2011

As the Legislature enters its second half, there has emerged a disturbing pattern of ignoring many of Florida's core values. Over the last half-century these values have given Florida government—whether in Republican or Democratic hand—a stability and predictability that is now threatened.

What are some of those at-risk values?

Florida is a treasure which we have the privilege of enjoying with the responsibility to preserve and enhance that treasure for future generations.

For most of Florida's history, up until the mid 1960s, our state was treated like a commodity. If you didn't like it you changed it: land into water; water into land. The business of the state was business, and our enormous natural resources were just another input. The quality and safety of our coasts, fresh waters, open lands and the Everglades were regularly and enthusiastically sacrificed on the altar of growth.

Riding over the horizon were two merging armies. Emerging Democratic leaders, such as Reubin Askew of Pensacola and Lawton Chiles of Lakeland, who were in the vanguard of the recently reapportioned Legislature, joined forces with young Republicans like Nathaniel Reed of Hobe Sound and Warren Henderson of Sarasota, who were appalled at the change they had seen in their newly adopted state.

These armies had a common mission: to reverse the damage commoditization had done to Florida and replace it with a culture of conservation and intergenerational responsibility.

The markers of success of the united armies of Florida are many.

Florida has one of America's most esteemed state park systems. Our state has seen dramatic improvements in air and water quality. The Florida Everglades are now the American Everglades with Congress agreeing to partner with the state to preserve this unique treasure for our grandchildren's grandchildren and beyond—a public-private partnership for quality development rather than lowest common denominator.

In the next month all of this will be threatened. The Florida Forever Act and its predecessor land-acquisition programs, which have saved almost 9.4 million acres of our most environmentally sensitive lands for the public is, after 44 years, being zeroed out of the budget. The proposed cuts to Everglades restoration are so deep it is doubtful the crucial goal of salvaging this world treasure and protecting the water supply for more than 6 million Floridians will be realized. If Florida walks out on Everglades restoration, Congress won't be far behind. Comprehensive planning for future land and water use, which has elevated growth to a new standard of quality, is under all-out assault.

Florida is a dynamic state which requires vision to assure that future opportunities and needs are anticipated and met.

Since World War II that vision has largely been focused on understanding and responding to Florida's incredible growth.

Florida was the least affected of America's large population states by the Industrial Revolution. Our economy today—service, agriculture, tourism—is not much different than it was a century ago. What has substituted for traditional industry and has served as the fourth leg of our economic stool has been growth. Since the 1960s Florida has grown consistently by 3 million new residents each decade. It almost did so in the first decade of this new century but stagnant growth in the last years of that decade held it below the historic standard.

This is not a blip or statistical anomaly. There are several factors that have converged to slow growth, but three should particularly concern us. The current economic recession has shaken many Americans nearing retirement as to whether their defined contribution pension will support a move to Florida. Talk of major changes to Social Security and Medicare heightens that anxiety. Other states, especially in the Southeast, have emerged as stiff competitors for the attention of families at or near retirement. Fewer young families are choosing Florida as their home.

Now, new vision is required to prepare Florida for an era in which, yes, there will be growth, but it will be likely be at a reduced rate and reduced capacity to carry our economy.

So what do we do about it? Get serious about attracting the technology industries which are shaping and will shape the world's future. This will require a dual strategy: a renewed commitment to the protection of our competitive edge—Florida's environment—and building a world-class preschool through graduate school education system. The states which have benefited most by technology industries—such as North Carolina and Virginia—have done so not by selling themselves as the cheapest places to do business but rather as states that have built the infrastructure and the educational institutions which will most help businesses achieve sustained profitability.

In addition to a potential return to the Florida as a commodity policy of the early 20th century, this Legislature is on course to erase decades of investment and progress in education. Hopefully the Legislature will reject a proposal of a 10 percent per student cut in primary and secondary schools. Less likely is a change in the downward trajectory of support for higher education. Since 1990, in inflation-adjusted dollars, per student funding of the state university system from general revenue has dropped by about $4,000. These savage cuts to education expose a lack of vision for Florida's future.

Florida aspires to fundamental fairness for all its citizens.

Traditionally Florida's tax system was based on three principles: adequacy: sufficient revenue to support education and other services to the people; resilience: a stable revenue stream matched to needs so that the effects of business cycles are mitigated; and fairness: Floridians pay taxes according to their ability to do so.

These principles have been mangled by changes in the last decade, most of which were advanced as necessary for economic growth.

Since 1999 there has been a stream of tax reductions to make the state more attractive for investment. Absent these cuts, state revenue in 2011 would be $4 billion greater. This would have avoided the need for the deep cuts now being considered by the Legislature.

The stunning truth is that on virtually all fronts—the Legislature, the executive budget office, academics—there has been a failure to subject these cuts to the basic question: Did they work?

Without specific analysis we are left to answer that question based on data reflecting the impact these cuts had on jobs: How many jobs have been created and what did they contribute to the quality of life of working families?

The increase in jobs from 2000 to 2010, after the economic development stimulating tax cuts began taking effect, was 606,798. This increase was substantially less the in the two decades prior to the tax cuts: 1980–1990: 1,998,833; 1990–2000: 1,530,936.

Those statistics describe the quantity of jobs created before and after the tax cuts. In terms of take-home pay, what was the quality of those jobs? Florida first achieved a long-sought goal of exceeding the national average of per capita income in 1983 when Floridians earned 100.3 percent of the national average. State workers reached a peak in per capita income in 1987 at 101.7. By 2010 that relationship reversed and Floridians earned only 96.8 percent of the national average.

After 12 years of tax cuts, there is no evidence in these numbers that the cuts have achieved their purpose of accelerating quality jobs.

If that is the case, what have we done? All of the tax cuts, particularly the total repeal of the tax on stocks and bonds, primarily benefited the upper 5 percent of Floridians, thus contributing to the enormous disparity in wealth in the United States: The top 5 percent of Americans claim 63.5 percent of the nation's wealth, while the lowest 80 percent get only 12.8 percent. In more recent years, Florida politicians have regressively shifted the cost of state services from the richest Floridians to those working hardest just to make ends meet. If the Legislature remains committed to adequacy, resilience and fairness as the foundation of our tax system, serious reconsideration should be given to these tax cuts and the harm they have done.

As a lifelong Florida Democrat, I consider myself to be a conservative man in my personal conduct and political philosophy. I believe in respecting traditions which have proven themselves in the real life of our state. I hope this Legislature will pause, reassess the consequences of its decisions on the future of Florida, reject extremist ideologies, and recommit to Florida's heritage of commonsense values.

## An Ill-Advised Toss of the Dice

Bob Graham

*St. Petersburg Times*, December 29, 2011

Yogi Berra said "if you come to a fork in the road, take it."

There are those who feel we can follow Yogi's advice on the casinos proposal for Florida. We can have casinos and expand our economy beyond its traditional bases. But in my judgment, if we accept this siren call we are not taking the fork in the road; we will be selecting a path that will foreclose the far wiser one we have pursued for the past half-century.

A quick economic history of Florida:

In the 1880s Florida declined to participate in the Industrial Revolution, directly leading to an economy today that rests on a three-legged stool of agriculture, tourism and services.

Since 1960, those services have met the needs of the 3 million new Floridians who moved to the state each decade. Transformations including mosquito control, air conditioning, Social Security and other defined benefit retirement systems, the commercial jet airplane and Fidel Castro stimulated this growth.

During this period there was a growing recognition that Florida needed to add a fourth leg to its economy—ideally a high-tech, knowledge-based industry. The effort began paying off in the 1970s and 1980s, fueled by developments such as the Cape Kennedy space program; pharmaceuticals and electronics in South Florida; and military industries in Central and North Florida.

Florida had been one of the poorest states in the South. It was a signal achievement when in the 1980s, for the first time, Floridians exceeded the national average in per capita income, not once but in five years of the decade. Jobs increased annually more than 210,000.

Economic growth declined slightly during the 1990s and hit the wall in the middle of the last decade: From 2005 to 2010 the state lost almost 220,000 jobs. By the end of the decade, per capital income was 95.7 percent of the national average, about what it had been 35 years earlier.

I cite those statistics to illustrate that in 25 of the last 30 years the state had robust economic expansion. We should not be seduced into embracing casino gambling with its long-term economic and social consequences based on a five-year out-of-the-norm economic slump.

This is not a decision just for two South Florida counties. When parimutuel gambling was authorized in the midst of the Great Depression, it, too, was to be confined to a corner of the state. Today there are parimutuel facilities in every section of Florida. Already leaders in Lee, Duval, Orange and Pinellas counties are asserting that to be a competitive tourist destination, they must have casinos.

Let me ask a few questions:

Has anyone seen a substantial high-tech industry in Biloxi, Miss.; Atlantic City, N.J.; or Las Vegas? Would you like to be the CEO of a high-tech startup attempting to convince your board of directors that the place to locate was Las Vegas? The answer to all these questions is no.

Why is fairly obvious: Knowledge-based industry is attracted to places that offer a high quality of life for families, superior education, an ample workforce with a strong work ethic, and access to capital with a high risk tolerance. The ethic of high tech is incompatible. With the "high roller success by chance" culture of a community that has bet its future on casinos. Like oil and water, they don't mix.

Our success in the 1970s and '80s shows it is realistic for Florida to aspire to diversify its economy through knowledge-based enterprises. But aspiration will not become reality just because casinos are rejected. Their rejection is necessary but not sufficient to achieve that goal.

What else is required? Florida can learn a lesson from one of its own: Jeff Bezos.

Bezos is the stepson of Miguel Bezos, a Cuban-American who came to the United States as an adolescent. While Jeff was a young teenager the family moved to Florida. He graduated from Miami Palmetto Senior High School in 1982, the same year in which he received a Silver Knight award for academic excellence. Four years later, Jeff graduated from Princeton with honors in electrical engineering. After about five years on Wall Street he decided to strike out on his own. In 1994 after surveying the country, Jeff Bezos decided to locate his startup in Seattle.

Thus, Amazon was born.

Why didn't Bezos come home to Florida to start his knowledge-based company, which in 2010 employed 33,700 people? And almost 18 years later, what could we learn from him? Some of the reasons he settled in Seattle answer the question:

A high quality of life. But doesn't Florida have that also? Yes, but. The 2011 Legislature rolled back 40 years of bipartisan commitment to protecting one of the most blessed patches on Earth. It vacated decades of smart environmental and growth management policies.

Education. In Seattle, Bezos found a well-trained workforce and institutions that would assure a consistent flow of talented people to meet expanding employment needs and would collaborate in research and development. How about Florida? In 2011, the Legislature accelerated a declining commitment to education, spending almost 10 percent less per student in public schools and transferring even more of the cost of higher education to students and their families.

Available capital that encourages and fuels entrepreneurship. Most venture capitalists invest in firms within driving distance of their home to keep an eye on their investments. There is a symbiotic relationship between entrepreneurs and those with the risk capital to make them successful. The qualities which attract the latter, lure the former.

It doesn't seem we have learned much from Jeff Bezos.

When the destructive casino proposal is behind us, these are the topics that should be the subject for serious thought and action. Gov. Rick Scott has indicated a willingness to reverse the damage which was done to Florida's capacity to protect its environment and he has proposed a billion more dollars for the elementary-secondary school budget. He should add to those initiatives by convening Floridians to consider and recommend steps to achieve enhanced opportunity and prosperity for our people through knowledge industries.

And just maybe that next Jeff Bezos studying in a Florida school today will come home.

## Voting Rights Are Hindered in Florida

Bob Graham

*South Florida Sun-Sentinel*, January 29, 2012

This month the Florida Joint Center for Citizenship released its civic-health index for 2011. The report is based on a nationwide study by the National Commission on Citizenship. It was not a pretty picture for Florida.

In the 2010 report, Florida ranked 46th in its civic-health index based on factors such as registration and voting, volunteerism and working with neighbors to solve a community problem.

The 2011 report card focused on the Millennials, Floridians aged 18 to 29, and comments, "The extent to which these young men and women organize, volunteer, vote and petition their representatives ultimately will determine how well Florida is governed." Some of the highs or lows of the report:

21 percent of Florida Millennials voted in 2010—34th among Millennials in all 50 states.

18 percent volunteered for any group—44th.

2 percent attended any public meeting—46th.

2 percent worked with neighbors to fix a problem—44th.

While by no means the only gauge of a state's civic health, voting is the most fundamental and visible.

Florida, became a national laughingstock after the gaffes in 2000, resulting in the most contentious presidential election in modern history. Former Gov. Jeb Bush led the effort to reform Florida's system. In 2004 he described the progress: Early voting "was another reform we added that has helped provide access to the polls and provide a convenience. And we're going to have a high voter turnout here, and I think that's wonderful."

Gov. Bush was right. In 2000, 55.9 percent of eligible Floridians voted. In 2004, the turnout was 64.9 percent. A citizen might conclude Florida was on its way to a rejuvenation of its civic health.

That's not what happened. In spite of the dismal 46th place among the states in 2010, the Florida Legislature in 2011 took a giant step backward in laws governing registration and voting. Millennials were singled out for especially harsh treatment.

Voter registration was made more difficult: Organizations that have traditionally assisted Floridians in registering now must return registration forms within 48 hours of signature or face a fine of up to $1,000. The restrictions on volunteer registration efforts are much more onerous than under previous law. Among others, this has caused the Florida League of Women Voters to suspend its 72 years of nonpartisan registration drives.

Same-day address change was restricted: By long-standing tradition, Floridians who had moved within the state were allowed to update their addresses at the polling station on Election Day and cast a regular ballot. To facilitate this process, Florida has spent millions of dollars on a central voter database. The new law requires those who have moved from county to county and need to update their addresses to cast ballots provisionally.

Early voting was shortened. In 2011, the Legislature reduced the number of days of early voting from 14 to eight. The Sunday before Election Day, which in much of Florida was the early voting day on which the largest number of African-Americans voted in 2008, was eliminated.

An opportunity for increasing access was missed when the Legislature rejected the proposal of county supervisors of elections to allow a wider range of choice in locating early-voting sites.

And why did the Legislature do so? To avoid fraud in the election system. But as state Sen. Mike Fasano, R-New Port Richey, said, "No one could give me an example of all this fraud they speak about."

What is especially sad about this retreat is it turned the clock back to the 1930s. Similar Jim Crow laws were used to restrict voting of African-Americans and poor whites. The poll tax, which required voters to pay a tax for the right to vote, was the most pernicious. In 1937, as a freshman state senator, my father sponsored legislation that repealed the poll tax in Florida.

Another Floridian, U.S. Sen. Spessard Holland, made repeal of the poll tax in federal elections a lifetime crusade. In 1964, he was rewarded with adoption of the 24th amendment to the Constitution which did so.

We should hope the 2012 Legislature would honor that proud legacy and turn its back on a 21st-century version of the poll tax in Florida by repealing the voter-suppression laws enacted last spring.

## Rigging the Game

David Colburn

*Gainesville Sun*, May 13, 2012

The battle over redistricting legislative seats in Florida has once again resolved itself in a way that limits the voice of many Floridians.

Republicans have drawn House and Senate districts with the goal of maintaining their super majorities in both houses and appear to have been successful in doing so.

The new districts are much better than the old ones and certainly more compact. Moreover, according to the State Supreme Court, they meet the FAIR constitutional amendment standards.

But that does not mean they reflect the will of all the people. Indeed it is curious that, in a state roughly split between Democrats and Republicans, both houses appear likely to retain GOP super majorities.

So how has this come to be?

District lines are drawn by the party in power, and in Florida that means the process falls to Republicans. Most experts acknowledge that the party in power today has an enormous advantage in drawing these districts, because computer models allow the dominant party to draw lines that will secure their political advantage.

Democrats had hope to have a greater say in drawing the districts so that they could rebuild the party's standing at the state level and ensure a full voice for its constituents. As it now stands, the party has a significant plurality of registered voters, but it needed a district plan that makes it possible for them to be competitive in these legislative contests.

That did not happen as Republicans isolated black voters, perhaps the most important and certainly the most loyal Democratic constituency, into largely black districts. With most black voters excluded from the remaining districts, Republicans have been able to carve out a voting majority in them.

Such political machinations over districting are nothing new for Florida. Since World War II, efforts to control this process and thus the Legislature have been standard fare following every census. This was no less true in 1952 than it is in 2012.

Sixty years ago, the districting process was equally intense even though

Democrats held all but one seat in the state Legislature. The conflict then took place between rural North Florida and rapidly growing urban South Florida over which region would set legislative policy and thus direction of the state.

Following World War II, Florida's population increased substantially, with more than 2 million new residents entering the state between 1945 and 1955. Much of that growth occurred in Southeast Florida. Rural Democrats, fearful that northeasterners who settled in Southeast Florida had a different vision for the state, balked at redistricting the Legislature to reflect the growth of that region.

Their fears were not ill-considered. In the 1948 presidential election, Florida voters helped elect Harry Truman president, when South Florida residents overwhelming voted for him. By contrast, rural voters in Florida cast their ballots for Strom Thurmond, the candidate of the States' Rights Democratic Party, because of his commitment to segregation and state rights.

In the aftermath of the 1948 election, rural legislatures stonewalled reapportionment in Florida at every turn. By 1955, only 8 percent of Florida's voting population elected a majority of state representatives, and 17.1 percent elected a majority of state senators.

This skewed representation ensured a legislative majority in both houses that opposed the U.S. Supreme Court's school desegregation decision in Brown v. Board of Education of Topeka in 1954 and threatened Florida's future by pursuing extremist racial policies for the rest of the decade. Only the veto of Gov. LeRoy Collins prevented Florida from creating a private school system to avoid desegregation and jailing teachers who taught desegregated classes.

For the next 13 years, rural legislators blocked passage of reapportionment, despite the continued growth of urban, South Florida. Finally in 1967, in Swann v. Adams, the U.S. Supreme Court ordered the reapportionment of Florida to reflect "one man, one vote." Within months a new Legislature was formed that oversaw the modernization of state government, the abandonment of segregation and the rise of the Republican Party.

Today's political battle over reapportionment pales next to that of the 1950s and 1960s. But efforts to draw district lines to ensure the dominance of one political party and one political philosophy at the expense of the other is equally misplaced.

Even when districts meet new, tougher state constitutional muster, they remain suspect when they freeze out one party and, by extension, nearly half the voting populace. This is no less true today than it was in the 1950s.

## Florida Fiasco, Part 2

Bob Graham

*Tampa Bay Times*, August 28, 2012

Only 12 years ago, Florida was embarrassed by a voting tornado. As the nation became familiar with hanging chads and butterfly ballots, Florida was the State That Couldn't Vote Straight.

Fellow Floridians, we have a similar humiliation headed for us now. Different from a tornado—which appears almost without warning—this menacing hurricane has been lumbering toward us for over a year. Here's its track to date.

In 2011 the Legislature passed and the governor signed the most sweeping changes in Florida's election laws in decades. The alleged rationale was the prevention of voter fraud, although no or only trivial instances of irregularities could be identified. The lingering suspicion was that the real reason was suppression of voting by specific groups of Floridians.

Of all the changes, the most inexplicable were those to the early voting process. This post-2000 reform was heralded by Gov. Jeb Bush as contributing to increased voter participation. There was not the tiniest evidence of inappropriate use.

In spite of this, the days for early voting were reduced from a maximum of 14 to eight. The Sunday before Tuesday's Election Day was eliminated as an early voting date. The 67 county supervisors of elections were given the discretion to set the total number of early voting hours at between 48 and 96.

As five of Florida's 67 counties are under the federal Voting Rights Act, approval by the U.S. Department of Justice or a federal appellate court is required for any change in election procedure in those five counties. At the request of the state, the appellate court for the District of Columbia was the venue for this review.

On Aug. 17 the court ruled: "Florida is left with nothing to rebut either the testimony of the defendants' witnesses or the commonsense judgment that a dramatic reduction in the form of voting that is disproportionately used by African-Americans would make it materially more difficult for some minority voters to cast a ballot." This conclusion was based in part on the finding that in 2008, African-Americans cast 22 percent of the total early vote, even though blacks are just 13 percent of Florida's registered voters.

The state was given a limited get-out-of-jail-free card. If the supervisors of election in the five Voting Rights Act counties would agree to use the 96 maximum hours, the state could petition the court to be allowed to reduce the number of early voting days to eight.

Gov. Rick Scott immediately contacted the supervisors urging them to do so. Four have agreed. But not Republican Harry Sawyer of Monroe County, the Florida Keys.

The governor cajoled Sawyer to fall into line. Sawyer refused based on his knowledge that the voters in his community were working people, at home for dinner, not likely to use the hours late into the night. According to Sawyer, more early voting days is what would encourage more voting in Monroe County: "We're supposed to make it easy for voters, not hard."

Scott intimated he might remove Sawyer from his post of 24 years. Sawyer stood his ground; he would abide by the federal court's opinion.

The governor, probably inadvertently, took on the wrong man from the wrong place. Scott might not have been aware that 30 years ago in a dispute with the federal government over border patrol, Monroe County seceded from the union and raised the flag of the Conch Republic. For several joyous weeks the citizens of the world's newest republic tweaked their former masters in Washington, requiring visas for officials to enter its territory (visas which were routinely denied) and preparing to send its minister of foreign affairs to Buenos Aires to settle the Falklands/Malvinas war through shuttle diplomacy. All of this was to the beat of Jimmy Buffett songs and a not-inconsiderable number of margaritas.

Governor, this is not a bunch that is going to lie down and surrender.

While this latest rebellion is going on in Florida's southernmost county, the supervisors of election in the other 62 counties are deciding how many hours of voting to authorize. This means Florida is likely to have numerous forms of early voting and almost as many potential outcomes.

This unequal treatment will also be a gold mine for statisticians, political scientists and lawyers. The result from these different systems will be scrutinized, analyzed and subjected to regression analysis to reach an empirical determination as to whether the federal appellate court was right when it concluded the reduction of early voting days "would make it materially more difficult for some minority voters to cast a ballot."

A central issue in Bush vs. Gore, which declared George W. Bush president of the United States, was whether the equal protection of the laws was violated by the variation among Florida counties' election and recount procedures. It took the better part of six weeks the settle the 2000 elections. If this year's election in Florida is as close as it appears it will be, unfold your favorite lounge chair. It's going to be a long time before this one is settled.

The governor deserves congratulations for the manner in which he managed the preparation for Hurricane Isaac. He has the time and legal authority to avoid the next hurricane before it slams into Florida on Nov. 6.

## Bring Back Florida's Second Primary

**Bob Graham and George LeMieux**

*Tampa Bay Times*, March 27, 2013

Good government in Florida has become prisoner to several self-inflicted electoral wounds. The cumulative effect is a less representative democracy with too many elected officials holding narrow views and the belief that to compromise is to surrender core values. Think of the debacle of the federal government's sequester.

One self-inflicted wound, which passed with inadequate attention, is the elimination of the second primary in the selection of party candidates. From 1899 to 2001, if no party primary candidate received a majority in the first election, there was a second primary between the two top vote-getters. In 2001 and 2003, the second primary was suspended for the following year's primary elections and permanently repealed in 2005. Cancelling the second primary has resulted in candidates with high name recognition or a strong appeal to a narrow constituency becoming a party nominee with a small fraction of the first and now only primary voters.

Florida's second primary system produced some of our state's most notable and respected public servants. If not for the second primary, LeRoy Collins and Reubin Askew may never have been governor, Lawton Chiles a U.S. senator, or Bob Butterworth an attorney general. They were all the runners up in the first primary but prevailed in the second. Indeed, Florida's 1978 gubernatorial race was won by a co-author of this article, who placed second in the first primary.

This is the way representative democracy should work. People choose from a field of many in an elimination round. Then, the top two vote-getters face off in the nominating round where a majority vote is required for the best candidate to move on to the final November contest. Think of it as the playoffs. In college basketball there's a season to determine the top-tier teams, then elimination rounds culminating with a final contest, the championship. But the way Florida's elections are currently constructed, there's a season and a championship but no playoffs, and zero guarantee the two contestants facing off in November represent the broadest consensus of approval within their own party.

Reinstating Florida's second primary is not difficult, and by using existing technology neither cost nor burden should become an eliminating factor. To ensure our elected leaders actually reflect our values, we simply must follow an extended timeline for holding elections, just like Alabama, Georgia, Louisiana, Mississippi and a number of other states. The Legislature could easily set the first primary, for example, in early June and the second for early September. This schedule would provide more than ample time for the electorate to process their choices.

Our view is the second primary process engages more of the electorate, makes our political parties more relevant, promotes more representative candidates, and honors majority rule, a core principle of representative democracy. It achieves these qualities by giving people more opportunity to review and evaluate candidates, and choose among those who they think will best reflect their sentiments in local government, Tallahassee or Washington.

It is no secret lawmakers from both parties have hobbled the federal government with entrenched and extreme views. Instead of leading the world as its superpower, we limp from crisis to crisis, pushing off permanent solutions in favor of temporary fixes in part because the single primary process has produced elected representatives to whom the words tolerance or reasoned compromise are an anathema.

Making candidates win a true majority will help solve this problem. It dramatically reduces the chances of fringe, unvetted and unqualified candidates sneaking by their party's electorate. Most important, it produces policymakers with views that more accurately represent the majority of people who propel them to victory. A broken election system contributes to a broken government. It's time to begin fixing things. A return of the second primary would be a good place to start.

---

George LeMieux is a former US Senator and former chief of staff to Florida Governor Charlie Crist.

# 4

# The State, Region, and Nation

Issues that affect ordinary Floridians on a daily basis are not limited to the state itself. The interconnectedness of state, region, and nation provides the basis for the op-ed pieces in this section. They speak to concerns about the efficacy of government and the relationship of individuals to the broader world around them. The articles address the complexities and complications of modern life and how they relate to more personal matters. They also tie into many of the themes associated with the 2020 presidential election. By addressing the very meaning of citizenship and the reciprocal relationship between citizens and all levels of government, these articles examine the current status of Florida and what can be done to improve it. In recent years it has become fashionable to opine that government at all levels is broken, maybe irrevocably, and little can be done to fix it. While Graham and Colburn do not deny that governments have difficulties, the essays in this section often focus on solutions rather than problems. They talk about how ordinary people and seemingly hidebound institutions can work together to change society for the better. Yet, as the 21st century progressed, they had to grapple more and more with the distrust and cynicism of the Tea Party movement, which saw government at all levels (but particularly the federal one) as the enemy. Both Colburn and Graham viewed the 2016 election and the ensuing Trump presidency as watershed moments in American history. In 2016, David Colburn wrote, "Americans may not agree about much politically these days, but most would agree that they have never seen an election quite like this one in their lifetimes." However, I'm sure David would have agreed that, in light of the 2020 election, the previous statement could stand significant revision. Two years after Colburn penned that, Bob Graham also expressed concern about the fragile state of our democratic process. "We are at an inflection point," he wrote, "in which the foundational principles of our democracy and our national security interests are at stake." The pieces in this section point out how vital citizen input and involvement are to our democratic process. They also show how significant Florida has become to the American political process itself. By examining the increasingly important connections between Florida citizens and government at all levels, they provide insight into both our past problems and our future possibilities.

## Government Inept?

**Incorrect assumption governs debate**

David Colburn

*Orlando Sentinel*, October 9, 1995

Can the government do anything right these days? Few people seem to think so.

After 60 years during which the American people looked to the federal government for everything from military defense to public health to the arts, voters have finally said, "Enough."

Today's national mood promises to dismantle the massive bureaucracy that was established at the time of the New Deal and expanded under the Great Society of the 1960s. It also raises important questions about the very nature of government in American society.

The irony about the present debate is that 60 years ago the public was convinced that the private sector was responsible for all the ills of society, including the Great Depression.

Today it is government itself that is the perceived villain.

Both then and now, rhetoric rather than reason have [*sic*] forged the national discussion.

Indeed, the problem with the present debate is that there really isn't one. It starts with the incorrect assumption that government is essentially inept and ends up offering uncritical praise for privatization and the decentralization of government programs.

Many voters are decidedly uncomfortable with congressional efforts to dismantle the federal government, and rightly so.

They remain committed to government leadership in several areas of society. Few, for example, are willing to close down such agencies as the National Park Service or the Environmental Protection Agency, and fewer still favor substantial downsizing for the Centers for Disease Control, the Department of Defense, or the Federal Reserve.

Rhetoric rather than reason forges the national discussion.

Political leaders on both sides of the fence have distorted the national discussion about the role of the federal government by alleging that state governments are closer to the people and, therefore, better able to respond to their needs than are the distant Washington bureaucrats.

Some of this may well be true. It is quite clear, for example, that the federal government has interceded in areas that were better left alone. But state governments as well have not shown themselves historically to be any more efficient or responsive than federal bureaucrats.

Moreover, lurking within this decentralization argument is the belief by advocates that this will ensure the downsizing of government for three reasons.

In the first place, the states are not going to get enough federal dollars to manage these programs effectively and will be forced to choose among them.

Secondly, most states lack the bureaucracies to handle such programs, and thus they will be abandoned because they cannot be managed effectively.

And finally, lobbying organizations for these various programs lack the resources and staff to maintain public enthusiasm for them in all 50 states.

If this is the aim, then the public ought to understand it, and it should be part of this national discussion.

Clearly government needs to be reformed, but American society still depends on it to resolve the competing needs of the private sector with the well-being of its citizens, which are not always one and the same. What sort of balance should exist between government and the private sector is the question.

A debate that begins with the false premise that government programs have repeatedly failed the American people and, therefore, ought to be privatized or decentralized distorts the history of this country and ill-serves all of us in this important and much-needed discussion.

## Florida—In but Not Of the South

David Colburn

*Gainesville Sun*, July 26, 1997

"We're a southern state and damn proud of it," a resident of Taylor County commented in 1993, as he sat in his pickup truck.

But 300 miles to the south, a resident of Dade County looked thoroughly bewildered when asked what it meant to be a Southerner.

For much of its history, Florida has been two states.

One extends south from the Georgia border to Ocala. It has identified with the South and its social, political and racial traditions.

The other extends north from Key West and Miami, with a heritage that has little connection to the South. It has historically had a diverse and ethnic and racial population, and has viewed the state as part of a national and international economy.

To understand Florida's political and constitutional development in the 20th century, one has to be aware of this division and the way its citizens and political leaders have responded to it.

The Deep South association of Floridians grew out of the large migrations of people from Alabama, Georgia and South Carolina in the early 19th century.

These Southerners developed economic activities, including the plantation system and timber and turpentine industries, that reinforced social and political ties with their southern neighbors.

As the nation moved closer to a bloody division in 1861, there was little doubt where the loyalties of Floridians stood. By joining the Confederacy, Florida was forced to share the costs of the conflict and the burden of military Reconstruction.

It was a painful period for Floridians and they remained isolated from the national mainstream and mired in rural poverty for much of the late 19th and early 20th centuries as a result of this decision.

### Limiting leadership

The state Constitution of 1885 grew out of the political and racial developments of the Civil War and Reconstruction.

Consequently, it offered a decidedly conservative approach to government.

The delegates to the state constitutional convention took deliberate aim at the powers that had been granted to the governor in the 1868 Constitution and which enabled him to assume a prominent role during military Reconstruction.

The 1885 Constitution provided that members of the state Cabinet were to be elected independently of the governor and would be eligible for re-election.

That constitution and the cabinet system dominated state politics for the next 80 years. Governors in the late 19th century found that the restrictions of the constitution and the public's general animosity toward executive leadership gave them little opportunity to assert their leadership.

Throughout this period and well into the 20th century, Florida was a frontier state. Entire areas were literally uninhabited and many others had but a few families.

### The new South

When the promise of "the New South" appeared at the turn of the 20th century, Floridians eagerly embraced this reform movement, hoping it would mean economic growth and development.

They temporarily suspended divorce laws to keep Henry Flagler happy and doled land out to Hamilton Disston and others.

The New South bypassed Florida, but the land and tourist boom of the 1920s offered tangible promise. Cities and counties threw caution to the wind as each tried to wrest the golden goose from West Palm Beach and Miami.

Most ended up deeply in debt or bankrupt, constructing road and tourist facilities in the belief that if you build them they would come.

They did not, and by 1926, Florida was in depression where it would remain mired for 15 long years.

### War brings change

The state's rebirth commenced in the 1940s with massive federal expenditures and the migration of more than 2 million men and women into the state for military training.

Air-conditioning and effective mosquito control during this period made the state even more appealing to new arrivals and awakened some to the state's enormous economic potential.

And with new roads, Florida became accessible to the middle class as well as the wealthy.

The war gave the state a much-needed economic stimulus and its leaders moved quickly to capitalize on the changes taking place.

Gov. Millard Caldwell (1945–1949) dramatically expanded the activities of the Florida Department of Commerce to attract new business and visitors to the state.

Florida's sales pitch to prospective businesses and residents was essentially the same throughout the period from 1945 to 1980: Low taxes, a healthy environment, cheap land and a pro-business political climate.

With better roads and better automobiles, snowbirds from as far north as Canada came in search of the fountain of youth and warmth.

While Florida and its state political leaders basked in the post-war boom of its economy, they kept a wary eye on racial developments.

## Segregation ends

Business leaders and residents came predominantly from the Northeast and Midwest and had no intention of having their interests jeopardized by a commitment to a long-dead southern past.

All this worked against the efforts of the rural, North Florida-dominated Legislature to preserve segregation. Racial and social traditions were steadily eroded by policies that emphasized economic development and population growth.

In 1964, Washington removed the civil rights issues from state control by adopting the Civil Rights Act of 1964 and the Voting Rights Act of 1965. They abolished segregation voting restrictions based on race.

The Supreme Court also ordered the implementation of the principle of one person, one vote in Florida in 1967, and, with the stroke of a pen, dismantled opposition to reapportionment of the state Legislature.

## Forget the States—Let the Regions Pick the Candidates

Bob Graham

*New York Times*, August 8, 2007

Florida's governor, Charlie Crist, signed a law in May that moved the state's 2008 presidential primary to Jan. 29, one week after New Hampshire's. The idea behind this move was to put Florida in the national spotlight and force candidates to pay more attention to the state's issues.

As a Florida native who spent almost 40 years serving the state in Tallahassee and Washington, I have never been concerned that Florida—the largest swing state, with 27 electoral votes—would be ignored in 2008. But in front-loading the primary calendar, Florida and the other states that have moved their contests to Feb. 5 or earlier have unintentionally damaged the presidential election process.

In the 22 days from Jan. 14 to Feb. 5, voters in more than two dozen states—including California, Illinois and New York—will cast primary and caucus ballots. Their zeal to stand at the front of the line will poke irreparable holes in a political screen that has served Americans well: the living rooms of Iowa and New Hampshire.

As a presidential candidate four years ago, I stood in many of those living rooms and met highly knowledgeable voters who wanted to judge candidates up close and personal. They demanded substantive, well-reasoned answers to specific questions about issues from Iraq to health care to agriculture.

In these Iowa and New Hampshire living rooms, presidential contenders meet a substantial percentage of the people who vote in those states. Several times, voters in living room audiences told me that they would have to reserve judgment on my candidacy because they had met me "only once." I withdrew from the presidential race before the Iowa caucuses and New Hampshire primary and didn't have the opportunity to win their votes, but Iowans and Granite Staters won my deep respect for their diligence and seriousness.

Iowa and New Hampshire are not perfect, but they are more likely to eliminate flawed candidates than states where voters see only television commercials. In 1972, Ed Muskie, a former vice presidential candidate and Maine senator, was supposed to trounce his Democratic rivals in New Hampshire. But voters picked up on Muskie's tendency to wear his temper on his sleeve. He barely won a contest that should have been a cakewalk. His candidacy soon ended.

Twenty-four years later, Iowa caucus-goers killed the hopes of Sen. Phil Gramm of Texas, another early favorite. In the 1996 Republican contest, Gramm dazzled insiders and pundits with his money-raising prowess. After Iowans met the acerbic Gramm face-to-face, they voted him fifth in the caucuses. He dropped out of the race.

Although Iowa and New Hampshire will not lose all influence in 2008, Sioux City and Nashua may become little more than stopovers on the way to San Francisco and New York. The two candidates who win their parties' nominations will do so with less of the rigorous inspection performed in Iowa and New Hampshire living rooms.

In our new political environment, Iowa and New Hampshire are unlikely to reclaim the role they once played in screening our future presidents. Too many other states are eager to influence the process, too.

So if we can't recreate the past, what would be the next best screen? Some have wryly suggested a political version of "American Idol," with voters sizing up candidates from living rooms across the nation and eliminating one candidate per week until the party nominee is chosen. I think the better analogy is college football's Bowl Championship Series, which rotates the title game from year to year among the traditional bowl games.

A series of five regional primaries, spaced three weeks apart and rotated every four years, would give voters from Miami to Maui to Manchester opportunities to be first in the nation. Candidates could spend more time with citizens of neighboring states and less time on coast-to-coast flights. Because the primaries would be stretched out over three months rather than three weeks, reporters and other political scorekeepers could not rush to declare a national winner.

Regional primaries are not as intimate as living rooms in Cedar Rapids and Portsmouth. But they might accomplish what the 2008 primary season probably will not: a comprehensive and meticulous screening of the men and women who would be president.

## How to End the Gridlock

Bob Graham

*Washington Post*, January 30, 2008

For much of the past two decades, Americans have watched in frustration as presidents and members of Congress have repeatedly achieved deadlock rather than consensus on issues that are critical to our nation. The results of this partisan traffic jam are frightening. For example:

** Almost seven years after the Sept. 11 attacks, we still have huge gaps in national and homeland security. Our military is stretched thin, and our nation remains vulnerable to catastrophic terrorism.

** Almost 50 million Americans still have no health insurance, and the number of the uninsured rises every year.

** As evidenced by the bridge collapse in Minneapolis last August and the crumbling levees in New Orleans, we have recklessly neglected our infrastructure.

** Gas prices remain high, but we still have no real energy policy.

** Worst of all, we are betraying the fundamental American aspiration that future generations achieve more than those that came before. Seven of 10 Americans now believe that our children will be less well off than their parents.

Many factors have contributed to these ills, but the chief cause is the rampant partisanship that has paralyzed Washington. Early this month, I joined with former Sen. David Boren and 15 other experienced public officials from both parties to discuss prescriptions for overcoming the stalemate. Our primary focus was the presidential election. The next president will have a clean slate and the burst of enthusiasm that accompanies any new occupant of the White House. He or she has an opportunity—and an obligation—to attack the disease of partisan hostility and to set the tone during this election.

We suggested a few initial steps. Each presidential nominee should commit to appointing a truly bipartisan Cabinet that would include the most qualified people available, regardless of their party affiliation. Presidential candidates should be pressured to clearly describe how they would establish a government of national unity. Since results matter more than words, we would also press both major-party nominees to lay out specific strategies for reducing polarization and reaching bipartisan consensus on our agenda of national challenges.

The next president can't do it alone. If we are to break the cycle of partisan gridlock, others who have contributed to the disease must also help with the cure. To this end:

** Congress must restore and modernize the campaign finance reforms enacted after Watergate. Today, a presidential candidate accepts public financing at the risk of being discounted as weak and irrelevant.

** The media must insist that future presidential debates each focus on a single issue. Candidates can hide behind sound bites when a debate covers every and all subjects. But when candidates must spend a full 90 minutes discussing healthcare or national defense, voters will learn who is for real and who isn't.

** Political parties must fundamentally reform the dysfunctional presidential primary system. We need a better process in 2012—one that empowers all Americans. My preference would be four regional primaries, held at three- to four-week intervals from January to April.

** Our citizens must be educated to use their powers for effective participation in the political process. Democracy was never intended to be a spectator sport.

History tells us that bipartisanship is possible. In the 40 years after World War II, nine presidents—four Democrats and five Republicans—worked side by side with Congresses of both parties to contain the Soviet Union and strengthen the free world. We can resurrect that healthy condition, but it starts with cutting out the cancer of hostile partisanship. It's time to use the knife not to injure political opponents but to cure.

## Let's See You Top This, South Carolina

David Colburn

*Gainesville Sun*, July 11, 2010

In the past, whenever Florida ranked near the bottom of a national poll or one of our political leaders mortified us in front of the national media, we used to say sheepishly, "Thank God for Mississippi."

Those were the good old days when Mississippi was at the bottom of the barrel in most categories and its politicians were from Pluto.

Unfortunately, we can't use this slogan any longer because Mississippi now has political leaders who make sense, at least occasionally.

Ah, but what about South Carolina you ask? Can't we Floridians at least say, "Thank God for South Carolina?"

Jon Stewart calls South Carolina the "nation's whoppee [*sic*] cushion," and a Republican operative in the state refers to it "as the mudpit of Republican politics."

But can we Floridians really thump our chests and point to South Carolina as the real national embarrassment? Sure South Carolina might have U.S. Senate candidate Alvin Greene who stands accused of showing pornography to a University of South Carolina student, but we have Republican gubernatorial candidate Rick Scott.

Scott headed Columbia/HCA, the nation's largest for profit health care company that bilked taxpayers and the federal government for billions in Medicare fraud. Columbia/HCA admitted its guilt and paid a fine of $1.7 billion.

Scott says he was unaware of the Medicare fraud while he was CEO. Sure Rick!

Wait a second, you say. South Carolina has Nikki Haley, formerly Nimrata N. Randhawa, as its Republican nominee for governor. Haley seems like a lovely person with very little political experience. Not what South Carolina needs after its last governor, Mark Sanford.

Nikki wants South Carolina's government to be run like a business. Now there's an interesting idea; perhaps we can model our governments along the lines of Lehman Brothers or Enron or WorldCom or General Motors . . .

Nikki may look good and have great ideas, but she is no Charlie Crist.

Charlie has been governor for four years, while Nikki was a lowly member of the state legislature, and one would be hard-pressed to identify what Charlie accomplished. He did run most of the insurance companies out of Florida, largely ignored the housing and commercial real estate crises that have nearly bankrupted the state, and appointed Jim Greer to head to state GOP. Greer currently faces charges of felony grand theft, fraud, and money laundering!

And yes, Charlie was slow to recognize the impact of the oil spill on Florida's beaches and fragile environment. But he's on it now!

So what else has South Carolina got in its political closet? Have they got a Jeff Greene, Democratic candidate for the U.S. Senate seat in Florida?

Jeff has great connections to media celebrities like former heavyweight boxing champ Mike Tyson, who served as the best man at his wedding, and Heidi Fleiss, a convicted Hollywood madam, who was once his housemate. Top that South Carolina.

And Jeff made millions, maybe billions, by investing in credit default swaps and betting that Floridians would fail to meet their home mortgage obligations. Now there's a candidate who may have no confidence in us, but who would surely represent our best interests in the U.S. Senate.

Let's not forget Marco Rubio either, the Republican candidate for the U.S. Senate. Marco had a Republican Party credit card that he used to buy his groceries, wine, and repair the family van. I wonder if Marco plans to have the federal government balance its budget with the Republican Party credit card.

Hey Jon Stewart—South Carolina politicians may look good on paper, but do they really stack up to this remarkable array of political talent in Florida or to the profundity of their vision for the state? Not hardly.

So while we might mutter "Thank God for South Carolina" as we listen to Jon Stewart roast those Gamecocks, we'd have little basis for doing so.

## Revolution Is in the Air

**Social media outlets have given voice to the voiceless, despite the efforts of repressive regimes to silence them**

David Colburn

Gainesville Sun, January 15, 2012

While much has been made of the past year, most are just grateful that it is over. Charles Dickens's opening sentence in "A Tale of Two Cities" was written over 150 years ago, but his words could well have applied to 2011: "It was the best of times, it was the worst of times."

The world's economy muddled through a deep recession with no end in sight. All was not doom and gloom, however. At the same time, people in many different parts of the world embraced freedom, throwing off the shackles imposed by their oppressive, corrupt and long-serving political regimes.

Few places in the world escaped the financial and economic woes of the United States and Europe. Most economies were stagnant at best, and unemployment and home foreclosures devastated many individuals and families.

But people everywhere were also inspired by Mohamed Bouazizi, a fruit and vegetable seller in southern Tunisia, who immolated himself in despair after corrupt local officials seized his produce and his means of supporting his family on Dec. 17, 2010. His seemingly solitary act was captured on a cellphone and quickly went viral through social media outlets in the Middle East. His desperate act unleashed a revolutionary outburst that turned the region upside down.

The economic recession and the Arab Spring were linked in ways that have only partially been understood. Young people in various parts of the world, frustrated by the economic devastation wrought by the greed of banking and financial institutions, were inspired by the actions of a lowly individual in Tunisia against those forces controlling his life.

These developments remind us, as few others can, how intertwined our lives have become in this global and technological age.

Using social media, young people took up the banner of Bouazizi's cause, mobilizing friends and sympathizers against some of the most hard-bitten and longstanding regimes in the world. Not only did they overthrow Zine El Abidine Ben Ali in Tunisia, but they joined forces with others to remove Mubarak in Egypt and Gaddafi in Libya. These three had dominated the lives of their citizens in North Africa for 96 years. Within a few months, all had been removed from power.

Dickens' words again spoke to this movement for freedom and human dignity in ways no others have: "it was the epoch of belief, it was the epoch of incredulity; it was the season of Light, it was the season of Darkness."

There is every reason to believe these movements will continue to make their presence felt throughout the world, giving voice to the young and the most disadvantaged people. Events in Syria underscore the ability of people to communicate their message to the world, under the harshest and most brutal of regimes.

In just the past month, we have witnessed hundreds of thousands of Russians marching into Red Square to protest the corruption in the recent election. Despite efforts by the government to block these demonstrations, the leaders, mostly young and college educated, mobilized their forces through social media websites.

In China, the elders in the town of Haimen knelt on the road to block the expansion of a coal-fired power plant which, they claimed, contributed to a substantial rise in cancer cases and heavy pollution in the seas in which they fished. Their protests were captured by cellphones and circulated on social media sites throughout the world.

In the United States, many young people have embraced the Occupy Wall Street movement in anger over the greed and exploitation of Americans by the nation's elite.

Where exactly are these protests taking us? No one can say with certainty, but it seems clear that there is great dissatisfaction over the inability of individuals to control their own lives.

It is the most remarkable development of 2011 and, so far, of this century. These social media outlets have given voice to the voiceless. And despite the efforts of the most repressive regimes to silence them, they persist and promise to challenge traditional dogma at every step.

And no nation and no institutions are immune to this, as we have seen. Dickens again wrote perceptively in 1860, "it was the spring of hope, it was the winter of despair; we had everything before us, we had nothing before us."

In 2011, the social media outlets and the human aspiration for freedom have combined to offer hope and placed everything before us.

## The Truth about Those Medicare 'Cuts'

Bob Graham

*Tampa Bay Times*, October 21, 2012

Hiram Johnson, governor and senator from California, wrote, "The first casualty when war comes is truth." The political war that is the campaign of 2012 has wounded the truth about Medicare. The charge that $716 billion was ripped from Medicare to pay for the Affordable Care Act (ACA) is not accurate. Get a cup of coffee and find a comfortable chair while I explain the details. This is not going to be short or simple. But it is important that you understand the truth.

First, my credentials: As a Democratic senator from Florida I served on the Senate Finance Committee—the committee responsible for Medicare. Representing Florida and its many Medicare beneficiaries, I have been immersed in its history and participated in more than a decade of changes.

Although I retired from the Senate before the ACA was enacted, I am well versed in the sections of Medicare that are now alleged to have been raided of $716 billion to fund ACA. Since retiring from the Senate, I have served on the board of directors of a health insurance firm. For 10 years I have been a Medicare beneficiary.

* * *

Fact One: Of the $716 billion "taken" from Medicare, there are no cuts to the services that patients themselves receive. Let's go through the four major areas of savings, which account for 83 percent of the total. (The other 17 percent comes from myriad smaller items. Unless otherwise indicated, all statistics are for the 10-year period 2013–2022).

1. $284.3 billion comes from reduced payments to Medicare Advantage, a 2003 addition to Medicare. This provision has an interesting and illuminating history. Up until 1982, Medicare was virtually a fee-for-service program. You went to your health care provider, received services, and Medicare paid the bill up to 80 percent.

In that year insurance companies convinced Congress they could provide better services at 95 percent of the fee-for-service cost. This option was named Medicare+Choice. Medicare beneficiaries were given the option of staying with the fee-for-service coverage or joining an insurance plan. In 1997 about 5 million, or 14 percent, of Medicare beneficiaries opted for the latter.

By 2003 that had declined to 10.9 percent of beneficiaries. The insurers then returned to Congress with the request that their reimbursements be increased from 95 percent to a percentage that varied by county across the United States, but averaged out to 114 percent (104 percent in Florida). Thus Medicare Advantage was born.

By 2009 about 25 percent of Medicare beneficiaries elected the Medicare Advantage option. The average cost to Medicare for Medicare Advantage was an additional $12 billion per year. In the ACA, Congress elected to phase out Medicare Advantage over six years with additional fees and bonuses for enhanced quality of care, which resulted in the projected savings.

2. $220.5 billion is a reduction in payments to providers such as hospitals, ambulatory surgery centers, skilled nursing facilities and home health agencies through an annual productivity adjustment. A financially significant but little-known aspect of Medicare is that it has been used to fund activities that were outside the ambit of medical services to older Americans and the disabled. One of those was to compensate medical providers for changes in overall productivity and not that productivity which relates only to Medicare beneficiaries.

This compensation has been in the form of annual increases in the reimbursement rates for selected services rendered by providers. It is anticipated that other changes in Medicare, such as expanded access to preventive care and the cost-control incentives in the ACA, will increase the efficiency of providers and reduce the historic level of annual reimbursement increases.

3. $55.8 billion is saved through fraud suppression. For years politicians have said that budgets could be balanced if only we would reduce waste, fraud and abuse. Here we have a chance to do it. The ACA shifts emphasis from pay and chase (seek out the thieves after they have stolen taxpayers' money) to prevention (stop the thieves from getting close to your money in the first place).

The ACA requires a higher level of screening for applicants to secure a permit to provide goods or services to Medicare beneficiaries; enhances the use of surety bonds; outlines tougher penalties on those caught stealing from Medicare; and provides additional funding for medical fraud strike forces. Sadly, Florida has been at the epicenter of Medicare fraud. Currently one of the largest Medicare fraud cases in the history of the program is under prosecution with alleged cheats in Florida as its primary targets. The Medicare program and its Florida beneficiaries will be especially rewarded by these antifraud initiatives.

4. $30.8 billion will be taken from payments to hospitals which serve a disproportionate share of low-income Medicare and Medicaid beneficiaries. These payments will be less needed because through the ACA there will be fewer people without insurance and thus fewer unable to pay for their health care.

* * *

Fact Two: The Medicare program is a direct beneficiary of a substantial portion of these policy changes.

About $30 billion will be reallocated to eliminate the doughnut hole in prescription drug benefits. Think of a glazed doughnut and focus on the hole. The beneficiary munches through one side of the doughnut receiving prescription drug benefits of as much as $1,897.50 and out-of-pocket co-payments of $632.50 for a total of $2,530.

Then he or she falls into the hole where there is no Medicare payment for prescription drugs until the beneficiary has spent out of his or her own pocket an additional $1,137.50. Then the beneficiary climbs out of the hole and continues to chew through the other side of the doughnut with Medicare paying 95 percent until the end of the year when the beneficiary gets a fresh doughnut and starts again. In 2011, the ACA reduced the hole in the doughnut 50 percent for brand drugs and 7 percent for generics. The doughnut becomes a jelly roll in 2020. It is estimated the elimination of the doughnut hole will save the average beneficiary $4,200.

* * *

Fact Three: Accessibility and affordability of Medicare preventive care will be dramatically increased.

Before the ACA, beneficiaries paid deductibles and/or co-payments for preventive services such as bone mass measurement, hepatitis B vaccines, pap tests, pelvic exams, mammography, and most colorectal cancer screenings. Beginning this year, these life-saving measures as well as an annual wellness exam are free to Medicare beneficiaries.

* * *

Fact Four: Future additional preventive services covered by Medicare will be determined by science, not politics.

Many Americans can tell a story of a family member or friend who passed away unnecessarily because a treatable condition went undiagnosed. Mine is about a friend, not yet eligible for Medicare, who died of colon cancer. He neglected to have a colonoscopy every 10 years as recommended. When he was finally diagnosed the cancer had become terminal. My grief caused me to ask if Medicare would have paid for a beneficiary's early medical attention. The answer, to my dismay, was no.

The only means to expand Medicare services was for Congress to amend the law and add the service. I introduced legislation to do so, and all hell broke out. Instead of this being a scientifically based discussion of the benefits and cost of this addition to Medicare, it became a food fight among various providers about different colon diagnostic procedures. I can tell you the U.S. Senate was totally disarmed in its ability to make an informed judgment, particularly when the combatants began weighing in with substantial campaign contributions.

This experience convinced me there needed to be a better way to decide the efficacy of current and proposed preventive services. For several years I introduced legislation to set up a panel of medical experts to make these decisions. All these efforts failed in the face of resistance from congressional prerogatives and industry competitive advantage.

Medicare will now do exactly that, although it has been characterized negatively as putting a bureaucrat between grandmother and her doctor. This is a decades-old process, used in the military, where experts make judgments as to the need for closure or realignment of military bases with Congress making a non-amendable up or down vote. Likewise, the ACA establishes a panel to review Medicare services and report recommended changes. If Congress fails to act within seven months, the change becomes law. Whom would you rather have deciding what services will be available to you: the chairman of a congressional subcommittee or the dean of a prestigious medical school?

* * *

Fact Five: Changes to Medicare and the adoption of the ACA will extend Medicare's solvency. The year in which the receipts coming into the Medicare trust fund will be less than expenditures going out will be extended by eight years, from 2016 to 2024.

Thank you for staying to the end. These facts, based on my experience and knowledge of Medicare, have convinced me that the ACA has enhanced Medicare, not ravaged it. Now, it is up to you to decide.

## Florida's Future a Complex Challenge

**Floridians lack a sense of community, a mythic identity and knowledge of the state's past**

David Colburn

*Gainesville Sun*, December 16, 2012

So what is the biggest challenge facing Florida in this century? There are many possible answers, including: global warming, drinking water, economic growth and opportunity, immigration. And the list goes on.

The state's major challenge, in my view, is building a strong and healthy Florida and creating "one out of the many" who choose to live here.

For the first half of the 20th century, Floridians had a clear sense of themselves and their state. But it was not a society we would want to replicate—Floridians were racially polarized and the state struggled to provide a future for its residents.

Since World War II, Florida has changed dramatically, first being discovered by northerners and then by Hispanics. For the past 40 years, people have arrived in extraordinary numbers, but they have also departed for other places in very large numbers. An average of 3 million entered the state in the decades since 1970. From 2000 to 2010 alone, 2.8 million people moved into Florida, despite the Great Recession. But an estimated 900,000 also departed during that time.

Today, as a result of this demographic upheaval, 48 percent of Floridians were born in another state, 19 percent in a foreign country, and 33 percent in Florida. The percent of native born is the lowest in the nation, while the percent of foreign born among the highest.

Is it any wonder that Floridians lack a sense of community, a mythic identity, and a knowledge of the state's past?

Finding ways to bridge the ethnic, age and racial divisions and to develop a citizenry that is informed, engaged and has an appreciation of what it means to be a Floridian is difficult at best in this highly mobile society.

For those seniors who reside only half the year in Florida, understanding the problems facing the state and its young families does not come easy. Seniors will remain the single-most influential group of voters for the foreseeable future, and their numbers will be bolstered by the generation of Baby Boomers, those born from 1946 to 1964, who choose to settle in Florida. The challenge facing Florida is to engage these seniors, many of whom are part-time residents, in ways that will encourage them to look beyond their self-interest to the welfare of others and the state.

Further complicating this situation, seniors are overwhelmingly white, while young families are increasingly of color. Approximately 77 percent of those over 65 are white, compared to 13.3 percent for Hispanics and 7.38 percent for African Americans in 2012. This age and ethnic divide does not lend itself to addressing respective concerns and needs.

For immigrant groups, especially those in this hemisphere, the ability to move back and forth has been made easy through air travel, and it has, in turn, complicated the development of a cohesive citizenry. Most Hispanics have arrived in the last two decades and their identity remains principally with their homeland and with people from their homeland who have moved to Florida.

What seems certain about Florida's immediate future is that, as the Great Recession eases its grip, population growth, dominated by the Baby Boom migration to the south and Hispanic immigration to the north, will reassert itself and shape the state for much of this century.

Florida's complex racial, ethnic and age diversity, together with its dramatic demographic changes, promises to compound further its lack of identity and to make consensus on public policy difficult. Carl Hiaasen says of Floridians that they are unpredictable because they don't know or remember the past. But it is not just senior citizens who are memory-challenged. In a state as dynamic as Florida, where change is a daily occurrence and where traditions find little traction, Floridians struggle to find community.

While diversity of this sort is a tremendous obstacle to building community and achieving understanding, diversity has also enabled the state to compete globally and to be enriched by the diverse cultures immigrants have brought with them.

The task confronting the state is how to preserve the benefits of diversity and also find ways to draw us closer so that we can forge a meaningful future together. We need to start that conversation.

## Federal Government as Enemy? Not So Fast

David Colburn

*Tampa Bay Times*, March 14, 2013

In the last decade, a political ideology has surfaced that depicts the federal government as a millstone around the neck of the nation. If you have followed the sequester debate, for example, you will have heard this expression used so frequently that it has become almost common parlance.

But is it accurate? Let's just focus for a minute on one state—Florida—and the role the federal government has played in its development. By any measure, the evidence underscores the point that Florida's postwar growth and development would not have been possible without the active intervention of the federal government.

Take World War II as an example. The investment the federal government made in Florida to train American GIs for the war in Europe and Asia ended 14 years of brutal economic Depression in the state. Those years make the recent Great Recession seem like a cakewalk. More than 25 percent of the population was unemployed in an era when most women did not work. Florida's cities teetered on the edge of bankruptcy throughout the 1930s. Key West actually went bankrupt.

War mobilization launched the state's economic recovery—it built roads, air facilities and ports—and introduced hundreds of thousands of Americans to Florida for the first time. These federal investments in the state laid the foundation for its postwar population and economic boom.

Okay, so the naysayers among you contend that World War II necessitated federal action to protect the nation and defeat our fascist enemies. It was a unique series of developments in your view, not to be duplicated in another era.

Only 10 years later, however, the state's future was seriously tested by the civil rights revolution. A majority in the Florida Legislature opposed public school desegregation and integration in the public sphere.

Gov. LeRoy Collins urged legislators and Floridians to accept the changes ordered by the federal courts and federal government, but he got nowhere. Legislators promised to close the public school system if integration occurred. Even as Florida's economic development slowed, legislators refused to yield. Only the actions of the federal courts in the

1950s and 1960s and the federal government through the Civil Rights Act of 1964 and the Voting Rights Act of 1965 led Florida to abandon its racial traditions and ultimately preserved its postwar economic prosperity.

If you remain unconvinced, consider the resistance of North Florida to equitable representation in the state Legislature.

From 1945 to 1967, representatives from North Florida refused to apportion the state Legislature to reflect the dramatic growth of South Florida and largely ignored the interests of residents in that region.

In a battle royal over who would control state politics and the future direction of the state, North Florida legislators refused to relinquish control for 23 years. By 1955, 8 percent of the population in rural Florida controlled a majority of seats in the state Senate and 17.1 percent controlled a majority in the state House.

It took the action of the U.S. Supreme Court in Swann vs. Adams (1967) to force the state to redraw its districts and bring about an equitable reapportionment of the state Legislature. Without such action, it is not clear when the Legislature would have reflected the will of all Floridians and particularly the needs of those in South Florida.

These actions by the federal government were essential to Florida's modernization. Without federal action, Florida would have remained mired in the politics and racial policies of the 19th century, and the dynamic population and economic growth of the post-1945 era would have been stymied.

Moreover, the federal highway system that made Florida accessible to middle-class Americans, the development of Cape Canaveral that spurred space exploration, federal assistance to Cuban immigrants that ensured their access to freedom in Florida and this nation, and the construction of military bases and ports throughout the state are just some other important examples of federal action that ensured Florida's economic prosperity.

So before we go jumping on the anti-federal government bandwagon, imagine how Florida would look today without it. Florida would certainly not be a place of nearly 20 million diverse people who have made the state a microcosm of the nation and who have extended its reach throughout North and South America.

## Americans Are Turning Their Backs on Civil Debate

David Colburn

*Gainesville Sun*, December 7, 2014

Remember when Americans discussed politics without screaming at one another or without dismissing those on the other side as perverters of our democracy? Many of us are old enough to recall periods like this and to wish for their return.

Today, our political language has become so intense and extreme that it keeps us from trying to find common ground, and worse, it polarizes us to such a degree that some among us think that violence is an acceptable solution. These fanatics insist that civil conversation should not be pursued with people whose actions endanger the basic values of our democracy.

Are we on a tortuous path that bears an eerie resemblance to the decade of the 1850s, when compromise ceased and violence dominated our interactions with one another? In the run-up to the Civil War, Americans turned their backs on civil debate, congressmen ranted at one another, and people from North and South increasingly turned to violence to settle disputes.

John Brown's murderous raid on Harper's Ferry was but one example of the extreme divisions that permeated American society in the 1850s. Brown was convinced that his actions in October 1859 were essential to "protect our persons, property, lives and liberties, and govern our actions." Robert E. Lee, who captured Brown and his disciples, believed John Brown was insane.

But was Brown any more fanatical or troubled than Eric Frein, who 155 years later (in mid-September of this year) concocted a plan to murder Pennsylvania state police officers? Like Brown, Frein was inspired by political events and the extremism of his time. He confessed to law enforcement officials in Pennsylvania that he wanted to foment "a revolution" in order to reclaim "the liberties we once had."

Two months later, a man with anti-government views very similar to Frein's deliberately set fire to his house in Tallahassee in order to trap officers who came to rescue him and his home. He murdered one officer before he was killed.

Shortly thereafter, Larry Steven McQuilliams, assaulted police headquarters, a federal court and the offices of the Mexican government in Austin, Texas. Austin Police Chief Art Acevedo said he thought the shooter's violent anti-government behavior came from the vitriolic debates in American politics. "Our political discourse has become very heated and sometimes very angry, and sometimes the rhetoric is not healthy," Acevedo commented.

The week before McQuilliams assault, Sen. Tom Coburn, R-Okla., one of the more responsible leaders in Congress, warned that President Obama's executive order on immigration could spark "instances of anarchy" and "violence." Coburn's insinuation about what might result from the president's decision ignored the fact that previous Democratic and Republican presidents had done much the same thing.

Republican U.S. Sen. Ted Cruz added to the cascading condemnation of Obama by announcing to The Washington Post that the first order of business of the new Congress "should be a series of hearings on President Obama, looking at the abuse of power, the executive abuse, the regulatory abuse, the lawlessness that sadly has pervaded this administration."

These and other comments are couched in language that implies our government no longer represents our best interests and is out to suppress our liberties. The 24-hour news cycle and the news political commentary on MSNBC and Fox feed the public's political paranoia, and the radio stations are worse.

If this is a special nation with a special heritage, and I think it is, shouldn't we debate the important issues facing us in a reasonable and intelligent manner? And shouldn't we take the time to listen respectfully to one another?

For the sake of our democracy, I suggest we begin doing so.

## Florida Has Gone from Obstacle to Asset in National Politics

David Colburn

*Gainesville Sun*, April 5, 2015

Florida has received more national attention for its election debacles than it has for producing viable presidential candidates. Perhaps that has something to do with a state where everyone is from somewhere else, or perhaps it has to do with not being able to take a place seriously when its residents wear flip-flops and shorts for most of the year.

But here we are in 2015, and two of its most prominent political figures—Jeb Bush and Marco Rubio—are considered front-runners for the 2016 Republican presidential nomination.

So why now and not at some earlier period?

Prior to World War II, not a single political figure from Florida rose to the ranks of those considered for the presidency or vice presidency. During much of this time, Florida had a very small population—for a time the smallest in the South—and its six to eight electoral votes counted for little in a presidential contest in which 266 electoral votes decided the outcome. Its chief executives also cast a very small political shadow because they were limited to one term in office.

In the aftermath of the war, Florida assumed greater and greater national prominence as its population soared by nearly 2 million per decade from 1950 to 1970 and 3 million per decade from 1970 to the present. Between 1944 and 2012, Florida's electoral vote grew from eight to 29, making it a required stop for any serious candidate and its political leaders ripe for presidential consideration.

In the 1960s, Gov. LeRoy Collins was the first to be mentioned as a serious vice presidential candidate. Collins gained national attention for his progressive leadership during the tumultuous days of desegregation in the 1950s. Almost single-handedly Collins kept Florida from descending into political chaos. But neither Collins nor any other southern governor was given serious consideration for the presidency as long as race defined the region's politics and social mores.

Lyndon Johnson's ascendency to the presidency, following the assassination of John Kennedy, changed all that overnight. With the implementation of the Civil Rights Act of 1964 and the Voting Rights Act of 1965, Johnson transformed the region and helped recast it as the New South—an economically and socially dynamic place—where creative leadership began to take hold.

Among the most prominent figures to emerge in this period was Reubin Askew, governor of Florida from 1971 to 1979. Askew, who was a disciple of LeRoy Collins, became widely respected for his leadership on race relations, judicial reform, open government, environmental reform and expanded public school funding. If he had sought the Democratic nomination for president in 1976 when Georgia Gov. Jimmy Carter launched his candidacy, Askew might well have been the party's choice.

But, as they say in politics, timing is everything. When Askew waited until 1984 to throw his hat in the presidential ring, he had been out of office for four years and his record was largely forgotten.

Following the Askew years, only Bob Graham, twice governor and three-term U.S. senator, commanded any serious national attention before 2015. Al Gore may well have won Florida and the national election if he chose Graham as his running mate in 2000. Four years later, health issues derailed Graham's presidential aspirations.

Even with their state and national prominence, neither Askew nor Graham attained as much traction for the presidency as Jeb Bush and Marco Rubio. For Bush and Rubio, their success has benefited significantly from Florida's political and demographic changes. Bush came to power alongside the Republican Party and, together they fashioned a conservative revolution that extended Bush's influence well beyond Florida. Rubio, a Cuban American, emerged from the ethnic caldron of Miami and used it as a base to capture a U.S. Senate seat in an increasingly diverse state. He has come to epitomize a new Florida and a new America.

Where the state once served as an obstacle to the national aspirations of its political leaders, it is today an asset. In place of what was once a small, isolated and segregated state, a demographic and political juggernaut has emerged. At the same time, Florida has become the nation's major swing state, where its 29 electoral votes are vital to the election outcome and where presidential candidacies are increasingly launched.

## Trump Recalls Populism and Dark Side of Politics

David Colburn

*Gainesville Sun*, October 29, 2016

Americans may not agree about much politically these days, but most would agree that they have never seen an election quite like this one in their lifetimes. Even if we go further back in time to the turn of the 20th century, it is difficult to find a counterpart to 2016.

The personal nature of the attacks by both candidates, and especially by Republican Donald Trump, have set a new low. His persistent derogatory references to immigrant groups, Muslims and women are without precedent. Trump could not get away with this, however, if he did not have significant support. And he clearly has that.

So what's going on?

If the distinguished American historian Richard Hofstadter (1916–1970) were alive today, he would attribute this campaign and the populist nature of it to the "dark side" of American politics, where paranoia emerges full force and drives the political engagement of one group of voters. According to Hofstadter, populism depicts elites as trampling on the rights, values and voice of the legitimate people. The majority of Americans who lacked both money and influence became particularly fearful about their place in the nation, the future of their children and the role of "others"—particularly those from minority ethnic or racial groups—and the wealthy. Hofstadter did not see much good in the emergence of populism or anything constructive in its political activism throughout American history.

Not everyone has agreed with Hofstadter's interpretation, especially when the debate focuses on the Populist movement of the late 19th and early 20th centuries. That movement mobilized the populace in rural and urban America to organize against the "money power" in the United States, which not only controlled the economy but also dominated the political leadership of the nation to the detriment of the poor, working class and middle class. The political agenda of the Populist movement during that era was quite successful and gradually worked its way into the fabric of American political system. In short, the benefits of Populism waged against the robber barons of that era arguably outweighed its negative aspects.

A re-interpretation of the dark side of populism emerged in the 1950s when historian Richard Hofstadter and sociologist Daniel Bell compared the anti-elitism of the 1890s Populists with that of Joseph McCarthy. Although not all academics accepted the comparison between the left-wing, anti-big business Populists and the right-wing, anti-communist McCarthyites of the 1950s, the term "populist," nonetheless, came to be applied to both left-wing and right-wing groups that blamed elites for the problems facing the nation.

George Wallace, four-term governor of Alabama, led one of most successful populist movements which was principally based on race, the exploitation of the anxieties of working-class whites and a denunciation of liberal values. He carried five states and won 13.5 percent of the popular vote in the 1968 presidential election.

Throughout U.S. history, populism struggled to find a leader who could take the movement national. Joseph McCarthy and George Wallace came closest. But neither had a national following.

The tea party movement failed in a similar manner until Trump came along. Even though their objectives have not always been aligned, both the tea party and Trump appear to need one another. For its part, the tea party advocates a reduction in government spending, fewer regulations, lower taxes, the repeal of the Affordable Care Act and the selection of Supreme Court judges who adhere to the original interpretation of the Constitution, positions that Trump claims to support. Trump has built a movement with a significant following and the tea party loyalists have found someone whose name and reputation appear to support many of their positions and thereby give them greater national visibility.

The downside for tea party activists is that Trump made the movement negative from the beginning of his involvement. He has branded people of color, minority groups and immigrants, as well as people of certain religious faiths, as the source of the nation's problems. He has even chosen to objectify women instead of trying to sell his brand of populism to them. Moreover, Trump has switched positions on various policy issues over the years, thus making him less dependable as a potential tea party ally in the long term. He also has touted the importance of making deals. The tea party has been known for its steadfast position on various issues that do not brook compromise, hardly compatible with the basic tenets of Trump's "The Art of the Deal."

Although at first blush, Trump seemed the answer to tea party national aspirations, his repeated tendency to throw thunder bolts at opponents and his lack of preparedness and candor have overshadowed tea party concerns about issues most important to its adherents.

It remains to be seen whether Trump has served the needs of the populist tea party movement or taken it down a path to political humiliation.

## The Cure for the Post-Election Blues Is to Hold the Government Accountable

Bob Graham and Chris Hand

*Time*, December 22, 2016

At the end of The Candidate, when underdog U.S. Senate candidate Bill McKay (played by Robert Redford) upsets a heavily favored opponent, he pulls his campaign manager into a side room and asks a single panicked question: "What do we do now?"

In the weeks since the November 8 election, some people have chosen to answer that same question by taking their concerns to the streets. While we respect the right to peaceably assemble, and understand the worries that have motivated the protests, demonstrations alone are not the answer.

The answer is to fully embrace our rights and responsibilities as citizens in a democracy. Whether you are pleased or dismayed by the November 8 outcome, the election was not the end of the story. It was the beginning of an opportunity to flex our citizenship muscles and make government work for us.

Let's start with the victors. Polling suggested that Donald Trump won the Republican nomination because voters believed that government no longer listened to everyday Americans. A Rand Corporation survey in January 2016 found that 86.5% of primary voters were more likely to vote for Trump if they believed that people like them didn't have any say about what government does.

Both the general election outcome and Senator Bernie Sanders' strong showing in the Democratic contests prove that feeling of alienation from public institutions is even more widespread—particularly in parts of the nation that have not shared in the economic recovery. But that feeling won't go away just by voting for candidates who speak to those frustrations. Empowerment does not occur vicariously. Those Americans who voted in hopes that President-elect Trump and other candidates would upend the political and economic status quo now need to hold victorious elected officials accountable.

Similarly, the feelings of disappointment that many Hillary Clinton supporters or Donald Trump opponents have experienced after the election won't go away on their own. While there are no permanent victories or defeats in politics, rejuvenation does not occur organically. Those who view the results with concern need to get up off the turf, dust themselves off and use the skills of effective citizenship to move the political and governmental processes in their direction.

Identify a problem. Do your homework. Join with others who share your goals. Gauge public opinion and spread the word through traditional and social media. Pick the right timing. Find the necessary financial resources. Persuade decision-makers. Demand a return to the foundation of democracy—the teaching of civics and active citizenship in elementary and secondary schools, as well as colleges and universities, to help students become successful advocates.

You may be skeptical that citizens can make government respond. Many people believe that, as the saying goes, you can't fight City Hall. But Americans have repeatedly demonstrated over time that such a cynical sentiment is incorrect.

Don't take our word for it. Ask the unlikely alliance between leaders in the Georgia Tea Party and Georgia Sierra Club. Working with solar power advocates, they persuaded regulators and state legislators to help Georgians use solar energy over the objections of politically powerful utility interests.

Ask the grieving women who sat around a table in Sacramento, California, and channeled their sadness into the founding of Mothers Against Drunk Driving. Less than five years later, they had established hundreds of local MADD chapters around the nation and transformed federal and state law.

Ask the University of Missouri football players who took a stand and refused to play until their concerns about racism on campus were addressed. Faced with a possible boycott and the resulting loss of revenue, the university president seen as indifferent to those concerns had no choice but to resign.

Ask the LGBT advocates and business leaders who formed coalitions in places as far-flung as Indiana, North Carolina and West Central Florida to insist that public leaders—including Vice President-elect Mike Pence—oppose discrimination and ensure equality.

These American patriots have reaffirmed that each of us holds the most important title in American democracy: citizen. As former Illinois governor, presidential candidate and ambassador Adlai Stevenson once said, "As citizens of this democracy, you are the rulers and the ruled, the law-givers and the law-abiders, the beginning and the end." Now is the time to embrace that exalted status.

---

Chris Hand is co-author with Bob Graham of *America, the Owner's Manual: You Can Fight City Hall—and Win* and was chief of staff for the consolidated City of Jacksonville, FL, from 2011–2015.

## Will Trump and Tea Party Partnership Last?

David Colburn

*Gainesville Sun*, May 5, 2017

In 2009, I was in Akron, Ohio, and happened upon a tea party rally nearby. I had read about the tea party movement but I had not seen or attended a gathering of its supporters. So, I decided to take a few minutes before dinner to see what the fuss was all about.

A speaker was denouncing the policies of the Obama administration and the dismal state of the national economy. Almost all of those in attendance were white and looked to be struggling financially. They were people I could relate to since my family had been working class and I had worked alongside them unloading trucks and trains in Providence, Rhode Island, to pay my way through college.

My first impression of the movement in Akron was not positive. The few speakers I listened to had little to offer but complaints about the federal government for ignoring the plight of the working poor. But they offered no specific plans to ease the unemployment rate or combat declining salaries and called on the crowd to join them "in throwing the bums out of Washington."

From what little I observed at the rally, I thought this was a movement that would struggle to be successful and I mentioned that to those I had dinner with that evening. They generally agreed with me.

But the tea party would go on to prove us wrong. Aided by Republican strategists and spokesmen who saw the tea party as a way to re-energize the Republican Party, activists gained additional traction among other whites who were attracted to the populist appeal of the tea party.

This modern-day Populist movement sought to mobilize working class voters against the "money power" in the United States, which they felt controlled the economy and dominated the political leadership of the nation to the detriment of the working class.

Tea party members and Donald Trump's campaign joined forces in support of a reduction in government spending, a stronger economy, fewer federal regulations, lower taxes, the repeal of the Affordable Care Act and tighter immigration controls. Their collaboration proved instrumental in Trump's election as president in 2016, turning out their working class political base in record numbers.

While the affiliation with Trump energized the tea party and enhanced its visibility, it also had its downside. Trump was not a dedicated tea party loyalist. His book, "The Art of the Deal," made clear that he was prepared to compromise if it would secure those programs he valued most.

By contrast, the tea party has been known for its steadfast position on various issues and would not brook compromise on its principles. In his first 100 days, Trump switched positions so frequently that many tea party leaders were not sure what he stood for and some concluded he was unreliable.

How long this partnership lasts remains to be seen. So far most white workers seem willing to stick with Trump, even if he frustrates them on many of their core concerns. His distortion of events and repeated accusations of fake news, however, are a shallow foundation on which to maintain a coalition, much less secure a better future for the working class.

## We Are Former Senators. The Senate Has Long Stood in Defense of Democracy—and Must Again.

### Bob Graham with 43 other former senators

*Washington Post*, December 10, 2018

Dear Senate colleagues,

As former members of the U.S. Senate, Democrats and Republicans, it is our shared view that we are entering a dangerous period, and we feel an obligation to speak up about serious challenges to the rule of law, the Constitution, our governing institutions and our national security.

We are on the eve of the conclusion of special counsel Robert S. Mueller III's investigation and the House's commencement of investigations of the president and his administration. The likely convergence of these two events will occur at a time when simmering regional conflicts and global power confrontations continue to threaten our security, economy and geopolitical stability.

It is a time, like other critical junctures in our history, when our nation must engage at every level with strategic precision and the hand of both the president and the Senate.

We are at an inflection point in which the foundational principles of our democracy and our national security interests are at stake, and the rule of law and the ability of our institutions to function freely and independently must be upheld.

During our service in the Senate, at times we were allies and at other times opponents, but never enemies. We all took an oath swearing allegiance to the Constitution. Whatever united or divided us, we did not veer from our unwavering and shared commitment to placing our country, democracy and national interest above all else.

At other critical moments in our history, when constitutional crises have threatened our foundations, it has been the Senate that has stood in defense of our democracy. Today is once again such a time.

Regardless of party affiliation, ideological leanings or geography, as former members of this great body, we urge current and future senators to be steadfast and zealous guardians of our democracy by ensuring that partisanship or self-interest not replace national interest.

Max Baucus (D-Mont.), Evan Bayh (D-Ind.), Jeff Bingaman (D-N.M.), Bill Bradley (D-N.J.), Richard Bryan (D-Nev.), Ben Nighthorse Campbell (R-Colo.), Max Cleland (D-Ga.), William Cohen (R-Maine), Kent Conrad (D-N.D.), Al D'Amato (R-N.Y.), John C. Danforth (R-Mo.), Tom Daschle (D-S.D.), Dennis DeConcini (D-Ariz.), Chris Dodd (D-Conn.), Byron Dorgan (D-N.D.), David Durenberger (R-Minn.), Russ Feingold (D-Wis.), Wyche Fowler (D-Ga.), Bob Graham (D-Fla.), Chuck Hagel (R-Neb.), Tom Harkin (D-Iowa), Gary Hart (D-Colo.), Bennett Johnston (D-La.), Bob Kerrey (D-Neb.), John Kerry (D-Mass.), Paul Kirk (D-Mass.), Mary Landrieu (D-La.), Joe Lieberman (I-Conn.), Blanche Lincoln (D-Ark.), Richard Lugar (R-Ind.), Barbara Mikulski (D-Md.), Ben Nelson (D-Neb.), Sam Nunn (D-Ga.), Larry Pressler (R-S.D.), David Pryor (D-Ark.), Don Riegle (D-Mich.), Chuck Robb (D-Va.), Jay Rockefeller (D-W.Va.), Jim Sasser (D-Tenn.), Alan Simpson (R-Wyo.), Mark Udall (D-Colo.), John W. Warner (R-Va.), Lowell Weicker (I-Conn.), Tim Wirth (D-Colo.)

# DIVERSITY

# 5

# Race Relations

It has often been said that "Florida is in the South, but not of the South." Nothing, however, could be further from the truth, and the articles in this section verify the fact that Florida's long history of problematic race relations places it squarely alongside Georgia, Alabama, and Mississippi. In January 1861, Florida became the third state to secede from the Union, and it had the highest per capita lynching rate of any state in the country. Between 2020 and 2025, we mark the somber anniversaries of Florida racial incidents that match anything that happened in other Southern states. These include the centennial of both the Ocoee massacre and the destruction of Rosewood, the 75th anniversary of the Groveland Four case, the 70th anniversary of the still-unsolved assassination of Harry T. Moore, and the 60th anniversary of the St. Augustine civil rights demonstrations. In the essays in this section, David Colburn recognizes the importance of racial matters to Florida's history and the continuing impact those issues have on the state today. Colburn points out that Florida has made efforts to confront its racist past, particularly in providing state-funded financial compensation to the descendants of those who lost their lives or their homes in the 1923 Rosewood massacre. But he is also aware that the stain of racism still marks Florida and that we are nowhere near the post-racial society we thought we had achieved with the election of Barack Obama as president in 2008. These pieces also remind us that while matters of race affect society at large, they also impact specific individuals in many ways. The personal stories told here allow readers to understand just how important (and insidious) racial problems can be, and how the efforts of ordinary Floridians can make a huge difference in bridging the racial divide. There are no simple answers given here, no magic cures or solutions suggested. However, the articles tell readers that recognition of past evils is a necessary first step in confronting the racial problems Florida, and the nation as a whole, still face today. The questions broached in this section underlie many of the concerns that are examined in other sections, particularly those examining politics and leadership. They recognize the insight of W.E.B. DuBois in his seminal 1903 *The Souls of Black Folk* when he wrote, "the problem of the twentieth century is the problem of the color line." They also let us know that this problem has not yet been solved in the 21st.

## Campus Crossroads: Black vs. White vs. Understanding

David Colburn

*Orlando Sentinel*, June 14, 1993

Spray-painted signs saying "N****** Go Home" appear on buildings, and a statue of Martin Luther King Jr. is defaced repeatedly with swastika symbols. Elsewhere, a gang of teen-age blacks randomly assaults whites, sending several to a hospital.

It is an all-too-familiar scene in the nation's cities in the 1990s. But this hostility and violence is taking place on college campuses, where the minds of the nation's "best and brightest" historically have been opened to new ideas and to tolerance between different peoples.

It is distressing enough to see such confrontations in the nation's cites, but what does it say about us as a people and our commitment to interracial cooperation if this intolerance infects even our institutions of higher learning?

It was just 30 years go [*sic*] that King launched a crusade against racial intolerance in Birmingham, Ala., in an effort to make the South and the nation live up to the ideals expressed in the Declaration of Independence. Aided by college students and faculty, the demonstrations in Birmingham pricked the conscience of a nation, and together with the death of President John Kennedy resulted in the overthrow of legal segregation. In the three decades since, the nation has witnessed the integration of its public schools, the elimination of racial restrictions on voting, and widespread progress by black Americans in the private and public sectors.

Despite these achievements, they have not resulted in the sort of interracial understanding and cooperation that many, including King, had sought.

Indeed, today's African-American citizen believes that discrimination remains widespread and that it constitutes a major obstacle to fairness, justice and opportunity. Most white citizens have almost an entirely different view. They believe that the special federal programs for minorities violate norms of fairness and equality and have occurred at their expense. Ironically, although both groups have similar aspirations, each has come to view the other as an obstacle to its own progress.

Compounding these divisions, interracial communication has seldom been worse. White and black students refrain from talking to one another on campus. Moreover, black and white citizens are almost completely divided over President Clinton's withdrawal of Lani Guinier to head the Justice Department's civil-rights division, and black and white Floridians are similarly at odds over the not-guilty verdict in the trial of former Miami police officer William Lozano.

Academic leaders on college campuses actually have contributed to the deteriorating racial climate. At City University of New York, a black scholar laces his lectures repeatedly with anti-Semitic and anti-white remarks, while a white scholar on another campus alleges the genetic inferiority of blacks. When faculties meet to discuss issues of race, they often end up shouting at one another, or worse. In the past two years, scholars have begun pairing off into groups that embrace or denounce the new political correctness, but there is little discussion and even less communication.

If these intellectual leaders of society cannot communicate with one another, how we can we expect more of their students and the larger society?

Disagreement among academicians has intersected with divisive racial perceptions that make the "common ground" difficult to find. Whites identify the disintegration of the black family with the cause for much of the nation's social ills and for the violence in the nation's cities and suburbs. Blacks believe that whites still refuse to accept the principle of equality and that the economic policies of the federal government and the white elite have kept blacks in a subservient position and led to the problems confronting the urban poor.

Lost in the anger and rhetoric are a number of positive developments, which have seen whites and blacks working together to improve public schools, housing and opportunities for children, and to heighten racial awareness and sensitivity on campuses. Unfortunately, these achievements are submerged beneath the racial classes and vitriol, seldom receiving the attention of the public.

The mounting racial division threatens the future of this diverse nation, whose continuing success requires us to balance society's need for unity with respect for individual and group difference. It is a delicate balancing act that requires considerable moral and intellectual leadership of the kind provided by King and scores of faculty and students in the 1960s.

That the balkanization of American society has spread to college campuses is particularly disconcerting. It suggests that such divisions may influence this country for some time to come and that they are so emotionally felt that, even within the hallowed halls of the nation's universities, they undermine rational discourse.

## A Chasm between Whites, Blacks on Memory of Rosewood

David Colburn

*Orlando Sentinel*, March 2, 1997

John Singleton's new movie, Rosewood, has received critical acclaim and been cited for its historical accuracy. But although it purports to be based on the true story of Rosewood, which was destroyed by racial violence in 1923, Singleton's version more often reflects the director's personal interpretation than it does reality.

But the truth about Rosewood is not an easy matter. Various myths have grown up around events there, and they have taken on a life force of their own.

The reality is that there are many details that are unknown, and perhaps unknowable, about Rosewood. For example, what led to the killing and the destruction of the community? No one can be sure. The sexual assault of Fanny Taylor may have been the immediate cause, or it may have resulted when Taylor tried to shield her white lover from her husband by screaming that she had been raped by a black man.

How many people died? Eight deaths—six blacks and two whites—can be accounted for, but many more may have died at the hands of a heavily armed and intoxicated white mob. These and many other questions about Rosewood remain unresolved.

In fact, the details about Rosewood and the historical memory regarding the events there took divergent paths in the days and weeks immediately following that horrific first week in January 1923.

The white accounting and the early white memory alleged that Taylor had been assaulted, that black residents of Rosewood hid her assailant from law-enforcement officials, and that the destruction of the community was the direct result of efforts to protect her attacker. So it was reported by white newspapers in Florida and recounted by whites in Levy County as they recalled the events at Rosewood.

Black newspaper reports and black memory took a quite different perspective. From the outset, the black narrative portrayed Fanny Taylor as a liar and Sylvester Carrier as a hero for standing up to the assault on his mother's home by Klansmen. It also depicted a local white population that was jealous of the success of Rosewood's residents and a political and legal establishment that supported the destruction of the town.

The fact that such divergent stories developed in the immediate aftermath of Rosewood suggests that events there had great significance for both white and black communities. As with the two O.J. Simpson trials, black and white citizens viewed Rosewood differently for a reason. Events in Rosewood were central to each of their views of American society.

Black residents were convinced that the violence in Rosewood could not have occurred without the cooperation of the white establishment. Moreover, they knew that none of this would have been tolerated if it happened to a white community. Their heroic depiction of Sylvester Carrier was meant to challenge this society in a most fundamental manner.

The white recounting of events at Rosewood was intended to reinforce segregation and racial distinctions in an age of rapid change and heightened insecurity. Any challenge to the fundamental tenets of Southern racial patterns in this era required, according to custom, a peremptory response from whites, as occurred in Rosewood.

During the next 50 years, the white version of events at Rosewood would lose its legitimacy. After the civil-rights movement, few could defend what happened at Rosewood. And in place of this memory, residents developed an amnesia about Rosewood. Like many native Germans who contended they knew nothing of the Holocaust, whites in Levy County remembered little about Rosewood and were sure that no locals had been involved.

But the survivors of Rosewood never completely forgot what had happened, try as some might. And when the family reunions began in the early 1980s, the Rosewood men and women gave renewed voice to the black memory of events in 1923. And black Americans, angered over police harassment in the 1990s and a court system that seemed unjust, if not racist, embraced that memory as if it were their own.

The historical memory of Rosewood has become symbolic of the chasm between white and black Americans in the 1990s. Whites want to put it behind them, and blacks find it representative of the persistent discrimination they face in American society. Singleton's portrait passionately embraces the black narrative. Although acknowledging that there were decent white people in and around Rosewood, Singleton's movie asserts that whites and blacks at the time of Rosewood and in 1997 live in a racist society.

It is a troubling movie and a troubling legacy. Rosewood cannot be ignored, and yet it also cannot bring us together.

Memo: David R. Colburn is professor of history at the University of Florida. He was the co-author of the Rosewood Report that was submitted to the state Legislature in 1993.

## Abandon Busing? Hard-Won Gains Would Be at Risk

David Colburn

*Orlando Sentinel*, March 22, 1999

In a little less than two months, the nation will celebrate the 40th anniversary of the Brown vs. the Board of Education of Topeka, Kan., decision and the end of segregation in its public school system. It would be more than a little ironic if we did so while simultaneously abandoning busing, which has made school integration possible. Yet don't be surprised if this, in fact, happens.

On May 17, 1954, the U.S. Supreme Court stunned the nation and sent the South into convulsions by ordering the dismantling of segregated public schools.

Sixteen more years passed, however, before the decision was fully implemented, because Southern politicians used every weapon at their disposal to undermine the decision.

Now, little more than a generation later, public officials throughout the nation and in Florida—including Orange County—seriously are considering an end to busing, and effectively an end to the integration of public schools as we have come to know them.

What happened to the nation's commitment to integration and to integrated schools? How can a country that underwent one of the most traumatic social revolutions in its history consider reversing itself?

During the past decade, several developments have converged to mobilize support in both black and white communities for an end to busing and a revival of neighborhood schools.

Within the black community, two movements on opposite ends of the spectrum—one nostalgic and the other radical—have become intertwined and together have enhanced support for neighborhood schools. The two movements are influenced, in part, by the alleged failure of integrated schools to improve significantly the academic achievement of black children.

The nostalgic effort pictures the black segregated school as a place where children benefited from a teacher, mentor and neighbor all wrapped into one. This view alleges that black teachers cared more for black children, and, as a consequence, the children did at least as well in school as they are doing today and felt much better about themselves in the process.

The radical argument calls for black control of schools, so that black children can avoid the intellectual and cultural oppression of white, capitalist, Eurocentric America. Contained within this viewpoint is the growing belief in many quarters in the black community that black children also are being academically and psychologically isolated in integrated schools and denied knowledge of their own heritage.

At the same time that these developments have occurred in the black community, the white commitment to integrated schools has eroded steadily. Most whites have never been enthusiastic about busing, but they have adjusted their lives to the school bus.

Where support for busing particularly has declined is among middle-income whites. These people increasingly are concerned about the lack of funding for public schools and believe that the funds diverted to busing could well enrich the academic environment for their children.

There is also an unstated belief in the white community that public schools would be far safer if the children of the black poor went elsewhere. Although tinged with racism, this view goes beyond race, because most of these white parents have no objection to their children attending schools with middle-income black children.

Aligning themselves with those favoring an end to busing are several of the nation's black mayors, who are searching desperately for sources of funding that would aid their administrations in addressing other urban problems, and school reformers, who believe neighborhood schools will increase parental involvement and consequently the educational advancement of children.

Mayor Freeman R. Bosley Jr. of St. Louis opposes busing because he believes integration will occur only when neighborhoods are integrated. But he and others like him also want the funds for busing so that they can address such pressing needs as crime, drugs, dysfunctional families and limited job opportunities.

All of these arguments have varying degrees of merit, but should we throw out the academic and societal advancements that have come through integrated schools in order to achieve them?

Despite the contention of busing critics, we do know that the people of this nation were racially isolated one from the other before 1954, and we do know that certain social and cultural assumptions were widespread because of this separation. A recent Lou Harris poll reveals that fewer Americans harbor racist attitudes than at any previous point in our nation's past. It would be impossible to argue that integrated schools have not been the critical component in this change of attitudes.

Moreover, despite the contention of those nostalgic for the past, black schools fared poorly in educating children in the 1940s and 1950s, and conditions in these schools were inadequate at best. Even today, predominantly black schools still suffer from poor facilities because most are located in lower-class neighborhoods.

Although Mayor Bosley may be right in arguing that integration will occur only when neighborhoods are integrated, the statistics do not reveal that this will occur any time soon. Does it make sense in the meantime to abandon integrated schools?

It is easy to criticize the academic failings of our public schools and to argue that funds for busing could be better spent elsewhere. But how do we isolate the problems in the schools from the other social developments that affect them, and will these problems disappear with the end of busing? Not likely.

The authors of the Brown decision sought to fulfill the promise of the preamble of the Constitution by using the schools to create a more perfect union among the people of this nation and also to advance the educational process for white and black children. Are we now prepared to turn our back on this commitment? Are we prepared to say integrated schools don't work?

If so, what are we saying about ourselves as a society?

## Florida Stands at a Racial Crossroads

David Colburn

*Orlando Sentinel*, August 29, 2010

In just 50 years, Florida has gone from being a very traditional biracial, southern state in which race defined both the social and political environment to one of the most racially and ethnically complex states in which color and diversity seem to be the new norm.

Of the 18.5 million people now residing in the state, 76.7 percent are white, which mirrors the national percentage of 74.3 percent. But 15.3 percent of Floridians are African American (compared to 12.3 nationally) and 20.5 percent are Hispanic (compared to 15.1 percent nationally).

Moreover, when you examine the white percentage closely, you realize that the figure is misleading because a significant percentage of Hispanics identify themselves as both Hispanic and white.

The complexity of Florida's population is further underscored by the fact that 18.7 percent of us are foreign born (compared to just 12.5 percent nationally), and 25.8 percent speak a language other than English at home (compared to 19.6 percent nationally).

Spanish is the dominant second language, but Creole is spoken by a large Haitian population. And a host of other languages can be heard at coffee houses in any of Florida's large cities.

Unlike the first half of the 20th century when color was a liability, Florida's diversity has been an asset to political candidates like Bob Martinez, a grandson of Spanish immigrants, who was elected governor in 1986, and Mel Martinez, a Cuban refugee as a child, who was elected U.S. senator in 2004. And former Gov. Jeb Bush and his wife Columba, who was born in Mexico, mirrored within the state's first family Florida's new multi-ethnic society.

Despite the diversity of Floridians and despite the ways in which state leaders promote Florida's diversity internationally, racism and anti-ethnic sentiments occasionally rear their head (such is the case in Gainesville at the moment). Such occasions result in part because much of the state's history was dominated by race.

Some of it also has to do with Florida's inexperience as an immigrant-receiving state until 1959. Unlike New York and Massachusetts, Florida had little contact with immigrants prior to the arrival of Cuban refugees. This historical confluence of experiences has occasionally been daunting and resulted in discrimination and occasional violence against immigrants and people of color.

Fortunately, a long line of governors from Reubin Askew to Bob Graham, Bob Martinez, Lawton Chiles, Jeb Bush, and Charlie Crist have repeatedly condemned such acts and have publicly embraced the image of a multi-racial and multi-ethnic Florida.

Florida has also enjoyed a strong and expanding economy during much of the period from 1970 to 2007, which helped alleviate racial and ethnic divisions, because there was opportunity for all.

But the Great Recession of 2008–09 has opened up wounds that were only sporadically present in the past as residents lost their jobs and their homes, and their general optimism about the state's future. Suddenly, for some Floridians, "the others" among us have been accused of being part of the problem.

Calls for restrictions on immigration and for English to be required in public schools and in public places have emerged with new energy. Tea Party members, who are overwhelmingly white, express angst over the direction of American society and by implication the changing face of America and the growing prominence of people of color in all walks of life. Less than one percent of Tea Party members are black or Hispanic, and Tea Party supporters attribute affirmative action programs for minorities and the nation's immigration policies as reasons for their economic difficulties.

In the just completed Republican primary race for governor, both Attorney General Bill McCollum and his victorious opponent, businessman Rick Scott, turned their backs on the policies of recent state leaders to curry support among those angry over the state of immigration, both legal and otherwise, in Florida. Barely two weeks before the primary McCollum tried to one-up Scott's support of the Arizona law by proposing a Florida version that would be even more restrictive.

Their hard line has opened up old wounds and created dissension even among Republicans.

Marco Rubio, the son of Cuban exiles and a Republican nominee for the U.S. Senate, has refrained from embracing such an immigration policy and ignored calls to ban citizenship for children of illegal immigrants. Rubio knows personally that such a proposal threatens to polarize Floridians and will do little to remedy the state's economic woes.

So what happened to the enlightened Florida that welcomed people from all backgrounds and to those Floridians who viewed the state as a beacon of hope for all? Have we become, as Rick Scott and Bill McCollum seemed to imply during the GOP primary, two-faced about our diversity? It's fine as long as whites are gainfully employed and have access to good jobs.

Or are we ready to embrace the "new Florida"; a place of ethnic and racial complexity that struggles with its diversity as it seeks to create a better place for all?

We stand at a crossroads.

## Remember Our Local Civil Rights Heroes, Too

**David Colburn**

*Tampa Bay Times*, February 1, 2018

In their initial years, Dr. Martin Luther King Jr.'s birthday celebration and Black History Month broadened our understanding of the nation's racial heritage and paved the way for a major, much-needed revision of American history text books [*sic*]. "Remembering King," however, overshadowed many aspects of the civil rights movement and its multifaceted history, especially after his assassination. As a result, too many Americans learned only part of the story: a history told from the top down.

Nowhere was this more evident than in St. Augustine, where Dr. King and his nonviolent army launched their civil rights campaign in the spring of 1964. St. Augustine was one of the four major campaigns of the Southern Christian Leadership Conference. The first was in Albany, Ga., in 1961 and 1962; followed by Birmingham, Ala., in 1963;St. Augustine in 1964; and Selma, Ala., in 1965. While all these campaigns were local in nature, they were intended to mobilize nationwide support for desegregation and voting rights.

At the outset of the campaign King and his aides branded St. Augustine as "the oldest segregated city in America," to highlight how deeply embedded segregation was in this historic city, a symbol of the nation itself. King's depiction of St. Augustine reflected his media savvy and brilliant grasp of public relations.

Nevertheless, SCLC's successes in these communities owed much to the work of local civil rights activists who campaigned for years to bring about racial change and mobilized a substantial network of supporters. This history often got overlooked in most early studies of the civil rights movement, which focused principally on King and SCLC. St. Augustine, for example, had an active chapter of the NAACP well before SCLC arrived, which was led by two women who lobbied white city leaders to provide equal access and equal facilities for black citizens and their children. They also championed efforts to register black citizens to vote.

Over time these two women recruited local black teachers, black professionals, city workers and students at Florida Memorial College to the movement. Dr. Robert Hayling, a local dentist, became the most prominent of the new members. He became frustrated with the pace of racial change and pursued a progressively more activist approach in response to the stonewalling by city leaders and the violence of local white militants. It was Hayling who led the efforts to recruit King and SCLC into St. Augustine.

Despite the critical role played by the local NAACP and Hayling and his supporters, white leaders at the state and local levels contended that civil rights demonstrations did not begin until King and SCLC entered the city on Easter Week 1964. This twist on history dominated the St. Augustine civil rights story for many years.

That changed permanently, however, when Ms. Gwendolyn Duncan, a drug-prevention specialist and substitute schoolteacher, decided enough was enough. She wanted young people to know the real story and to be aware that the movement owed a great deal to local leaders who came from families like their own.

Together with local historian David Nolan, Duncan organized two conferences in 2007 and 2009 for teachers, counselors, activists and historians to illuminate the full story of civil rights in St. Augustine. Duncan also formed an organization called Anniversary to Commemorate the Civil Rights Demonstrations (ACCORD), and with Nolan established a civil rights museum that featured the local movement, developed a city Freedom Trail, and brought former civil rights leaders like Dr. Hayling back to the community to be celebrated and interact with residents, teachers, and students.

Hayling died in 2015 at the age of 86. But by keeping his and other local civil rights stories alive, Duncan, Nolan, and others in communities throughout the South have enabled that history of local leadership to be told, from textbooks to tram tours, in all its complexity for the benefit of future generations.

This February as we remember King and our nation's racial heritage, let us also celebrate the work of local volunteers who helped guide us on the tortuous path to racial justice.

## Florida Events Hastened Racial Change in the Nation

David Colburn

*Gainesville Sun*, February 2, 2014

When we celebrate Black History Month this month, Floridians should take a few moments to reflect on the monumental historical events that redefined the state's racial heritage, and in doing so, hastened racial change in the nation.

Two such events that immediately stand out are: the destruction of Rosewood and the civil rights movement in St. Augustine. This year marks the 91st anniversary of the racial violence at Rosewood, Fla. (January 1923), when this predominantly black community was destroyed. It is also the 50th anniversary of the decision by the Southern Christian Leadership Conference and the Rev. Martin Luther King Jr. to bring their national civil rights campaign to St. Augustine (during the spring and summer of 1964).

The events at Rosewood during the first week of January 1923 highlighted the pervasiveness and horrific consequences of racism in Florida. The entire black community was destroyed following an allegation of rape against a black man who was never identified. Several residents were also murdered by white mobs, and others were driven from their property forever. In reflecting on these developments and subsequent life, one resident observed: "Nothing was the same after Rosewood."

During the intervening 91 years, Rosewood became a transformative event as the state and nation began to hear stories about individual black survivors, initially in an article by Gary Moore in the July 1982 issue of The Floridian, the Sunday insert of the St. Petersburg Times, then in an episode of "60 Minutes," and finally from survivors themselves and former white residents.

As the events of Rosewood became public knowledge, it sparked a state and national campaign to compensate survivors for the loss of their property and the damages they suffered. Led by state legislators Al Lawson and Miguel DeGrandy, an intriguing alliance between a Democrat and Republican and an African-American and a Cuban American, Florida compensated each of the survivors in 1994—the only racial incident of its kind in the nation's history in which a state acknowledged its complicity and in which survivors were compensated.

In the case of St. Augustine, it was 50 years ago that the city found itself at the epicenter of the civil rights movement. In the spring of 1964, Dr. King and his fellow ministers from SCLC joined forces with local civil rights activists to do battle with city and county leaders over the community's widespread segregation policies. In between SCLC campaigns in Birmingham (1963) and Mississippi (fall, 1964), King viewed the St. Augustine movement as a way to keep the issues of segregation and racial discrimination before Americans and to maintain pressure on Congress to adopt the pending Civil Rights bill of 1964.

Despite being only 35 years of age, King was already a veteran of three major civil rights campaigns, the nation's leading spokesman for racial change and a gifted organizer with the ability to mobilize people from all walks of life behind the movement. Calling St. Augustine "the Oldest Segregated City in America," he drew the national press to the city to cover the protests and recruited an army of supporters.

Local white leaders fought King at every turn and worked closely together to defeat civil rights protesters. They also privately encouraged the violence perpetrated by white extremists against the demonstrators.

Paradoxically the actions of local leaders and militants played into the hands of King and supporters of civil rights reform. Events in St. Augustine unfolded on the national news and in the nation's newspapers, mobilizing public and congressional leaders behind the civil rights bill. The bill became law on July 2, 1964, and ended segregation in the nation. The demonstrations by young and old in St. Augustine had been instrumental in its adoption.

As we celebrate Black History Month, we need to remember that Florida's place in the nation prior to 1964 was circumscribed by racism and segregation policies that crippled its advancement and oppressed an entire race of people. It took the courageous actions of individuals in Rosewood and St. Augustine to expose this and to help secure the nation's democracy for all its people.

## As the Last Rosewood Survivor Dies, Let's Remember What We Did

David Colburn

*Tampa Bay Times*, May 13, 2018

Mary Hall Daniels was a child of 3 when a white mob destroyed her home and the predominantly African-American community of Rosewood in Levy County in 1923. The last survivor of what came to be known as the Rosewood massacre, Mrs. Daniels died on May 2 at the age of 98. Her passing has raised concerns among many that our knowledge and understanding of Rosewood and the pervasiveness of racial violence in Florida's history might well be lost with her.

The tragedy at Rosewood during the first week of January 1923 not only highlighted the prevalence of racism in America, but also subverted the nation's commitment to democracy and to a fair and impartial judicial system. The black community was destroyed after a false allegation of rape against a black man who was never identified. Several residents were also murdered by a white mob. Others were driven from their property forever.

Black citizens throughout the nation asked what had happened to the nation's commitment to make the "World Safe for Democracy" when it entered World War I in 1917. Didn't Rosewood and other acts of racial violence and discrimination usurp this promise?

The white response to this question was unambiguous. The editor of the Gainesville Daily Sun underscored the views of other whites when he proudly proclaimed in December 1922, on the eve of Rosewood, that he was a member of the Klan. He even singled out the organization's many noble qualities.

Ruthless and inhumane actions against black citizens became the accepted response in the South and increasingly in the North when they protested segregation. During the period from 1918 to 1927, Klan members and lynch mobs nationally took 454 lives, 416 of whom were African-American. In Florida, 47 black citizens were lynched during the same period. It was open season on African-Americans, with any violation of southern racial codes sufficient to warrant torture and execution.

Indeed, Florida was among the worst states for violence in this period. In addition to the 47 blacks who died by lynching, the highest per capita rate in the nation, whites destroyed the town of Ocoee in November 1920 when two black men attempted to vote. In Perry, four black men were murdered for allegedly killing a teacher.

In the 1980s, when the events of Rosewood finally came to light from this dark and distant past, it sparked a state and national campaign to compensate survivors for the loss of their property and the damages they suffered. State legislators Al Lawson and Miguel DeGrandy formed a cross-party, cross-cultural alliance—between a Democrat and a Republican and an African-American and a Cuban-American. Joining them was Gov. Lawton Chiles, five state historians and Florida's leading law firm, Holland & Knight, which gathered the historical and legal documentation detailing the history of Rosewood.

The legislative investigation turned on the testimony of Leslie and Ernest Parham, two white residents of Sumner, adjacent to Rosewood, where Ernest delivered ice frequently. Both asserted that the residents of Rosewood were good people, owned their property and were law abiding. Ernest emphasized to the state commission that "They did not deserve what happened to them."

In spring of 1994, Gov. Chiles and the state Legislature agreed to compensate each of the survivors. Nine survivors shared $2 million in what remains the only racial incident of its kind in the nation's history in which a state acknowledged its complicity and in which survivors were remunerated.

Why should we worry about Floridians forgetting this era after the state took the extraordinary step of compensating the victims? First, the story of Rosewood was covered up for seven decades by whites who denied any knowledge of or participation in the town's destruction. Second, there were many other horrific events in Florida and the nation that are seldom referred to in history books. Third, Florida's population has changed so dramatically since the survivors' compensation that few know of Rosewood today.

So, yes, we are in danger of forgetting this tragic past. But moving forward on race requires that we hold on to our history and continue to honor the victims of Rosewood and other racial violence. The nation's new lynching memorial in Montgomery, Ala., is an important step. Researchers with the Equal Justice Initiative have identified the lynchings of more than 4,000 U.S. citizens between 1877 and 1950, including 19 in Alachua County and eight in Levy County, home of Rosewood. The memorial consists of hanging columns arranged by counties, each with the names of victims from that county. Each county can bring home a duplicate column to display. Another possibility could be building something simple and powerful, echoing the feeling of the Vietnam Veterans Memorial.

We owe it to all victims of racial violence; to all survivors; and to the future, to acknowledge past injustices. Mary Hall Daniels' life spanned the tumultuous period from Rosewood's destruction in 1923 to the apology and compensation from the state in 1994. Let us pledge to her, and the other residents of Rosewood, that we will never forget their history—and ours.

# 6

# Population Diversity

Since the first Europeans made contact with the area they named La Florida, the state has always had a diverse population. It is not coincidental that in the 19th century, Florida sent the first Hispanic person to the U.S. House of Representatives (Joseph Hernandez) and the first Jewish person to the U.S. Senate (David Levy Yulee). By 1900, Florida had the largest immigrant population in the South, fueled by significant Cuban, Spanish, and Italian migration to the burgeoning cigar manufacturing community of Ybor City. Buoyed by low taxes, inexpensive housing costs, and year-round warm weather, newly retired senior citizens flocked to the Sunshine State in the post-World War II era, making Florida a haven for the elderly. In the 1950s, the population of persons over 65 increased by an incredibly 132 percent—at a time when only four other states saw an increase of more than 50 percent. By 2019, almost 21 percent of the state's residents were over 65, representing an important voting bloc often concerned about very different political issues from those of Florida's younger citizens. Florida's population is also exceptionally diverse ethnically, racially, and culturally, which can lead to a lack of political unity. Colburn concludes that "Florida's complex racial, ethnic, and age diversity, together with its dramatic demographic changes, promises to compound further its lack of identity and to make consensus on public policy difficult." While the articles in this section discuss the political problems inherent in a diverse polity, they also talk about the importance of embracing this very diversity to ensure a better future for the state. A 2001 article in the Fort Lauderdale *Sun-Sentinel* verifies this dichotomy; it concluded that Florida has "a population whose diversity is both an asset and a challenge." And the population continues to get more diverse. No longer is Florida's Hispanic population almost exclusively Cuban. Significant numbers of Venezuelans, Columbians, and other South and Central Americans have turned south and central Florida into a polyglot region whose political leanings are up for grabs. Over one million Puerto Ricans called Florida home in 2019. Other Caribbean migrants, particularly from Haiti, add to Florida's diverse mix of people. And while The Villages, the largest retirement community in the country, remains a bastion of Republican support, the same amenities there that appeal to mature conservative residents also attract older gay and lesbian couples. What can this population diversity mean for Florida's future? David Colburn said it best in a January 1, 2017 *Tampa Bay Times* op-ed. "So here's wishing," Colburn wrote, "that Florida continues to embrace the future in 2017 and to include all its people in that embrace."

## Younger vs. Older Voters

**Ominous implications for nation, especially for Florida**

David Colburn

*Orlando Sentinel*, July 26, 1992

Senior citizens believe they have paid into the system and are only receiving their fair share in return. The young worry that health care and Social Security needs of the elderly are helping to drown the federal budget in a sea of red ink.

In a recent survey of Florida voters, two political scientists reported dramatic findings: The state's elderly were perceived by voters under 55 as variously "an economic burden, an economically selfish voting bloc, a generationally divisive influence, or an unconstructive community element."

Their findings reflected the consequences of the recent recession, which not only crippled the American economy, but also has created deep divisions within American society as individuals and groups compete for limited job opportunities and diminishing resources. It was not the first time that the country's laboring classes and its ethnic and racial groups clashed during a period of economic decline. But it was the first time in recent memory that generational conflict emerged between the nation's senior citizens and other voters.

In their study, Professors Walter Rosenbaum and James Button of the University of Florida argue that intergenerational divisions might well shape local and perhaps national politics for the remainder of this century and perhaps beyond. According to Rosenbaum and Button, such conflict occurs most sharply at the community level, "where the elderly are no abstraction but a daily reality."

The initial results of their research have ominous implications for the nation and especially for Florida, where nearly one in five residents is retired. This is a society that is continuing to gray rapidly and one in which governmental resources and entitlement programs are being increasingly earmarked for the elderly.

The massive baby boom generation of the World War II era is also fast approaching retirement, and this group is not being replaced in the workplace by an equal number of younger people. Where five workers formerly funded Social Security and health care programs for each retiree, only two workers will support one retiree in the near future.

Adding to the concerns and alienation of younger voters, the over-55 generation is a well-to-do group, controlling nearly 75 percent of the financial assets of American households. They have simultaneously become wealthier as a group and also a heavier financial burden on society. It is an ironic development to say the least, and one that has not escaped the attention of those who are being asked to fund special programs for retirees.

Although senior citizens believe they have paid into the system and are only receiving their fair share in return, the young are not so convinced. They worry that health care and Social Security needs of the elderly are helping to drown the federal budget in a sea of red ink and threatening state budgets, and that they will be saddled with these financial burdens for much of their careers.

The intergenerational conflict has been further dramatized by the political organization and lobbying efforts of the American Association of Retired Persons. In Florida, the AARP has mobilized entire retirement communities to vote for candidates who support its political agenda. It is, not surprisingly, one of the wealthiest and most influential political action committees in the United States, and its influence is further magnified in an era when fewer and fewer non-retirees are voting in state and national elections.

Rosenbaum and Button found that younger voters in Florida particularly resent the narrow agenda of the AARP and its lobbying for single-issue items that benefit only its members. The two authors note that this especially true in communities that have a high proportion of retired voters.

In this age of diminishing resources and declining job opportunities, tensions between groups are bound to increase. The American economic pie has dwindled in size and international economic competition threatens to reduce the United States to a low-paying, service-based economy. A crippling federal deficit, fueled by entitlement programs, adds to America's economic woes and further limits its competitiveness.

Should this pattern persist and should the elderly continue to be perceived as lobbying to protect and enhance their own interests at the expense of the general welfare, then younger voters will remain at odds with their older brethren. The consequences of such a clash would not be in the best interests of the nation or in the best interests of the elderly, but this is often the result when resources and opportunities are diminished and when groups compete for a narrower slice of the economic pie.

## Gray and Growing Grayer: The Elderly and Florida

David Colburn

*Orlando Sentinel*, February 14, 2000

Customarily a place of youth and beauty, Florida has more recently become a state for retiring and growing old.

It is a sea change in the way the nation views Florida and in the way Florida sees itself. Historian Gary Mormino notes, "No society had ever confronted or conceived a future in which a large part of its population lived for two or more decades after they stopped working."

This demographic development and its ramifications for Florida in the 21st century were the subject of this year's annual meeting of the Reubin

Askew Institute, which explores issues of statewide significance, at the University of Florida earlier this month.

The development of a large and dynamic senior population has been unfolding rapidly in Florida during the past 30 years. Seniors represented only 6.9 percent of Florida's population in 1940. Four decades later, that figure was 17.3 percent. By 1990, 10 of 11 of the nation's most-senior counties and 15 of the top 19 could be found in Florida. The state's retirees now are more than 18 percent of the population, or nearly 2.9 million people, and, by itself, this population is larger than that of 17 states.

Seniors exercise enormous political muscle in Florida because they vote in much larger numbers than do other constituent groups. The U.S. Census Bureau and Division of Elections found that, in the 1998 elections, seniors made up 18 percent of the state's population, 24 percent of the voting-age population and 27 percent of the state's registered voters.

Last year, Florida had the second-oldest population in the nation, behind West Virginia. And the Sunshine State will see its senior population expand significantly after 2010, with the retirement of the baby-boom generation. The so-called baby boomers, the children of the World War II generation who were born between 1946 and 1964, have been moving through American society like the proverbial pig through a python. As the nation enters the new millennium, they are fast approaching retirement. Indeed, there is a baby boomer turning 50 every seven seconds in this country.

By 2025, as many as 22 of the state's 67 counties are expected to have senior populations of 30 percent or more. And the number of senior citizens—those older than 65—is expected to be 5.4 million people, or 26.3 percent of the population. Florida will be the oldest state in the nation; by contrast Alaska will be the youngest, with only 10 percent of its population being older than 65.

By any measure, this group of seniors will be the single most influential group in the state. At the local level, these seniors will have the ability to decide most elections. Moreover, in statewide campaigns in non-presidential elections, seniors in 2025 could well determine the outcomes by themselves. There seems little question that they will shape the political agenda and the platforms of political candidates at all levels of government.

The social and economic demographics paint a generally positive picture for the next generation of Florida's senior citizens. With some exceptions, the baby-boom seniors are much better off financially as they approach their retirement years than their parents were. A generally strong economy and a booming stock market have strengthened their investments and retirement portfolios.

There is every indication, then, that the baby boomers in 2025 will be more financially secure and more active than any preceding it. Their wealth will be an asset to Florida. Although some experts argue that seniors are a drain on the state economy, recent studies dispute that. Between 1985 and 1990, for example, seniors transferred $8 billion in assets to Florida and transferred only $1.8 billion out of the state.

The continued expansion of this group also has significant implications for public policy, especially in the areas of health care, transportation, the workplace and social programs.

In health care alone, for example, the leading causes of death in Florida are closely related to the age of its population: Heart disease tops the list at 31.5 percent of all deaths, followed by cancer at 24 percent and cerebra-vascular [*sic*] diseases at 6 percent. Current statistics indicate that seniors live generally healthy lives until age 75, at which point physical disabilities begin to occur.

Nevertheless, longevity for seniors will continue to improve with advances in health care, diet and physical exercise. One of the largest increases among seniors in Florida, for example, has been among those who are 85 and older. That trend is expected to continue throughout the 21st century.

As Florida enters a new century, the evidence suggests that it will continue to struggle mightily with the dynamics of population growth and change. Seniors will be in a unique position to determine the political direction of the state, but Florida also will be faced with a higher proportion of both African-Americans and Hispanics as well as younger citizens who will want to see the state addressing their needs.

The 200 participants at the Askew Institute recommended that the governor and state legislative leaders take the lead in helping citizens of all ages understand these developments and their consequences for the state and in seeking constructive answers to them. Askew participants also proposed that historical notions of aging be reconsidered and that intergenerational connections be promoted at all levels of society to increase understanding and promote communication between elders and others [*sic*] citizens.

## Baby Boomers: A Big Part of the Graying of Florida

**Environment and weather attract seniors from other states**

David Colburn and Lance deHaven-Smith

*Gainesville Sun*, March 5, 2000

A Floridian asked her next-door neighbor, "Where do these people keep coming from?"

"I have no idea," responded the neighbor.

"Incidentally, how are your relatives in Chicago?" the neighbor inquired.

"Fine," she responded, "and yours in Rhode Island?"

This story is apocryphal, but it conveys the rapidity of population change in the state. If 10 Floridians were gathered in a room, seven would be from another state or nation.

Current population projections indicate Florida will rank first among the 50 states in the number of persons—approximately four million—added through net internal migration between 1995 and 2025.

They will be joining a substantial number of newcomers who have settled in the state since 1970.

A survey conducted for Leadership Florida found in 1999 that only one in four adult Floridians was actually born in Florida.

Over one-half of Florida's adult residents did not live in the state prior to 1980. One in four has moved to Florida during the 1990s.

As demographers assess the population projections for Florida over the next 25 years, they believe newcomers will continue to flock into the state, although the pace of growth will slow somewhat.

Growth will remain the dominant fact of life in Florida for most of the 21st century. The "Florida Dream"—a place of beautiful beaches, sun, youth and personal renewal—still resonates in the American fancy.

The state's strong economy during the period from 1994 to 2000 has added to its appeal among many Americans, Latin Americans and Europeans.

## An aging state

The most significant demographic development in Florida in the 21st century will be the growth of its retirement population. The emergence of a large and dynamic senior population has been unfolding rapidly in Florida during the past 30 years.

Seniors represented only 6.9 percent of Florida's population in 1940. Four decades later that figure had leapt forward to 17.3 percent.

By 1990, 10 of 11 of the nation's most senior counties and 15 of the top 19 could be found in Florida. The state's retirees presently constitute more than 18 percent of the population, or nearly 2.9 million people.

Traditionally a place of youth and beauty, Florida has more recently become a state for growing old and dying.

Eastern Airlines delayed its bankruptcy by delivering coffins from southeast Florida to various parts of the United States. Delta Airlines transported over 40,000 coffins in 1998.

Seniors first came to Florida because of the appeal of the weather, environment, low taxes and relatively cheap property.

The weather and the environment offered them a lifestyle that enhanced their senior years, and the tax structure enabled most to live comfortably on their fixed retirement incomes.

Historian Gary Mormino reminds us that "No society had ever confronted or conceived a future in which a large part of its population lived for two or more decades after they stopped working."

The state's seniors, currently larger by comparison than that of 17 states, have an influence that few other age groups can match.

## A political force

Seniors have made their presence felt at the state and local levels of government, taking an active role in the political process and voting at much higher rates than other voters. Quite conservative in their political views, they have helped spark the resurgence of the Republican Party in the state.

Seniors exercise enormous political muscle in Florida because they vote in much larger numbers than other constituent groups.

The U.S. Census Bureau and Division of Elections found in the 1998 elections that seniors constituted 18 percent of the state's population, 24 percent of the voting age population and 27 percent of the state's registered voters.

Political scientist Susan MacManus recently observed that exit surveys of the 1998 gubernatorial election revealed that seniors represented 32 percent of all voters.

And when those 60 and older were lumped together, they represented a staggering 42 percent of the voters.

Moreover, seniors are increasingly electing one of their own to local and county government posts.

Seniors constitute 29 percent of the city council members in Florida, compared to 23 percent nationally.

Senior citizens also have made substantial demands on the state's social and medical services while simultaneously pressuring state politicians to limit new tax initiatives and other revenue measures that might adversely affect their fixed incomes.

This, while they have supported programs to aid the infirmed, provide better health care and protect the elderly from crime, they have generally resisted new spending for other social programs, education and family-related issues.

## The boomers retire

The second oldest state in the nation in 1999 behind West Virginia, Florida will see its senior population expand significantly after 2010 with the retirement of the baby boom generations.

The so-called baby boomers, children of the World War II generation who were born between 1946 and 1964, have been moving through American society like the proverbial pig through a python. There is a baby boomer turning 50 every seven seconds in this country.

By 2025, as many as 22 of the state's 67 counties are expected to have senior populations of 30 percent or more. The number of senior citizens, those over 65 years of age, is expected to be 5,453,000 (or 26.33 percent of the population.) Florida will be the oldest state in the nation.

By any measure, this group of seniors will constitute the single most influential group in state politics. At the local level, they will decide most elections in many counties.

Moreover, in statewide campaigns in non-presidential elections, seniors in 2025 could well determine the outcomes by themselves. There seems little question that they will shape the political agenda and the platforms of political candidates at all levels of government. Candidates will find it virtually impossible to win without their support.

### Boomer politics

Although many Boomers have mellowed a great deal in middle age, they remain committed to many changes that occurred during their lifetimes.

Baby boomers are more likely than those in other age groups to define themselves explicitly as liberals.

Moreover, when compared to other adult Americans, boomers typically express less support for the military as an institution and for programs to increase military expenditures.

These attitudes are holdovers from the Vietnam era and the boomers' cynicism about the defense establishment.

### The elderly as an asset

The social and economic demographics paint a generally positive picture for the next generation of Florida's senior citizens.

With some exceptions, the baby boom seniors are much better off financially as they approach their retirement years than their parents.

A generally strong economy and booming stock market have strengthened their investments and retirement portfolios. There is every indicating, then, that the baby boomers in 2025 will be healthier, more financially secure and more active than any preceding them.

Their wealth will be an asset to Florida. Although some experts argue that seniors are a drain on the state economy, recent studies dispute that.

Between 1985 and 1990, for example, seniors transferred $8 billion in assets to Florida and only transferred $1.8 billion out of the state.

The continued expansion of this group also has significant implications for public policy, especially in the areas of health care, transportation, the workplace, and social programs.

Current statistics indicate that seniors live generally healthy lives up to age 75, at which point physical disabilities begin to occur.

Nevertheless, longevity for seniors will continue to improve with advances in health care, diet and physical exercise. More and more seniors will live longer and healthier lives in the future.

## A quality Florida

As seniors live increasingly into their 80s, 90s and 100s in the next century, they will insist that Florida have in place a good health care infrastructure.

They will also insist on state programs to provide transportation facilities and social programs to enhance the quality of their senior years. Many recent seniors have found the large retirement condominiums of South Florida unappealing. And as older seniors have begun dying, younger seniors have not moved in to replace them.

Moreover, even when younger seniors do move into condos with older seniors, they stay only briefly, often relocating further north.

Known as "halfbacks," these seniors have sought more dynamic communities in North Florida or in other Southern states that take them halfway back to their former states of residence.

As Florida enters a new century, the evidence suggests it will continue to struggle mightily with the dynamics of population growth and change.

Seniors will be in a unique position to determine the political direction of the state, but Florida will also be faced with a higher proportion of both African Americans and Hispanics as well as younger citizens who will want to see the state addressing their needs.

Florida government, which has been generally reactive in the late 20th century, must become more proactive in helping citizens understand these developments, their consequences for the state, and in seeking constructive answers to them.

How Florida addresses the needs and concerns of senior citizens and also speaks to the needs of other citizens seems certain to represent its major challenge in the 21st century.

---

Lance deHaven-Smith is professor emeritus of political science at Florida State University.

## Think Opportunity, Not Conflict, as Generations Mix

David Colburn

*Orlando Sentinel*, September 30, 2007

That Florida continues to change dramatically in the 21st century does not surprise anyone who lives in the state or visits it. That Florida has emerged as a national and international laboratory in which residents representing four generations interact with one another in the workplace and in the community is probably news to most.

Author Greg Hammill writes, "This is the first time in American history that we have had four different generations working side-by-side in the workplace." The vast migration of seniors into Florida, their greater longevity and the migration and immigration of young families and young adults have positioned Florida as a testing ground for how these four generations interact with one another and the consequences it has for both the workplace and the community.

No state has changed more than Florida during the post-World War II period. Massive population growth has transformed Florida from a rural, Southern state to one that is vastly more complex, more urban and more diverse. Today, two in 10 Floridians are Hispanic and seniors now constitute 16.4 percent of the population. Both groups are expected to increase significantly in the next decade.

Are there ways that Florida can avoid intergenerational conflict, develop approaches to strengthen its communities, and capitalize on the talents and wisdom of all age groups? Hammill observes, "Research indicates that people communicate based on their generational backgrounds. Learning how to communicate with the different generations can eliminate many major confrontations and misunderstandings. . . ."

Residential patterns in Florida, however, have created substantial obstacles to improving communication between age groups. When seniors choose to reside in enclosed towns like The Villages or in gated condominiums such as those that dot the landscape in Southeast and Southwest Florida, and when many minorities find themselves isolated in largely segregated urban neighborhoods, finding common ground is difficult.

Compounding this situation is the fact that most retirees, especially those who are well to do, are white, while those with young families are increasingly Hispanic and African-American. The 2000 Census, for example, revealed that whites constituted 83.2 percent of those over 65, while Hispanics constituted only 9.9 percent, and African-Americans but 6 percent. The potential racial and ethnic divide between the four generations poses a major challenge to Florida and its political leaders as they seek to address the needs of all groups. This becomes especially true in difficult economic times.

Moreover, the priorities of seniors are principally health care, low taxes, financial security, the environment and transportation, while for most young families the priorities are education, job growth and opportunity, housing and health care. Although there is some overlap, there is often a sense of competition for Florida's resources and legislative priorities.

But an AARP/University of Southern California survey in 2004, Images of Aging, offers some encouragement. It found that "most Americans (85 percent) felt that older residents help to improve the quality of life in their community, and half (49 percent) felt that the economic benefits older residents bring to their community make up for the amount local government spends on them."

Indeed, many of Florida's recent retirees are well-off financially, and projections for the baby-boom retirees suggest that they will be even better off financially than those born before World War II. The wealth of seniors also has advantaged the state significantly. Between 1985 and 1990, for example, seniors transferred $8 billion in assets to Florida. Seniors have also taken on many important volunteer roles in society. All these factors, as well as a strong state economy, have been instrumental in the general harmony between the age groups.

What can we, as Floridians, do to maintain and build upon intergenerational harmony? What should we be prepared for as the current four generations face their respective opportunities and challenges—for example, as more seniors opt not to retire or re-enter the workforce because of financial pressures (erosion of traditional pension plans and health care) and the need for self-fulfillment, and middle generations juggle the needs of both older and younger generations for care and support?

Perhaps the first step to improving communication is to make the four generations aware of the commonalities that exist among them. No matter what age, race, ethnicity or income status, all Floridians want safe, vibrant and livable communities in which services, health care and transportation are readily accessible.

A growing number of resources exist to help states and local leaders build strong communities and improve communication among residents. One of the important resources is the Viable Futures Toolkit focused on "Sustainable Communities for all Ages" developed with the support of the blue moon fund and the Annie E. Casey Foundation.

Finding solutions to the challenges posed by four generations living and working side-by-side is critically important for the future of the state. Florida has a unique opportunity to create a generational model for the nation. Are we prepared and willing to do so?

## Forge a Florida Identity

David Colburn

*Tampa Bay Times*, January 1, 2013

So what is the biggest challenge facing Florida in this century? There are many possible answers, including: global warming, drinking water, economic growth and opportunity, immigration. And the list goes on.

The state's major challenge, in my view, is building a strong and healthy Florida and creating "one out of the many" who choose to live here.

For the first half of the 20th century, Floridians had a clear sense of themselves and their state. But it was not a society we would want to replicate—Floridians were racially polarized and the state struggled to provide a future for its residents.

Since World War II, Florida has changed dramatically, first being discovered by Northerners and then by Hispanics. For the past 40 years, people have arrived in extraordinary numbers, but they have also departed for other places in very large numbers. From 2000 to 2010 alone, 2.8 million people moved into Florida, despite the Great Recession. But an estimated 900,000 also departed during that time.

Today, as a result of this demographic upheaval, 48 percent of Floridians were born in another state, 19 percent in a foreign country, and 33 percent in Florida. The percentage of native-born is the lowest in the nation, while the percentage of foreign-born among the highest.

Is it any wonder that Floridians lack a sense of community, a mythic identity, and a knowledge of the state's past?

Finding ways to bridge the ethnic, age, and racial divisions and to develop a citizenry that is informed, engaged, and has an appreciation of what it means to be a Floridian is difficult at best in this highly mobile society.

For those seniors who reside only half the year in Florida, understanding the problems facing the state and its young families does not come easy. Seniors will remain the single most influential group of voters for the foreseeable future, and their numbers will be bolstered by the generation of baby boomers, those born from 1946 to 1964, who choose to settle in Florida. The challenge facing Florida is to engage these seniors, many of whom are part-time residents, in ways that will encourage them to look beyond their self-interest to the welfare of others and the state.

Further complicating this situation, seniors are overwhelmingly white, while young families are increasingly of color. Approximately 77 percent of those over 65 are white, compared to 13.3 percent for Hispanics and 7.38 percent for African-Americans in 2012. This age and ethnic divide does not lend itself to addressing respective concerns and needs.

For immigrant groups, especially those in this hemisphere, the ability to move back and forth has been made easy through air travel, and it has, in turn, complicated the development of a cohesive citizenry. Most Hispanics have arrived in the last two decades and their identity remains principally with their homeland and with people from their homeland who have moved to Florida.

What seems certain about Florida's immediate future is that, as the Great Recession eases its grip, population growth, dominated by the baby boom migration and Hispanic immigration, will reassert itself and shape the state for much of this century.

Florida's complex racial, ethnic and age diversity, together with its dramatic demographic changes, promises to compound further its lack of identity and to make consensus on public policy difficult. Carl Hiaasen says of Floridians that they are unpredictable because they don't know or remember the past. But it is not just senior citizens who are memory-challenged. In a state as dynamic as Florida, where change is a daily occurrence and where traditions find little traction, Floridians struggle to find community.

While diversity of this sort is a tremendous obstacle to building community and achieving understanding, diversity has also enabled the state to compete globally and to be enriched by the diverse cultures immigrants have brought with them.

The task confronting the state is how to preserve the benefits of diversity and also find ways to draw us closer so that we can forge a meaningful future together. We need to start that conversation.

## Embrace Florida's Diversity Instead of Isolation

**David Colburn**

*Gainesville Sun*, September 30, 2018

Florida has long been distinguished as a place of astonishing beauty and complexity with its seductive beaches, lakes and rivers, and its diverse population. The sea of visitors who came to enjoy the state's natural beauty often stayed to become permanent residents, especially after World War II.

In a remarkably short time frame, they transformed Florida into one of the most ethnically and racially diverse states in the nation. Today's residents continue to arrive from nearly every corner of the globe and, in the process, they have strengthened Florida's economy, enriched its culture and advanced its place in the hemisphere.

What was a rural, isolated, impoverished and segregated state prior to 1940 became one of the most dynamic, multiracial and multi-ethnic states between 1950 and 2018. Florida stood at the epicenter of the population influx that redefined the nation.

Joining this diverse population were retirees from the north, whose children had left home in search of new jobs as the national economy boomed. Seniors thus found themselves free to begin a new life away from the harsh winters. The low taxes, inexpensive property and salubrious environment of Florida proved particularly appealing. These demographic changes transposed Florida's standing in the nation.

Seniors basked in the sunshine and enjoyed the outdoors for much of the year—prolonging their lifespan in the process. For many this was the Fountain of Youth portrayed by Ponce de Leon. Florida Historian Gary

Mormino, one of the state's leading scholars who followed the parade of migrants into Florida in the 1970s, described the state as a "powerful symbol of renewal and regeneration." The quality of life revitalized retirees and enriched it for immigrants in ways few initially imagined.

All the state needed to achieve a near-perfect environment was air conditioning and bug spray. By the mid-1950s, both became realities.

The appeal of Florida's environment became so widespread that residents feared the loss of the state's environmental beauty, and they looked for ways to secure their slice of paradise. But that goal proved unachievable as 3 million people per decade entered Florida from 1970 to the present, searching for their own slice of paradise.

Their numbers were so great—reaching nearly 21 million residents in July 2017—that the only way to preserve paradise was to exercise strict zoning restrictions over development. Most, however, had fled the north to escape intrusive government and taxes and had little interest in re-imposing them on Florida.

The state's population explosion was so dramatic that the majority of newcomers knew little about Florida's past and the challenges it faced as a result of the tremendous population growth. Initially residents resided in neighborhoods comprised of people like themselves. Seniors walled themselves off from "others" by residing in high-rise condominiums or in enclosed communities like the Villages, while immigrants lived in urban ghettos with others who looked and spoke like themselves.

As the population boomed in the 1950s, Democrats resorted to blatant racist campaigns that pledged to close all public schools to prevent desegregation. Then in the 1960s, state politicians organized to stop the massive influx of Cubans fleeing the Castro revolution, condemning them, in particular, for trying to establish a foreign country in South Florida.

In the late 1960s and into the 21st century, Republicans became the majority party by labeling the Democratic Party as liberal, pro-busing, pro-taxes and anti-business. These appeals made no attempt to educate Floridians about the opportunities provided by its immigrant and aging populations.

A state with a longer history and a stronger sense of itself might well have ignored such infantile appeals. But not in Florida, where so many people were new to the place and unfamiliar with one another—almost 20 percent were born in a foreign country and more than 50 percent were from another state.

In strong economic times, particularly the 1970s and 1980s, reason and substantive debate prevailed at the polls, but not after 2000 as the technology boom collapsed, the nation found itself mired in war in the Middle East, and the great recession of 2008 almost bankrupted Florida and the nation.

Still, Florida's future remains full of promise with a population that reflects the rich heritage and diversity of the nation, and an economy and culture that leads the hemisphere. But it will continue to struggle to achieve its potential if its political leaders persist in isolating us from one another and we accept their partisan drivel.

## Florida Has Been Greatly Enriched by Newcomers

David Colburn

*Tampa Bay Times*, April 6, 2019

There has been so much negativism of late around issues of diversity that a nucleus of white citizens, encouraged by President Donald Trump, have denounced racial and ethnic minorities as a burden to the nation and Florida.

The reality, in fact, suggests just the opposite. The nation and Florida have been greatly enriched by the nation's multiplicity of people, a resultant diverse and dynamic economy, and an advancement, not a diminishment, of the nation's liberties.

Today's social and demographic changes were rooted in the 20th century, and this transition proved arduous for the nation and particularly so for Florida. For much of this era race and ethnicity tended to divide rather than unify Americans. Florida was one of the poorest, most isolated states in the nation, with a citizenry that was deeply divided by race.

On the eve of World War II, the state represented little more than an intriguing footnote in the history of the United States. It was the place of the oldest European settlement in the nation as well as the oldest free black community, but few Floridians were aware of their history and lacked interest in celebrating it.

For the better part of 14 years, from 1926 to 1940, Florida was mired in the Great Depression, with no obvious way out. World War II would change the state's image as soldiers in training told relatives back home about the beauty of the place. Gradually a more progressive Florida took hold and the state readily opened its doors to people from all backgrounds.

During the following 70 years, Florida was transformed from one of the most regressive states in the South as well as one of the most backward to one of the most diverse, complex and dynamic states in the nation. Only California rivaled Florida's ethnic and racial complexity.

For once in modern history, Florida led the nation and Floridians welcomed the entry of people from throughout the Hemisphere, including Cubans, Puerto Ricans, Jamaicans, Haitians, Venezuelans and many others. With doors of the state flung open, ethnic and racial immigrants were welcomed in most of the service industries and regarded as essential to Florida's economic renaissance.

By 1990, sociologist John Shelton Reed observed that, as a result of these developments Florida had lost all of its Dixie characteristics with the exception of one small area in the Panhandle.

The dramatic demographic changes made Florida a richer, more complex and diverse state. By 2010 fewer than one-third of Floridians were native-born, while 46 percent were born in another state, and 17.6 percent in a foreign country. Hispanics constituted 22 percent of the population, an increase from less than 1 percent in 1940.

While Florida was a vastly different place in the 21st century, it was not adverse [*sic*] to persistent racial appeals and violence, particularly during economic downturns and racial clashes over such issues as Civil War monuments.

In contrast to the past, however, most of these encounters spawned a limited following, and black and ethnic people refused to sit quietly when they occurred. Most minorities were fully integrated into most walks of life in Florida.

According to the Census of 2010, Florida's African-American owned businesses ranked 4th nationally, Hispanic-owned businesses ranked 2nd nationally, and women-owned businesses stood 3rd. Such economic diversity served as a roadblock to racism.

If there is a message Florida offers the nation today, it is a remarkably progressive one: that all people have value and all have the potential to add significantly to the advancement of society, especially when opportunity is widely available.

It is that message which should be embraced and celebrated today.

## Heroism, Yes, but Also Hate

David Colburn

*Tampa Bay Times*, July 4, 2019

As we celebrate July Fourth, it is a good time to remind ourselves of the challenges that still face us as a nation. While we have enjoyed a remarkable history as the world's oldest democracy, it has not been achieved without discrimination and violence against many of our people.

Our treatment of African Americans and Native Americans is most notable. And yet from the inception of the nation, African and Native Americans fought alongside George Washington to secure the freedom of the nation from British oppression. In the aftermath of the American Revolution, however, both peoples were denied the rights of citizenship and forced off their property.

Much the same occurred in the Civil War when blacks and Irish immigrants joined the armies of the north to defeat the Confederacy, despite widespread discrimination and violence against them. Gen. Ulysses Grant acknowledged the importance of the contribution of both people, but the nation refused to end segregation and discrimination against them when the war ended.

And so it went.

In World War II, Japanese Americans on the West Coast were taken from their homes and placed in isolated internment camps for fear they would sabotage the war effort against Japan. Yet Japanese-American young men from these camps volunteered and fought bravely in Europe against the armies of Hitler and Mussolini. One of their units, the 442nd Regimental Combat Team, became the most decorated in military history. But after returning home, the soldiers and their families were denied the property taken from them when they were interned.

Despite widespread anti-Semitism in the United States before World War II, Jewish Americans also volunteered for service in record numbers

(1.5 million) to defend the nation against fascism. But in June 1939, when nearly 1,000 Jews from Germany attempted to dock aboard the ship St. Louis in Miami, they were turned away. Subsequent charges of espionage were used to deny entry to thousands more, many of whom were forced to return to Germany.

Black Americans also volunteered in record numbers and were initially assigned to quartermaster units because the military alleged they were not mentally fit to serve in the infantry. But when the Germans threatened to overrun the American forces at the Battle of the Bulge (1944–45), black soldiers were thrown into the battle by Gen. Dwight Eisenhower and helped stymie the German offensive. When they returned home with their war medals, however, they encountered widespread discrimination and violence if they spoke out against segregation.

We should never forget the heroism and contributions made by all Americans to the advancement and well-being of the nation. Our core values make us unique in the world, but they are only meaningful if we embrace them and exhibit them through our actions on a daily basis.

Following the murder of nine black worshippers at Emanuel African Methodist Episcopal Church in downtown Charleston (June 17, 2015), 20,000 residents came together at a mass unity rally held on the Arthur Ravenel Bridge. Charlestonians pledged to make this more than a one-time event. Since then, they have acknowledged and embraced one another, both friends and visitors, on a daily basis.

The action of Charlestonians is one way to acknowledge that we are one people, no matter our race, ethnicity or heritage.

Happy July Fourth, fellow Americans.

# PUBLIC POLICY

# 7

# The Economy and State Finances

State governments are about more than ideology and politics. At a basic level, they are about money—how to get it and where to spend it. Florida is no exception to this, and much of the political infighting in Tallahassee in the past half-century has taken place over taxes and spending. In 1924, in the midst of a land boom in which property values throughout the state skyrocketed, nearly 81 percent of the state's voters chose to amend the state constitution and outlaw a state income tax. Since the income tax ban is still enshrined in the constitution, leaving Florida as one of only seven states that do not have such a state tax, there is very little chance that Florida will ever enact such a revenue source. Graham and Colburn examine the state's financial concerns in this section, focusing on how state government weathered the financial and real estate crisis of the early part of the 21st century. They examine both the taxation and spending sides of state financial policy and find problems with each. In a state wedded to low tax rates and enormous corporate tax loopholes, they ask how Florida can provide even a basic safety net for the state's most vulnerable citizens. They also show how a tax structure predicated on unfettered real estate development and an unsustainable growth model is extraordinarily susceptible to the vagaries of the market, as shown in the great recession of the early 21st century. Tying issues associated with the previous section on population diversity to tax concerns, Graham and Colburn discuss how hard it is to convince diverse groups of Floridians of the need to have government spending provide services in even the most basic areas, like education and infrastructure improvement. They look at why and how attempts to restructure Florida's tax situation, such as Governor Martinez's 1987 intangible tax debacle, have failed so miserably. Finally, they attempt to analyze the issue of growth management and how that ties into concerns of taxation and expenditure. In the 1970s, Florida was the model for the nation with its planned program of government coordinated growth management and environmental protection. Graham and Colburn explain how this series of laws, regulatory agencies, and environmental support systems devolved into a governmental structure devoted to unrestricted growth. Most importantly, however, they advocate for a tax-and-spend system that will be fairer and will provide Florida with the financial resources necessary to support all its citizens.

## Florida Myth: Financing Future on a Shoestring

**David Colburn**

*Orlando Sentinel*, September 22, 1991

Gov. Lawton Chiles announced on Tuesday that he will not seek additional taxes to ease Florida's latest budget crisis but will, instead, continue his crusade to right-size government.

House Speaker T.K. Wetherell, a frequent critic of right-sizing, nevertheless agreed with Chiles, pointing out that "until Joe Lunchbucket decides that there is a problem out there, it isn't going to be fixed."

Florida's political leaders have not historically set a high standard for courage, and this latest development is certainly consistent with past practices. Expecting the Joe Lunchbuckets to ask for new taxes is a little like waiting for the Russians to beg for the return of Joseph Stalin. It will not happen.

Evidence from other states during the past few years has demonstrated that Joe Lunchbucket and his friends have a very cynical view of government and remain convinced that their tax dollars are misspent. This cynicism results from a variety of factors, some of them real, some of them imagined. The people have, nevertheless, supported tax increases when political leaders have educated them to the needs of the state.

As a Florida native, Chiles ought to realize that the Florida Lunchbuckets are generally more resistant to new taxes than their relatives to the north. After all, ever since World War II, when political leaders sought to diversify the state's agricultural economy and alter its frontier-like environment, new industry and new citizens have been recruited by offering low taxes, cheap land and abundant sunshine. As is self-evident, the appeal worked—some people say too well.

Cheap land is no longer part of the sales pitch, but people continue to be attracted by low taxes and a semitropical climate. In the last year, 26.5 percent of the 300,000 newcomers to Florida were 55 or older, the highest proportion in recent history, and many indicated they came to retire, enjoy the healthful environment and escape the high taxes in their former states. These people aren't likely to support new taxes without understanding the issues.

The mentality of these newcomers and those who have arrived since 1945 has been conditioned understandably by those factors that persuaded them to come in the first place. Moreover, many moved into well-protected, enclosed communities where they are often oblivious to the world around them. That they persist in believing Florida can finance its future on a shoestring should not be surprising. After all, hasn't it done so up to now?

And yet the people who continue to move into the state are not poor or ignorant. Figures for 1990 reveal that 45 percent have incomes of more than $35,000 a year, and 65 percent have incomes above $25,000. They also have the highest levels of education in the state's history. They are not dumb, nor are they necessarily insensitive to the needs of their new state, but they have to be made more aware of the future consequences of today's decisions.

During the past four decades, Florida has become one of the four largest and most politically influential states in the nation, and yet Floridians have still not accepted the responsibilities that attend the state's new status. Florida support for public schools, families, children and the elderly ranks among the bottom one-third of all states, and this was prior to the fiscal reductions in the spring of 1991.

How do you right-size these financial realities?

Until political leaders address the real human and social needs and the consequences they have for the future, the state will continue to provide little more than abundant sunshine to its citizens and newcomers. And Florida will continue to experience mixed results in attracting new businesses, many of which find the progressive leadership in states like

California, Illinois and Minnesota more attractive for themselves and their employees.

As Education Commissioner Betty Castor pointed out, Florida is in desperate need of political leadership. But it requires a unique kind of courage to lead in a crisis. Today's state leaders seem content to watch from the sidelines. This is particularly unfortunate, because the present debate involves much more than an economic crisis. It involves Florida's future.

## Trouble in Paradise

**Florida dream seems a pale representation of its former self**

David Colburn

*Orlando Sentinel*, December 6, 1992

In the wake of Hurricane Andrew and the economic recession, there seems to be trouble in paradise. What was once a land of hope and opportunity is suddenly viewed as a place with intractable problems that threaten not only the dreams of Floridians but the realities of daily life.

For most of the past 50 years, Northerners have rushed to Florida searching for the good life. And who could blame them? It remains, after all, a beautiful environment encompassed by the majestic oaks and crystal rivers of the north and stately palms and languid ocean beaches of the south.

Up to 1945, the summer heat and humidity kept people away, but air conditioning persuaded them to think of Florida as they had California. Few were disappointed with their decision as the economy expanded and the environment readily embraced them. Like Ponce de Leon before them, most felt they had found paradise.

Word passed quickly from family to friends about the unique qualities of Florida and more people came and continued to come, until their numbers reached nearly 1,000 a day in 1992. During this period, Florida became a beacon—a special place for those seeking political freedom and asylum and for those seeking an opportunity to pursue their dreams anew.

But the nation's newest Eden has suffered from the overabundance of humanity and from the social and environmental problems that their numbers have created. Suddenly, the realities of daily living have become a chore.

Hurricane Andrew not only highlighted but seemed symptomatic of the state's worsening social, environmental and economic problems. Crime, poverty, racial and ethnic polarization have all conspired to threaten the quality of life in Florida and to make it indistinguishable from these and other conditions that have so adversely affected Southern California.

It may be another generation or two before Florida is confronted with the magnitude of the problems that now face Southern California, but the line of progression seems unmistakable. Florida currently has the second-highest crime rate and the second-largest population on death row in the nation. During the next two years, it is estimated that every Florida prison will be completely filled with prisoners on mandatory sentences.

The Eden-like environment of Florida, which initially drew so many people to the state, is today confronted with the massive mercury poisoning of the Everglades and the closing of its public resources.

The Florida dream seems a pale representation of its former self. These developments have not escaped the attention of Gov. Lawton Chiles, who, as a native of Florida, understands more fully than most what has been lost.

Others in government, especially state Senate leaders Ander Crenshaw and Pat Thomas, also seem to realize that "politics as usual" cannot continue in the face of such conditions and that Floridians expect solutions, not more political bickering.

The problems facing Florida are not insurmountable, but they do require attention. The Netherlands, which has a larger population than Florida but only one-third the land space, has dealt successfully with similar problems for much of its recent history through rigorous planning and through investment in public and private sector areas that promise to enhance the future. There is no reason why Florida cannot do the same. The alternative to planning and to seeking solutions to the state's social, economic and environmental needs is to repeat the problems of Southern California or worse.

The Florida dream has always been a surreal image. Today, in the wake of Hurricane Andrew and the recession, that image seems even more distorted than ever before. Floridians need to realize that dreams do not become reality without much hard work and commitment. If Floridians truly value what they have had, they will make that commitment. If not, we will all be forced to embrace a dreary future and the permanent dismantling of the Florida dream. The choice is ours.

## Can Florida Defy Being Typecast?

**Economic challenge: Become a global leader**

David Colburn

*Orlando Sentinel*, September 5, 1999

When Europeans are asked to identify places in the United States, they most frequently mention New York, Washington, Los Angeles and Orlando. They know Orlando, of course, because of Walt Disney World. On visiting Florida, however, Europeans are often surprised by the diversity of the state and the fact that it is more than Disney World and more than one mammoth service economy.

Although Florida's economy has changed significantly in this century, agriculture remains a very important segment of it. Florida, for example, ranks first in the Southeast United States in farm income and third in the nation in farm profits.

But agricultural employment has decreased dramatically throughout the century as a result of farm consolidation and automation. Moreover, the amount of land devoted to farming also has declined, especially in South and Central Florida. There, urban sprawl and escalating land values have gobbled up prime agricultural real estate.

Despite the continuing prominence of agriculture in the state, the service economy has become the dominant sector and the principal source of employment in the second half of the 20th century. Florida now ranks fourth in the nation, behind only California, New York and Texas, in the total number of service establishments and fourth in the number of service jobs.

Not all service-oriented jobs are low paying, but most are. It is a sector that offers many entry-level jobs at near minimum-wage salaries, and it offers only limited opportunities for advancement because there are relatively few management positions.

These so-called dead-end jobs are crucial to this industry, which requires considerable manpower, but they are not conducive to the long-term economic prosperity of the state's citizens. In a 1997 issue of Florida Trend, a mother commented on some of the frustrations that Floridians experience in such a low-wage economy. She had decided to return to school when her daughter left home for college, and the two graduated from college at almost the same time. Both were able to find jobs in a salary range of only $21,000 to $22,000. The mother asked rhetorically why she and her daughter had bothered to attend a university when that was the highest pay that their degrees could command.

Florida's non-farm employment is projected to increase by more than 30 percent between 1993 and 2005, but income projections for the nation for the same period indicate that Florida salaries will remain low. The state will rank only 25th in the nation, reflecting the continuing dominance of service-oriented jobs.

It is a consequence of these developments that many of the nation's corporate leaders have typecast Florida as a low-wage, tourist economy, with a preponderance of unskilled workers who have limited educations and limited job skills. The widespread perception of an ineffectual public-school system has only confirmed this prejudice among corporate officials.

Although low wages and service jobs will remain commonplace in Florida, the state's overall economy is expected to remain a dynamic one well into the 21st century. Six of Florida's major regions will be among the top 31 in terms of employment expansion, with Orlando being the most prominent in the state and the second-most active in the nation.

Although the service economy will continue to shape the state's business sector for the foreseeable future, the emergence of a global economy and high-technology companies in Southeast Florida and in the Tampa Bay and Orlando regions promise the economic diversity that state leaders have long sought. Sixty percent of Florida's trade is with Latin America, and that trade has been steadily expanding for the past decade. The number of high-technology jobs has reached nearly 100,000 in Central Florida alone. Global trade and high technology also offer the greatest opportunity for improved salaries in the state, with jobs in this sector typically paying 25 percent to 33 percent more than those in the service sector.

The emergence of a global economy and high technology and the continued expansion of the service sector in Florida have had tangible benefits for Floridians of all ethnic and racial backgrounds. Florida, for example, ranks very high nationally in the number of black- (fourth), Hispanic- (third), and women-owned firms (fourth). The expanding global economy and the service industry, in which race and color appear to be an asset, have provided much greater access for women- and minority-owned firms than for most other economic sectors.

The continued substantial growth of Florida's population well into the 21st century suggests that economic opportunities will remain considerable. The question persists, however: Will Florida remain one large, service-driven economy or will it become a global economic leader as well?

Although the answer is uncertain at present, it is crucial for Florida's future and for Floridians.

## Florida Should Learn from Its Past to Chart Recovery

David Colburn

*Orlando Sentinel*, December 16, 2008

Property values in Florida plummeted, speculators fled for parts unknown, and the state's economy went into a free-fall. The image of Florida as a place of opportunity and renewed hope was quickly transformed into a land of desperation and discarded dreams. Left holding the bag were natives and residents who had no other alternative but to stay. Florida's cities and counties edged toward the precipice of bankruptcy with little hope in sight and inept political leadership to address it.

The history of the collapse of the land boom in Florida in the 1920s reads eerily like events of 2008. Flipping mortgages; egregious subprime, alternative A-paper and option ARM loans; and get-rich-quick schemes of the 21st century had their parallel more than 80 years ago. And the mentality driving the state toward economic disaster was much the same in both eras.

The crisis today pales next to that of the mid-1920s, when Florida entered an economic depression and only emerged from it in 1940 as the world went to war. But today's crisis appears to be by far the worst the state has experienced since then. From March 2007 to October 2008, Florida's construction industry lost 123,900 jobs, business services surrendered 52,900 positions, and manufacturing declined by 33,400 jobs. Florida's housing crisis may well be the worst in the nation. And state government now faces a nearly $6 billion deficit next year, with few prospects, other than draconian cuts to all segments of civic life, to balance the budget.

So what to do? In a recent essay, economist David Denslow of the University of Florida asked the pertinent question: Will the gaps left by construction, manufacturing, real estate and other declining sectors be filled only by tourist and other service jobs (in other words, is Florida doomed to having a third-world economy)?

During the land-boom collapse of the 1920s, no single group took responsibility to develop plans for post-Depression Florida. Political leaders argued about whether to cut taxes or to raise additional revenue to help those in need. In the end, they resorted to fisticuffs on the floor of the state Legislature and begged the New Deal for assistance.

Is that what awaits us in the special session of the Legislature and in the regular session in March? Not likely. Florida has better leadership at all levels than it had in the 1920s, but there is no sign that we are any better prepared to address the crisis before us or to make plans that will ensure a better future for Floridians. As of this writing, neither the Legislature nor any other group in Florida has considered how we got into this mess and how we can get out of it. No group is considering approaches that would offer the state and its citizens a better future.

The coming of World War II ultimately rescued Florida from the depths of the Great Depression in the 1920s and 1930s. And Florida built a strong postwar economy that relied disproportionately on population growth. It was a naïve policy, but it worked because more than 2.5 million people entered the state each decade following the war. But a state cannot build a future on growth alone, even massive growth, and this crisis, more than any, has demonstrated why.

Growth produces nothing but a demand for services, and it can fund those services only if that growth continues at a high rate. We have witnessed the short-sightedness of this policy for three decades. Our school drop-out rate is the highest in the nation, and our schools rank at the bottom nationally. Our universities and community colleges are overwhelmed with students and offer classes that are too large and too often taught by adjuncts. At the same time, we have one of the largest prison populations in the nation, and our infrastructure needs—from schools to water to roads to bridges—are massive.

There are no short-term or quick-fix solutions to the current crisis, but we need to be sure we know the causes, so we don't repeat them. And, even more importantly, we need to develop plans that will offer Floridians a future that is built not on growth but on a substantial investment in its people.

## Florida Needs to Take Bold Steps to Save Economy

David Colburn

*Orlando Sentinel*, January 22, 2009

In the early 1930s, during the worst of the Great Depression, Florida's political leaders threw up their hands in frustration, offering no solutions to the economic crisis confronting the state and its people. Instead, they petitioned President Franklin Delano Roosevelt to use New Deal programs to relieve Florida's economic distress.

Today, nearly 75 years later, it seems to be, as Yogi Berra once described it, "déjà vu all over again."

The state economy and the state budget are in dreadful shape. Unemployment has jumped dramatically from 4.4 percent in November 2007 to 7.3 percent in November 2008. Some counties have seen a 50 percent increase in the number of families receiving food stamps. The state deficit now exceeds $2.3 billion.

But that's not the worst of it. Amy Baker, the Legislature's chief economist, projects Florida will face another $4 billion shortfall in 2010.

So what's the solution? This past November, House Speaker Ray Sansom and Senate President Jeff Atwater promised Floridians that "all options will be under consideration, and we will work as quickly as possible to determine the best course of action."

But that was November. As of mid-January, the only solution seems to be, cut, cut and cut again. Cut public-school funding, cut higher-education funding, cut environmental programs, cut health care for children, and, oh yes, appeal to President Barack Obama to channel a proportion of the $825 billion economic-stimulus plan to Florida.

Republican Gov. Charlie Crist told reporters at the close of the special session, "I think it's very important that we support the new administration. Certainly it's [the stimulus package] going to help Florida, and I believe we'll see some progress there."

Is this the best Florida can do?

The governor and legislators assure us that, despite this economic downturn, Florida will recover, all will be right with the world, and we will once again have the funds to invest in education and compete globally.

Our leaders seem to have this fantasy view of the world that we can compete in a global economy on the cheap.

They are eager to denounce Obama for wasteful spending, but are more than willing to take our fair share of funds from his stimulus package. After all, we are the fourth-largest state in the nation and deserve our fair share.

Heaven forbid we should take any bold steps on our own. After all, this is a down economy we are told, and taxing cigarettes or Internet sales or removing the numerous sales-tax exemptions would be sheer lunacy in a down economy. The fact is that we are 46th in the nation in cigarette taxes (slightly higher than our public-school ranking, one should note), and we have no Internet sales tax for online companies that do not have a physical presence in the state (unlike 19 other states).

The current budget crisis places front and center the future of the state and tests our will to confront it. On the basis of this special session, it appears we have failed the test once again.

## Growth Management Didn't Cause State's Economic Woes

**Bob Graham**

*Orlando Sentinel*, January 12, 2014

In a recent widely circulated opinion piece, Wendell Cox, a St. Louis-based demographer, blamed Florida's growth-management laws enacted in the 1970s and '80s for the devastating effects of the 2007 great recession. Cox contends these laws restricted the supply of housing, contributing to the housing bubble, the financial crisis and great recession.

He further asserts the repeal of growth-management laws in 2011 was a key factor in the state's recovery.

As governor when Florida's 1985 Growth Management Act was passed, I'd like to share some observations regarding Cox's analysis.

In the 1980s, Florida was growing at the rate of almost 1,000 people a day, roughly the equivalent of adding a new city of Tampa every year. It was in this climate the Legislature overwhelmingly supported and I signed into law Florida's 1985 Growth Management Act.

In conjunction with land- and water-management legislation adopted in 1972, the act's four primary objectives were to protect environmentally sensitive areas from overdevelopment; ensure that the roads, schools and other infrastructure to support new development were properly funded and in place concurrent with the new growth; manage water resources for the public's benefit; and acquire conservation lands to protect Florida's natural resources, economy and quality of life.

From 1985 until 2007, Florida's economy flourished. Our population continued to grow, from 11.3 million in 1985 to 18.7 million in 2007. During the 1980s alone, Florida added 1.5 million new jobs and for the first time in the state's history, Floridians' per-capita income exceeded that of the average American.

The Financial Crisis Inquiry Commission, which investigated the great recession, did not find that growth-management policies such as Florida's were the cause of the collapse. Rather, the collapse of Florida's housing market—like those in other Sunbelt states—was driven by a variety of factors including rampant speculation, lax regulatory policies, weak underwriting standards and old-fashioned greed and fraud. These were the same causes of Florida's crashes in the 20th century, before the state's growth-management laws were enacted.

From 1990 to 2000, Florida added, on average, more than 100,000 housing units per year. But in the years leading up to 2007, housing starts exceeded 200,000 units per year and, between 2007 and 2010, 660,000 more residences of all types were authorized to be constructed, as well as more than 6 billion square feet of commercial and institutional space, most of which has not been built.

Florida's anti-government political order "seized the moment" in 2011, securing draconian cuts to conservation lands acquisition program and growth-management laws and sharp reductions in the budgets and staff of the agencies responsible for enforcing them. Like Mr. Cox, the blame for Florida's economic woes was pinned on these laws, saying they created an unfavorable climate for business.

Florida's growth rate is now well on track to return to the rate of 1,000 new residents a day. Florida's population grew by about 232,000 between 2011 and 2012, and it's projected to double and could triple to more than 50 million.

But due to the 2011 changes, Florida is less prepared to deal with the impacts of growth. Sound planning remains essential to protect Florida's economic health, natural resources and quality of life.

Throughout much of its history, Florida has been treated as nothing more than a commodity, to be bought and sold regardless of the consequences. Florida's laws calling for smarter, more compact development patterns brought more stability and predictability through the wise use of land and water resources.

Instead of being distracted by false diagnoses of the causes of the great recession and thus repeating those mistakes, it is time for Florida to learn from the past and prepare for the future.

Florida is a treasure that will continue to attract more residents. Our generation lives on one of the planet's most congenial peninsulas. We have an obligation to assure that our children, grandchildren and beyond can live in an even more prosperous and attractive Florida.

## Only True Reform Will Avert Another Financial Crisis

Bob Graham and Phil Angelides

*Sacramento Bee*, February 6, 2016

Five years after the Financial Crisis Inquiry Commission issued its investigative report into the financial meltdown, we have a long way to go to prevent a repeat of the crisis.

Congress and President Obama created the commission to look into the causes of the meltdown. We reviewed millions of pages of documents, interviewed more than 700 witnesses and held 19 days of public hearings across the country, including in communities hard hit by the crisis.

This two-year process confirmed that the crash was an avoidable tragedy, caused by widespread failures of regulation, reckless risk-taking on Wall Street and systematic breaches in ethics and accountability. Our inquiry exposed the urgent need to increase banking oversight and consumer protection.

Despite a furious attempt by some to rewrite history, the commission's findings have stood the test of time. In the years since, Americans continue to wonder whether anything has changed—and if their economic security is still at risk.

The answer isn't simple.

Obama and Congress took a major step forward by approving the Dodd-Frank financial reform law in 2010. That law mandated that banking regulators impose risk controls at the nation's 34 largest banks. It also established the Consumer Financial Protection Bureau (CFPB) to protect Americans from unscrupulous business practices. The bureau has forced the return of more than $11 billion to an estimated 25 million Americans that have been wronged by financial companies.

Although we have made some progress, it hasn't been nearly enough to match the magnitude of the crisis and what the country endured. Disturbingly, some members of Congress already are working to turn back the clock and return to the broken pre-crisis status quo that nearly brought down our economy.

Legislation backed by some in Congress would force regulators to roll back the improved risk controls at more than two-dozen of our largest banks. The Consumer Financial Protection Bureau also is under constant threat, as we saw during the recent fight in Congress over the omnibus spending bill, when some members tried unsuccessfully to change the agency's structure and prevent it from doing its job.

The Dodd-Frank standard requiring that lenders find that borrowers have the "ability to repay" has helped to ensure that mortgage loans are made more responsibly. But proposed legislation would return us to the dangerous pre-crisis way of doing business by weakening these standards and making it easier for lenders to prey on borrowers.

The crisis showed the importance of having regulators with backbone who are willing to stand up to Wall Street. But strong regulators alone aren't enough. They need the resources to do their job, and the American people's support when they act in the public's interest.

That's why it's been so disappointing to see Congress underfund the Securities and Exchange Commission and the Commodities Futures Trading Commission, which serve as Wall Street watchdogs.

The Commodities Futures Trading Commission has been given significant new responsibilities for policing a $400-trillion derivatives market. Yet, there was no increase in its $250 million budget this year, despite President Obama's request of $322 million.

The American people will never be truly protected from Wall Street wrongdoing until these agencies receive the resources they desperately need.

Since our report was presented, the Wall Street executives responsible for helping cause the Great Recession haven't paid any real legal, economic or political price for their actions. Fines and penalties still are treated as a cost of doing business. Violations often are settled for pennies on the dollar at the shareholders' expense, without any admission of wrongdoing. What's needed instead are real penalties for wrongdoing, including criminal penalties when warranted.

We have made progress since the commission's report. But building on these reforms will take political will, as revisionists continue to try to rewrite history, roll back progress, and prevent reforms from seeing the light of day.

---

Phil Angelides is former California treasurer and served as chairman of the Financial Crisis Inquiry Commission.

# 8

# Education and Civics Literacy

Both Bob Graham and David Colburn placed great emphasis on the value of education at all levels. As an elected public servant for over three decades, Bob Graham saw the value of an engaged, informed, and involved citizenry. When he left the U.S. Senate in 2004 after serving three terms in office, Graham could have easily transitioned to a high-paying D.C. or Tallahassee lobbying job and segued into a cushy retirement. Instead, he collaborated with the University of Florida to establish the Bob Graham Center for Public Service with the goal of (according to its website) "creating a community of students, scholars, and citizens who share a commitment to revitalizing the civic culture of Florida and the nation." For Graham, education is the key to that mission. David Colburn also shared Graham's passion for education. Colburn taught hundreds (maybe thousands) of UF undergrads and graduate students the basics of American and Florida history over his forty-year career as a professor and administrator. It was fitting that his last position at UF was director of the Graham Center on campus, where he could help implement Bob Graham's vision of producing college graduates who were well-versed in civic literacy. Both Graham and Colburn stressed primary and secondary education as well, and many of these articles reflect that interest. They bemoaned the politicizing of the educational system and pushed for more teacher input into the decision-making process regarding curriculum, testing, and technology. For them, the emphasis on STEM learning (science, technology, engineering, and math) is important, but has come at the cost of knowledge of basic civics and history. Their pieces on the value of online virtual learning seem especially timely in light of the educational transformation brought about by the COVID-19 pandemic. They are especially interested in educational improvement for all students, regardless of race or class. For that to be accomplished, they see the need for a renewed emphasis on public education, something they view as one of the great accomplishments of the American democratic system. That requires both more funding and a reallocation of resources to schools serving the neediest and most vulnerable students. As David Colburn wrote in a 2010 *St. Petersburg Times* op-ed article, "this demand for better schools and better educated children requires a school governance model that is professional, experienced, dedicated, and accountable to the public, students, and parents." The pieces in this section show the reader just how committed both authors are to high-quality education at all levels and how important they feel education is to a just and fair society.

## Better Schools: What Works, What Doesn't, Why We Must Try

David Colburn

*Orlando Sentinel*, February 2, 1992

Does anything work in the United States these days? Experts now contend that the educational system has broken down and needs a complete overhaul.

According to these critics, American education ranks far behind the rest of the industrialized world. A Newsweek survey in December, for example, found America languishing near the bottom in mathematics, science, reading and language study. Business leaders also complain that employees cannot write or do simple mathematics.

Confused and frustrated, parents and taxpayers ask how this can happen when the nation spends $5,500 per child per year for education, a figure that ranks above both Japanese and German expenditures.

Does the public educational system in this country, like the economy, stand on the brink of collapse?

Although some experts would have us believe so, there are several indicators that point to continuing strength in American education. The country presently provides equal educational opportunity for 41 million students who attend public elementary and secondary schools and enables more students to matriculate to college than any other industrialized nation. By all accounts, it is the most democratic system in the world.

And even with all the apparent shortcomings, American students have shown a capacity for ingenuity and creativity that is the envy of the Japanese.

The problems facing American education are complex, and despite the contention of some experts, there are no easy answers. Schools are faced increasingly with societal problems that have placed the family at enormous risk. The number of single-parent households has skyrocketed in this country, and so have households in which both parents work. As a consequence, children receive less attention, not only in the homes of the poor but also in those of the middle class. These children spend more time interfacing with a television set than interacting with their parents. This does not socialize them well for life or for learning.

But the schools are not without fault, as the Newsweek study makes clear. What annoys many people is that their tax dollars do not seem well spent. In the past three decades, for example, educational bureaucracies have grown like topsy, so that today's classroom teachers constitute fewer than 40 percent of all educational employees, down from 75 percent in 1960.

While some reforms are clearly in order, the public needs to be wary of educational gurus and grandiose solutions. American educational experts have had a fascination with curriculum fads, but very few have worked.

A recent "solution" would allow parents to use public school dollars to send their children to private schools. Although there are examples of private schools that offer a competitive educational experience for less money, there are numerous others that are either very expensive or that, to make a profit, provide inadequate faculty and poor facilities[.] An expanded private system might make public education more responsive to parents and to reform, but it is no cure-all.

And yet there are a number of reforms being debated that make good sense, promise positive change and would not cost millions to implement. Among these are programs to reduce the educational bureaucracy and to standardize the curriculum.

The former would also give teachers, rather than administrators, primary responsibility for structuring the curriculum. This modest reform has significantly enhanced teacher morale and effectiveness in several states.

Japan and Europe have had a nationwide curriculum since World War II, and it has strengthened teacher preparation programs, parent and student understanding of instructional goals, and state assessment of student learning. It has also helped to improve teacher quality.

There are many other more substantive reforms being debated that range from extending the school day from 3 to 5 p.m., lengthening the school year from 180 to as many as 240 days, as is the case in Japan, and requiring that schools play a greater role in the parenting and health-care process.

All of these proposals have been tried in one form or another elsewhere and apparently most work well, but they are not cheap and they may not result in the dramatic improvements that taxpayers want.

Whether we like it or not, schools are a reflection of our society, and until we strengthen the family and the child's environment at home, no amount of school funding and educational reform will enhance the achievements of our children. Teachers can make a difference, but they are not miracle workers.

## 8 Steps to Make Schools Better

David Colburn

*Orlando Sentinel*, August 14, 1994

Public schools will reopen in Florida and across the nation during the next few weeks, amid cries from many that public education is failing our children and dooming the United States to mediocrity. The critics, no doubt, have overstated the case, but there remains little question that public education warrants a major overhaul.

To dramatize their concerns, critics point to the following developments: comparisons of U.S. programs in mathematics and science with those of 13 other leading industrial nations that show American students finishing dead last; declining SAT (Scholastic Aptitude Test) scores, which have plummeted by nearly 80 points in the past three decades; and surveys by the National Assessment of Educational Progress—created by Congress to study student achievement—which disclose that more than one-fourth of all 17-year-olds are unable to do simple mathematics and that only 27 percent of them can write a basic letter.

This poor showing by American students continues to take place even though spending for public education has increased significantly in the past 30 years, from an average of $2,378 per child to $6,405 per child. The United States now has the second-highest per-capita investment in education in the world, trailing only the Swiss, and well ahead of the Germans and the Japanese.

Concerns about international competitiveness are the motivating force behind worries about public education. Business and government leaders contend that the United States must improve its educational system so that it can compete successfully in the global marketplace.

And even teachers admit that public education has deteriorated in this country. But although almost everyone acknowledges that the system must be improved, few agree about what can and should be done to reverse recent trends.

Nearly all experts agree that the most serious problem facing education today—the decline of the American family—is well beyond the scope of the schools. There is little question that, without parental support and stability at home, the odds against such children succeeding in school are enormous.

But while this remains the primary problem, there are some changes we can make to help all children—even those at risk—and we need to proceed with them now:

1. Offer school choice to parents on an experimental basis. The rhetoric surrounding this issue is so intense that few can discuss it rationally. School choice may not be the answer some suggest, but it may well upgrade many schools by forcing them to be academically competitive. How will we ever know unless we try?

2. Set national standards that emphasize academic, not social, change. Teachers and schools can do only so much. Once they become burdened with social responsibilities, the academic mission deteriorates. Unfortunately, all federal and state initiatives incorporate some social reform.

3. Develop accurate assessment criteria so that parents and children alike know which skills the children have acquired and what intellectual abilities they have developed.

4. Implement state-of-the-art vocational programs, such as those in Germany and France, that offer students who do not attend college a chance to acquire a skill and a meaningful job.

5. Reduce the educational bureaucracy; consider eliminating busing, and redirect those funds into neighborhood classrooms. At present, less than 40 percent of the funds allocated for education in this country actually find their way into the classroom. New York City, for example, has an educational bureaucracy larger than that for all of France. Polls now show that both black and white families favor neighborhood schools.

6. Either abolish colleges of education or redefine their mission. Teachers at the middle- and high-school levels do not need degrees in education. They require, instead, academic preparation in the disciplines that they will be teaching during their professional careers. Unfortunately, the educational bureaucracy is filled with people who have degrees in education and who continue to stonewall this reform at every turn.

7. Treat teachers as professionals and allow them to participate in the appointment of administrators and in the selection of textbooks and supplementary books for their classrooms. As part of this process, pay teachers accordingly, especially those who are consistently successful in advancing the educational talents of their students and those in critical-need areas, such as chemistry and physics.

8. Develop a meaningful disciplinary program that removes disorderly children from the classroom so that teachers can teach and students can learn without disruptions. Discipline has become the bane of education, and yet it constitutes the highest priority of administrators considering candidates for teaching positions. We have, in effect, allowed the tail to wag the dog.

The stakes have never been higher for rich and poor, for black and white. If we fail to be educationally, and therefore economically, competitive, all Americans will ultimately pay the price. And that price will be our standard of living and the future of our children.

## Florida Schools: In Search of a Miracle Worker

David Colburn

*Orlando Sentinel*, November 3, 1999

The failings of Florida's educational system have perplexed and frustrated more than a few political and business leaders. All realize that without a strong educational foundation, the state's future will be in jeopardy and its economic advancement will suffer.

Gov. Jeb Bush has initiated a fairly radical approach to upgrade the educational system by grading public schools and providing vouchers for children in failing schools to pursue their education elsewhere.

But will this approach solve the problems and offer the state and its children a more promising future?

Some critics allege that the educational shortcomings in Florida are a result of its massive population growth that has not only overwhelmed communities but has also created chaos in the public schools. In the past decade, alone, newcomers—from Northern states, South America and the Caribbean—have added more than 600,000 students to the state's 67 school districts.

Related to this population explosion, critics point out, is the extraordinary rate of mobility in and out of the schools. An examination of the Miami-Dade County school district, for example, the nation's fourth-largest and Florida's largest, most diverse and perhaps most dynamic system, suggests the magnitude of the problem. In the 1995–96 school year, 42,000 students moved into the district; 39,000 students moved within the school system; and 34,000 moved out of the system.

It is this sort of turnover and instability, experts contend, that accounts for many of the educational shortcomings in Florida's schools.

These same critics argue that the size of Florida's schools has also contributed to the educational deficiencies. Florida now has seven of the nation's 25 largest school districts: Miami-Dade County, Broward County, Hillsborough County, Orange County, Palm Beach County, Duval County and Pinellas County. Moreover, within these districts are some of the largest schools in the country. These schools, experts contend, create an impersonal environment that undercuts the classroom experience and the school's ability to focus on the needs of individual students.

Other critics argue that the family is the root cause of the educational problems in Florida and elsewhere. Children who come from strong family backgrounds do well in school, they note, and those who come from fragmented families and who receive little guidance at home do poorly.

The statistics for Florida's children suggest the magnitude of the problems confronting those who believe that simply changing the conditions in the schools will improve public education in Florida. As the curtain closes on this century, Florida ranks among the bottom 10 states in the nation in a host of categories that deal with the well-being of children. From death rates for children (ranked eighth) to violent death rates for teenagers (ranked fourth) to arrest rates for juveniles (ranked third), Florida children and teenagers appear to be a generation at great risk. Add to these statistics the fact that the state ranks third in the rate of single-parent families, by some accounts first in the rate of high-school dropouts, fourth in the rate of teenagers who are not in school and not working, and fifth in the rate of living in high-dropout neighborhoods, and one begins to understand the depth of the problems confronting Florida's schools.

How do you salvage, let alone educate, children who face such obstacles?

Two weeks ago, one of the failing schools in Gainesville invited all of the parents of its 500-plus students to attend a meeting to discuss an educational partnership between teachers and parents. The teachers called every parent; the school provided baby-sitting service; and Publix provided a free dinner for the occasion. Only 75 parents attended. Examples such as this repeat themselves throughout the state.

This educational morass is not going to be improved any time soon. Florida's growth rate for schoolchildren will not diminish for another four years, and it may not stabilize then. Although family conditions have improved slightly in this healthy economy, the single-parent rate has actually increased, rather than decreased, in the past four years.

The governor's proposals are certainly worth our effort. Schools can always improve, and so can teachers, but neither is a miracle worker. Clearly, more family-based programs are essential. Neither vouchers nor school grading can be expected to compensate for a home life in chaos.

## Enlist New Generation of Florida Citizens

**Graham, Frey: Teach civics**

Bob Graham and U.S. Rep. Lou Frey

*Orlando Sentinel*, February 4, 2007

Imagine living in a state where nearly 75 percent of public-school students reach the fourth grade without being able to identify the Constitution as the document that sets basic federal government rules.

Ninety-one percent of the students reach the 12th grade without being able to explain two ways that citizen participation in the political process benefits democracy.

More than 40 percent of the entire population cannot identify the three branches of government.

Less than 20 percent of voters bothered to turn out in recent primary election to choose nominees for governor and the U.S. Senate.

The state ranks 39th in average voter turnout and 49th in volunteering[.]

Sadly, these numbers are not a figment of the imagination but a reality of nightmarish proportions here in Florida. They suggest two disturbing trends that many Floridians are not motivated to participate in our state's civic life, and that even if they had the necessary desire, many Floridians would not know where or how to begin.

Unfortunately, our state dramatically underutilizes the one institution capable of building civic virtue: our public-school system. Several months ago, we assembled a bipartisan working group of educators and policy-makers to identify and recommend solutions of Florida's civics-education problems. Last week, we met with the governor and key state legislative leaders to present our five-part civics-education initiative.

First, Florida must make civics an integral part of the school curriculum. Right now, schools spend relatively little classroom time focusing on social studies like history, government, economics and geography. Even when civics-related subjects are taught, Florida's Sunshine State educational standards emphasize basic knowledge—learning names, dates and other facts—over the development of higher-level skills such as civic participation. We should use the scheduled 2007 revision of the Sunshine

State Standards to update civics guidelines so that students learn all of the skills they need to be effective citizens.

Second, civics knowledge and skills should be tested on the Florida Comprehensive Assessment Test. Like it or not, the reality of the FCAT is that subjects that are tested are taught. At present, Florida students are held accountable via testing for their achievements in reading, writing, mathematics, and even science—in short, every core academic subject but civics. Without assessment and accountability, civics will remain underemphasized.

Third, we need to empower educators who teach civics in Florida's public schools. Since students will not be transformed into active citizens without teachers who are properly trained, it is critical that we make civics instruction an essential discipline at the 33 Florida colleges and universities that offer certified teacher education. We must also help those teachers already in the classroom enhance their civics teaching skills and methods.

Fourth, Florida should lead the nation in textbook improvement. We have reason to be concerned about the quality of civics textbooks in Florida and across the country. Our educational policymakers must update academic standards, build instructional coalitions with other states and review our own textbook selection process to ensure that students have the right learning tools.

Fifth, we propose to establish a strategic center for Florida citizenship. For years, those students, parents, educators, elected officials, public-policy centers and advocacy organizations that are committed to transforming our students from children to citizens have often been on their own. A strategic citizenship center would support and help coordinate their efforts, monitor Florida's civic health, and keep us on track to produce educated and effective citizens.

In eulogizing Gerald Ford, former NBC News anchor Tom Brokaw described the late president as a key member of the "Greatest Generation," a group of Americans which, in Brokaw's words, was "accustomed to difficult missions, shaped by the sacrifices and the deprivations of the Great Depression, a generation that gave up its innocence and youth to then win a great war and save the world."

But, as Brokaw noted, what best defined that generation was its commitment to citizenship. When the Greatest Generation won World War

II, its members could have rested but instead "re-enlisted as citizens and set out to server their country in new ways, with political differences but always with the common goal of doing what's best for the nation and all the people."

Floridians who care about serving our state and doing what is best for its people have a similar mission: to enlist Florida's youngest generation as informed citizens who not only vote but also play active roles in shaping our government, building our communities and securing our future.

---

Lou Frey was a Republican congressman who represented central Florida from 1969 to 1979. A staunch advocate of civics education, Frey established the Lou Frey Institute of Politics and Government at the University of Central Florida. He died in 2019 at the age of 85.

## End Confusion about Who Minds the Store

**Graham, Frey: Courts will decide control of universities, tuition**

Bob Graham and U.S. Congressman Lou Frey

*Orlando Sentinel*, July 8, 2007

Our state university system has a problem: It has two bosses and both claim to have the legal authority to set annual tuition for Florida's 11 public universities. On Friday, we joined a group of concerned citizens and taxpayers in asking the courts to find that Florida voters empowered the Board of Governors—not the Legislature—with this critical task.

On June 27, Gov. Charlie Crist signed legislation that will permit three universities—the University of Florida, Florida State University, and University of South Florida—to raise tuition by 30 percent to 40 percent over the next four years. Legislators and the governor were wise to provide these universities with the financial tools to ensure that they are among the best in the nation.

But note the date of the bill signing. Universities had to wait nearly four months between the start of the 2007 legislative session and the bill signing to learn if they could raise desperately needed new funds for the fiscal year that started on July 1—four days after the bill was signed. As if that uncertainty weren't bad enough, the governor delayed the effective date until 2008 in hopes that the state could generate enough revenue to prevent tuition increases.

Apparently, these schools have decided they can't wait any longer. On July 2, citing a $30 million budget deficit, the University of Florida imposed a campus-wide hiring freeze. Florida State University recently capped student enrollment and reduced library and student computer-center hours. The University of South Florida is considering all of the above and more to close a deficit that may climb to $66 million.

It wasn't always this way. In the 1970s and 1980s, the Legislature and several governors committed to giving our state universities the resources needed to ensure financial stability. That stability powered academic excellence. By the mid-1980s, Florida state universities were close to being in the upper 25 percent of all U.S. public universities for both financial support and student performance. Even better, the results of this investment in stability extended beyond the classroom. While more than one factor contributes to prosperity, educational investments can have a powerful impact on economic success. From 1977 to 1987, Florida's per capita income rose from 94.4 percent of the national average to 100.1 percent.

Unfortunately, since the late 1980s, Florida has backed away from its commitment to financial stability in higher education. This retreat is especially obvious in our relative tuition revenues. Florida and Florida State are among the nation's 75 public "flagship" universities. A USA Today survey of college tuition and fees at these universities showed that Florida and Florida State had the lowest of all 75 flagship universities.

This disparity in revenues was complicated further by chaos in state university management. In 1999, then-Gov. Jeb Bush and the Legislature dissolved the Board of Regents, which had for almost a century regulated higher education spending among Florida's state universities. Suddenly, universities were mano-a-mano over scarce education dollars. Term-limited legislators took advantage of the situation and created expensive new graduate schools and other academic programs whether or not they were needed. A January 2007 assessment of the state university system said that the inflation of graduate programs will prove that Florida was either more visionary than other states or more undisciplined. We fear the latter is true.

This retreat from the fiscal commitment of the 1970s and 1980s severely impacted teaching and learning. But it also had statewide economic implications. In part because businesses recognized a disengagement from educational investment, many sought more stable climates elsewhere. From 1987 to 2002, Florida's per capita income dropped to 96.3 percent of the national average, a decline that erased almost all the gain we had achieved in the previous decade. The lesson was clear: We could not count on elected politicians to ensure that our state university system had the financial stability needed to foster academic and economic success.

In November 2002, more than 60 percent of Florida voters approved Amendment 11—the creation of an independent Board of Governors to oversee our 11 public universities. The constitutional amendment was designed to protect universities from undue political meddling that threatens academic freedom and financial stability. It preserved individual university trustees while providing that the board had the exclusive power to operate, regulate, control and manage of the overall state university system. As in states like California, Michigan and Minnesota, which previously established similar boards in their constitutions, our grant of authority from the people to the board included the power to set annual tuition and fees at state universities.

But the Legislature was reluctant to embrace the amendment despite its overwhelming support. In 2003, the House and Senate passed legislation to implement Amendment 11. Contrary to the amendment, the Legislature misguidedly attempted to preserve its previous tuition-setting powers. Consequently, the Board of Governors has spent the past four years hamstrung from doing the job the voters gave it in November 2002. As the recent debate over proposed tuition increases demonstrates, the Legislature continues to dominate state university governance—and our universities continue to be financially unstable.

In order to protect the state university system and its positive impact on our economy, we have asked the courts to dissolve any confusion and enforce voters' intentions. Our request is simple: Clarify that Floridians empowered the Board of Governors to operate and control the state university system, including the establishment of tuition and fees, and find that the Legislature's attempt to undermine the will of the people is unconstitutional. If the courts rule in our favor, Floridians may finally have a state university system with the true independence and financial stability to ensure that our children succeed academically and economically.

## Graham: Renew Sense of Citizenship

**Through new center, Florida must take lead**

Bob Graham

*Orlando Sentinel*, March 2, 2008

Former University of Chicago President Robert Maynard Hutchins famously remarked that "the death of democracy is not likely to be an assassination from ambush" but rather "a slow extinction from apathy, indifference, and undernourishment."

The current hype surrounding the 2008 presidential contest makes American democracy seem healthy. But the superficial glitz of the campaign only provides empty calories. At a much deeper level, basic citizenship—our personal commitment to engaging the democratic process—is starving for sustenance.

The numbers tell this story of undernourishment. In the most recent National Assessment of Educational Progress in Civics (2006), 70 percent of U.S. eighth-graders could not identify why the Declaration of Independence was written. Seventy-seven percent of high-school seniors tested could not describe two methods a citizen might use to change the law.

Florida also receives failing marks. In 2005, a statewide Florida Bar survey revealed that more than 40 percent of Florida citizens could not correctly identify the three branches of government. This lack of knowledge has metastasized into lack of action. Among the 50 states, Florida was 39th in average voter turnout in the 2004 general election. We are a woeful 49th in volunteerism.

The precarious position of American citizenship has many fathers:

• In an era when newspaper, television and radio station ownership are increasingly concentrated in the hands of a few, national news has crowded out the local stories most likely to stimulate civic activism. While partisan battles in faraway Washington rarely inspire anything but cynicism, a school board's decision to change graduation requirements or individual school boundaries can profoundly affect your children's lives. But try finding coverage of that issue on your local evening television news.

• Once upon a time, major political parties were eager to expand their reach. Today's parties often seem more obsessed with energizing their "base" voters—loyal stalwarts who will reliably cast ballots if motivated. Unfortunately, the messages that motivate base voters can alienate unaffiliated citizens whose participation would expand the electorate and strengthen democracy.

• In 1819, Thomas Jefferson declared that a primary purpose of education was to help Americans understand and exercise their rights and duties as citizens. For the better part of the next 150 years, schools fulfilled this mission. But then, the far right and far left each complained that civics instruction was biased against them. The two sides concurred on a solution—abolish civics from the curriculum—which they largely implemented.

• Academic subjects not tested are not taught and certainly not learned. In Florida, civics, history and other disciplines suffer because we do not include them in the Florida Comprehensive Assessment Test. But the problem is national in scope. The independent Center for Educational Policy recently surveyed 349 school systems to gauge the effect of the federal "No Child Left Behind" law enacted in 2002. Because that act mandates testing in reading and math only, most of the surveyed school districts have made significant cuts in classroom time devoted to other topics like social studies.

• In order to keep accreditation, colleges and universities are required to declare their institutional objectives. Nearly 75 percent list better citizenship as a goal, but many produce large numbers of graduates who never took a collegiate civics course.

When I left the U.S. Senate in 2005, I resolved to spend the rest of my public service career helping citizens reconnect with democracy. This week, the University of Florida will give that mission a home: the immodestly named Bob Graham Center for Public Service.

The Graham Center will work to reinvigorate citizenship in several ways. First, we will support the Legislature's wise decision to mandate civics education in middle schools. Thanks to a generous grant from the Helios Foundation, the Florida Joint Center for Citizenship—a partnership between our Center and the University of Central Florida's Lou Frey Institute of Politics and Government—will train middle-school teachers to mold active citizens.

Second, we will directly engage University of Florida undergraduates through our certificate program in public and civic leadership. In the classroom, these students will study ethics, communications, economics and history. They will also see civics in action through public-service internships and other hands-on, real-world learning experiences. We hope that the end result is a skilled and motivated group of young Floridians willing to dedicate at least part of their lives to the honorable pursuit of public service.

Third, the Graham Center will seek to elevate public dialogue by hosting a continuing series of lectures and debates on issues important to Florida, America and the world. The first of these exchanges will take place on March 6, with U.S Sens. Chuck Hagel, a Nebraska Republican, and Jay Rockefeller, a West Virginia Democrat, discussing the challenges that face our next president.

Former NBC news anchor Tom Brokaw has chronicled the "Greatest Generation" of Americans who overcame the Great Depression and defeated tyranny in World War II. As Brokaw has observed, what best defined that generation was its commitment to citizenship. When these Americans returned from war, "they re-enlisted as citizens and set out to serve their country in new ways, with political differences but always with the common goal of doing what's best for the nation and all the people."

In 2008, our nation must commit to the goal of enlisting a new generation of Americans who embrace the responsibilities of citizenship. Together, we can save democracy from the apathy and indifference that would kill it.

## Economy Relies on Educated, Smart Workers

Bob Graham

*Tampa Tribune*, April 30, 2008

With legislators cutting school budgets from kindergarten to college, the 2008 Florida legislative session hasn't been easy for public education. But only the House can prevent a bad situation from becoming much worse. This week, the House will decide whether to place on the November ballot a constitutional amendment with grave implications for Florida's educational system and future economic prospects.

Less than six years ago Floridians voted overwhelmingly to create an independent Board of Governors to oversee the state university system and remove pork-barrel politics from higher education. The hastily drafted 2008 constitutional amendment would suddenly undo this progress and make Florida the only state in the nation where legislative horse trading governs public colleges and universities. But the proposed amendment does not limit its destructive results to higher education. It would also make wholesale changes to elementary and secondary education that would favor politicians over citizens and educators.

The reasons why the House should oppose this ill-conceived amendment are many:

• Public debate on this proposal has been almost nonexistent, and legislators may not fully understand the catastrophic consequences of its adoption.

• Floridians created our current system through large majorities at the polls in the last decade. We do not need to change again when these reforms are in their relative infancy.

• If the amendment passes, state universities will experience the fourth organizational shift in less than a decade. No complex system—a business, the military, a governmental agency or a university—can lead effectively or function efficiently with such instability.

• Most important, at a time when Florida's ailing economy most needs well-educated and highly skilled employees and entrepreneurs, this proposed constitutional amendment would severely cripple the educational institutions charged with securing our economic future.

For good reason, Floridians are optimists. Florida has a proud history, but past progress does not guarantee future success. Our state is at a tipping point, and our actions now will determine whether Florida prospers today and tomorrow.

Florida's economy is primarily driven by national trends. Many Americans are suffering during this period of economic distress, and Floridians are among the worst afflicted. Our symptoms, which both these national trends and Florida's economic particularities have created, include the following:

• Florida is one of the three states where mortgage foreclosures and home property value losses have wreaked the most economic damage.

• The University of Florida Bureau of Economic and Business Research projects that our high population growth rate will collapse by as much as 50 percent during the next three years.

• The number of unemployed Floridians has reached its highest level in four years.

• In the last 20 years, the average Florida income has fallen from more than 100 percent of what a typical American earns to just over 96 percent. Had we not experienced that drop, Florida families would have earned, on average, almost $4,000 more each year.

During this downturn, how we manage our economy—and those institutions that directly affect the economy—will determine what kind of state we leave for our children and grandchildren.

We now live in an information economy that thrives on education. When modern CEOs make decisions on where to locate and expand their businesses, they choose communities that can provide a productive and flexible workforce. It is no accident that the states that have prospered most in this new economy—like California in the West, Massachusetts in the Northeast and North Carolina in the South—are those that have made the most sustained commitments to education.

The national business community's loss of confidence in Florida's commitment to education is a major reason why our economy is in trouble. If businesses see our state undermining and politicizing education, our ability to attract and hold high-paying information economy jobs will erode.

The Legislature's budget cuts are a step in the wrong direction. But the proposed constitutional amendment is a step off the edge of the precipice. This is a time for Floridians who understand our economy to step forward and demand the educational excellence that will power 21st century economic growth—and secure prosperous futures for Florida families.

## Democracy Withers If Civics Not Taught

Bob Graham

*Orlando Sentinel*, October 21, 2008

After a speech on education I gave as a state senator in 1974, I was approached by Sue Riley, a teacher skeptical of politicians who lacked classroom experience. How could we know what was best for students if it had been decades since we last stepped foot in a classroom?

Our conversation led me to spend a semester teaching civics at Miami Carol City Senior High School. The teaching experience was the beginning of what became the "workdays" program, through which I spent over 400 days working at jobs across Florida.

Thirty years later, the memory of teaching civics still motivates my work. Since my semester in the classroom, concern for political correctness plus a lack of institutional support, flexibility and funding have forced schools to de-emphasize civics. Most high schools today offer only one, often optional, civics course as opposed to the three courses that were the norm until the 1960s.

Not only has the quantity of civics education decreased, but there has been a steady decrease in quality. While older civics curricula emphasized civic participation and engagement in democracy, the current teaching is largely preparation for life as a spectator. In 2006, the National Assessment of Educational Progress reported that 81 percent of eighth and 12th grade students reported learning most about civics from watching television or in class videos. Only 18 percent and 25 percent, respectively, gained their insight by writing a letter expressing an opinion or helping to solve a community problem.

The results of this decline have been staggering. In 1972, the first year 18-year-olds could vote, more than half of the 18-to 25-year-olds turned out at the polls. In 2000 only slightly more than a third voted.

The data are even more jarring in traditionally disenfranchised communities. African-American, Hispanic and low-income students were twice as likely as their white counterparts to score below proficient on the

2006 NAEP in civics. How can government respond to the authentic voice of "we the people" if only some of the people speak up?

This week we got a discouraging but not surprising report card. The National Conference on Citizenship is developing indicators of civic health nationally and in the states. Based on public data and interviews with 506 Floridians, Florida's civic health was diagnosed as:

- 32nd in average voter turnout;
- 47th in average rate of volunteering;
- 49th in the percentage of Floridians who had attended a public meeting; and
- 40th in the percentage of Floridians who have worked with others in their neighborhood to solve a community problem.

Summarizing this information, Florida's Civic Health index for 2007 puts us at 47th in the nation.

Civic education can convert our democracy deficit into an abundance of civic knowledge and energy. This idea is not new. In describing the purposes of public education, Thomas Jefferson stated, "The objects of primary education . . . are to instruct the mass of citizens in these: their rights, interests, and duties as men and citizens . . . to understand his duties to his neighbors and country, and to discharge with competence the functions confided to him by either."

While much has changed in the two centuries since Jefferson wrote, his words continue to resonate. If we want future generations of Americans to sustain our democracy, we must educate them to be informed, skilled and engaged citizens.

The Florida Legislature has taken a first step. Today every middle school student is required to take one semester of civics. This summer a coalition of the Florida Bar, the League of Women Voters, the Lou Frey Institute of Politics at the University of Central Florida and the Bob Graham Center for Public Service at the University of Florida, with the generous support of the Helios Foundation, trained 133 middle school teachers to teach participatory democracy. More will be trained next summer.

Admittedly, our schools are being asked to educate students in everything from hygiene to driving a car. But there are creative ways to blend citizenship into other subjects. While an elementary student is learning the skills of reading, why not also start teaching him or her the content of American history? While high school chemistry students are focused on elements and compounds, wouldn't the course be more relevant if they also learned how science and civics have combined to make our air and water cleaner and safer?

In the age of high-stakes testing, a major advance will be the inclusion of civics in state assessments, such as the Florida Comprehensive Assessment Test, and the national No Child Left Behind student evaluation. The reality is if a subject is not tested, it tends to disappear from the curriculum. While not all policymakers agree with the current testing regimes, we should all be able to agree that if reading, math and science are tested, it does a disservice to our student citizens and our democracy if we fail to test civics.

Democracy does not automatically renew itself in each generation. Sustaining it requires a continued commitment to ensuring that all citizens have the knowledge, competence and motivation to make their mark on the American story.

## America Is Sleeping through an Education Crisis

### David Colburn and Brian Dassler

*Gainesville Sun*, July 12, 2009

In April of this year, McKinsey & Company, one of the world's leading consulting companies, released a report on public education in America titled: "The Economic Impact of the Achievement Gap in America's Schools."

Perhaps it is the title, but the report has gone almost unnoticed since its release three months ago. And yet, it is one of the most telling critiques of our public education system, and its consequences for this nation's economic success and its global competitiveness.

Consider this observation by McKinsey: "The longer American children are in school, the worse they perform compared to their international peers."

Or this one: "The persistence of these educational achievement gaps (between the U.S. and other advanced nations) imposes on the United States the economic equivalent of a permanent national recession."

The McKinsey report examined the economic dimensions of four distinct gaps in education:

1. Between the United States and other nations.
2. Between black and Latino students and white students.
3. Between students of different income levels.
4. Between similar students schooled in different states.

In each instance, the gap has come at an enormous cost, in the billions of dollars and even in the trillions of dollars (our new favorite sum), to the nation's economy and to its human capital. Just a narrowing of the gap in one of these four areas would mean hundreds of billions of dollars to the U.S. economy.

So why aren't we paying attention?

Is it because we have heard much of it before and are so frustrated that we don't want to hear it again?

Or is it that we are so caught up in the daily grind of this recession that we don't have time or energy to consider the impact of education or anything else on our future?

Or are we hesitant because race and ethnicity are prominently figured in confronting this challenge?

It may well be all of the above. But sleeping through the McKinsey report is inexcusable. It will only worsen an already unacceptable situation, and it won't resolve concerns about race and ethnicity if we opt to ignore them.

In 1969, the U.S. was a leader in high school graduation rates. Today, we have slipped to 18th out of 24 industrialized nations. In 2006, U.S. students, who were 15 years old, ranked 25th out of 30 nations in mathematics and 24th out of 30 in science. We only ranked above Spain, Portugal, Italy, Greece, Turkey and Morocco. And we ranked below such nations as the Slovak Republic, Luxembourg, Iceland and Hungary.

Since when did we start comparing ourselves to these nations? These are pleasant places to visit, but really.

What do these developments mean?

The folks at McKinsey have made it abundantly clear what it means. The educational gap over the past 40 years has already cost us somewhere between $1.3 trillion to $2.3 trillion in our Gross Domestic Product (GDP) or a 9 to 16 percent increase in GDP.

The report finds that the failure to help our young people achieve their academic potential is the economic equivalent of a permanent national recession; one substantially larger than the deep recession the country is currently experiencing.

If we had experienced that sort of increase in our GDP, there would be many fewer people of all races and ethnicities in poverty in this country and many fewer young people in prison. It led Al Sharpton to call school reform the civil rights challenge of our time.

But it is much more than just a racial or civil rights issue. School reform is at the heart of our nation's future and our political and economic security. Without it, we will founder as a nation.

Where should we begin?

Reading this report would be a good start.

Creating national standards and national requirements would be a good second step, so that we had comparable data across this nation and so that we could target states for improvement.

Third would be to take a good look at what is working. There are educational models at work in this nation right now that have achieved success for children from all backgrounds. They should be replicated!

Fourth, our school year was designed for an agricultural society. Why we persist in embracing it today makes no sense for the academic achievement of our students. No other advanced nation has such a short school year.

So let's take the McKinsey report to heart and do what this nation has always been good at, equipping all our people with the education and skills to ensure that they can out-compete other nations.

---

Brian Dassler was Broward County's teacher of the year in 2007 and founding principal of KIPP (Knowledge Is Power Program) public charter high school in New Orleans in 2008. In 2013, Dassler returned to Florida and was deputy chancellor of educator quality at the Florida Department of Education until his death in 2017.

## Guessing at the Best Teachers

David Colburn and Brian Dassler

*St. Petersburg Times*, August 23, 2009

As parents anxiously await the start of another school year and a new teacher for their child, two major national studies remind us that the single most important factor in a student's achievement is the quality of his or her teacher.

Reports by both the National Council on Teacher Quality (Increasing the Odds, 2005) and the New Teacher Project (The Widget Effect, 2009) concur in this finding, which probably surprises no one. Who does not remember a teacher who transformed their attitude about school and, in the process, their life?

So how do we find these teachers for our children? The question seems simple enough. But according to the authors of The Widget Effect, there is only one major problem: "Except for word of mouth from other parents, no one can tell you the answers."

Yes, that's correct parents, you are involved in a game of chance in identifying the best teachers for your child. Our system of education, which has been analyzed and re-analyzed innumerable times over the last century, offers you about as much chance of finding a great teacher as rolling dice.

A survey of 15,000 teachers and 1,300 school administrators by the New Teacher Project found, "A teacher's effectiveness the most important factor for schools in improving student achievement is not measured, recorded or used to inform decision-making in any meaningful way."

So what are these reports telling us that the public education system in this country has no rational process for measuring teacher effectiveness and provides insufficient, if any, mentoring programs to facilitate teacher success and thus the success of their students? Unfortunately, the answer appears to be a resounding "yes" to both.

Schools rarely collect data on effective teachers, and even when they do, the data are not used to help struggling teachers improve or reward those teachers whose effectiveness is making a difference in student learning.

Beginning teachers, and therefore the students of beginning teachers, seem to suffer most. They receive little or no guidance in their initial years in the classroom, and yet, the New Teacher Project study concludes, these beginning years are the most crucial in the development of teachers.

The evidence is also increasingly clear that ineffective teachers, those who don't make a difference in student achievement, are rarely told so. The National Council on Teacher Quality observed that "more than 99 percent of teachers receive the satisfactory rating." And "at least half of the districts studied have not dismissed a single nonprobationary teacher for poor performance in the past five years."

Both of these important studies debunk a number of other myths about teacher effectiveness.

You no doubt think that graduates of traditional teacher preparation programs, that is, schools and colleges of education, are more effective teachers.

Wrong. "Traditional routes into teaching do not appear to yield more effective teachers than alternative routes; there is no evidence to support policies that bar individuals from the profession because they lack such coursework."

You probably believe a teacher with a master's degree is a better teacher than one with an undergraduate degree.

Wrong. A teacher with a master's degree is no more effective in the classroom than one with an undergraduate degree. But the National Council on Teacher Quality reported that mathematics teachers who had additional coursework in mathematics education and science teachers who had advanced work in physics or chemistry were more effective teachers.

You also may believe that the longer a teacher is in the classroom the greater the success achieved by his or her students.

Wrong. The studies found no correlation between the length of service and the effectiveness of teaching.

## The Butcher, the Baker, the Candlestick Maker

### Bob Graham and Michael Weiser

*Washington Times*, September 20, 2009

Civic engagement is often thought of as simply volunteering or voting, but this definition limits our understanding of what is really happening in communities across the country. In response to these tough economic times, people are opening their hopes, their kitchens and their dining rooms to fellow Americans in need. Two important trends identified by this month's release of America's Civic Health Index, the nation's pre-eminent measure of civic engagement, help redefine citizenship and expand our characterization of this age-old term.

Taken together, these two trends tell an important story about the good heart of America and the willingness of Americans to solve problems in their own communities. We think these trends should be kept in mind as our elected leaders work to craft federal and state solutions to our economic hard times and business leaders work to revive our economy.

The index has been compiled since 2006 by the National Conference on Citizenship, the only organization chartered by Congress to focus on the quality of our civic engagement, and a group of leading social scientists that includes Robert D. Putnam, William Galston, John M. Bridgeland and Steven Goldsmith.

This year's index measures the effect of the deepest economic downturn since the Great Depression, and it clearly shows that Americans are turning inward. That's the first trend. The index finds that 72 percent of Americans report being less engaged in volunteering, participating in groups or performing other civic acts in their communities. What's more, 66 percent say they feel other people are responding to the current economic downturn by looking out for themselves.

Do these statistics really mean Americans are turning away from their communities? We think not. Fifty percent of Americans report that they gave food or money to someone in need who is not a relative and 11 percent have opened their homes to provide shelter for non-relatives. As we suggest above, this more intimate form of engagement is a new and broader definition, without the longitudinal data yet to prove the trend statistically. However, we can compare these numbers to the 40 percent of people who report volunteering in a more structured and traditional way, such as through a school, church or local club.

Beyond the fact that people are turning to this personal form of service, leading the way are Americans of more modest means, who are less likely to volunteer than more affluent Americans but more likely to provide food and shelter to others.

It's always easy to get lost in the statistics, but in modeling these behaviors, Americans seem to be saying that they are not turning away from their communities but refocusing their energies to help neighbors and others closest to them in more personal ways.

What seems to confirm that judgment is a second trend that measures whom Americans trust. The answer is "the butcher, the baker, the candlestick maker." Tough times are leading Americans to focus their trust on more personal institutions, with small or local businesses receiving the highest level of public trust. Organized religion—local churches, synagogues and mosques—jumped from fifth place in 2002 to second place in the 2009 survey, with 40 percent of those who "attend religious services frequently" reporting an increase in their civic activity. Bringing up the rear were Congress, the executive branch, banks and major companies, which occupy the basement of public trust. This is a complete reversal in the trust structure of Americans in the past five years, and it should have important implications for those who lead these institutions.

We think federal and state policymakers should take care to avoid making laws and regulations that frustrate the natural healing powers inherent in our communities. To the contrary, our leaders can enhance the good standing of the institutions they run by crafting public policies and business practices that rebuild public trust in the process.

We think legislators should engage citizens on the best ways to improve their communities. Instead of allowing town-hall meetings to devolve into angry sessions on health care reform, why not redirect this energy to solve more localized problems? Why not form social innovation funds that invest in people who rise up to solve local problems? Why not educate our people in the values and skills of participatory citizenship so that their natural inclinations can be more fully used in civic action for their neighbors and the country?

Americans are telling us they are ready, willing and able to act, but we need to meet them where they are. Why not put our trust in them?

---

Michael Weiser currently serves as chairman of the HistoryMiami Museum and chairman emeritus for the National Conference on Citizenship.

## Who Should Govern the Schools?

David Colburn and Brian Dassler

*St. Petersburg Times*, July 25, 2010

When asked to identify the most significant educational reforms of the last decade, most people identify charter schools, the grading of public schools, vouchers or virtual education. Left off the list and one of the most important in our view is changing the way schools and school districts are governed. In the past 10 years, the nation has seen more and more big-city mayors and state legislatures insist on assuming control of their school systems from local school boards. What accounts for these developments?

Mayors as well as state officials contend that schools are too important to the success or failure of a community and the state to be left to amateurs, volunteers or self-interested politicians. Mayors, like Rudolph Giuliani, former mayor of New York, have argued that voters hold them accountable for the successes or failures of their public schools. So why shouldn't they be in charge?

Michigan felt it had no choice but to take over Detroit's public schools when they were $318 million in the red and its students performed at the lowest level—compared to 18 of the nation's largest cities—on a fourth- and eighth-grade reading test.

Replacing this uniquely American custom of electing school boards has not been easy, as Giuliani, Michigan Gov. Jennifer Granholm and others have found out, and it has resulted in a hodgepodge of governance models.

So what accounts for the attack on school boards and do the newly proposed governance models have merit?

In our view school boards often include people with little knowledge or background in public education, or they include people with a built-in self-interest. Neither the well-meaning amateur nor the self-interested politician is a desirable school board member if this nation intends to re-establish its public schools as among the very best in the world.

How did such school board members get on a school board to begin with?

First, historically turnout for school board elections has been consistently very small, among the lowest for any elections in the nation. The result has been that certain key interest groups have been able to influence the outcome of these elections or, in some cases, to determine the outcome. These interest groups include school unions, companies with extensive business interests in education, and religious organizations that worry about the direction of the school curriculum.

The negative impact these interest groups can have was highlighted recently with Florida's Race to the Top application to the U.S. Education Department for $1 billion in additional support. This conflict of interest occurred when several school boards, whose members were closely identified with teacher unions, refused to challenge local union opposition to merit pay criteria and the teacher evaluation process required by the department.

Second, most school board officials are ill equipped by background and experience to address most major school funding issues, such as teacher salaries, insurance contracts, textbook and computers purchases, and the size and shape of classrooms. School districts are major corporations and require leadership with appropriate training—the issues are simply too complex for the well-meaning lay citizen.

Third, although abuse and corruption by school board officials remain relatively infrequent, there have been enough instances in Florida alone to call into question the quality and judgment of school board members. In 2008, for example, a Levy County school board member was arrested on charges of indecent exposure—he subsequently resigned. More recently, a Broward County school board member was convicted of bribery charges.

The substantial amount of local, state and federal dollars available to public schools suggests that greater professionalism and experience is essential to make sure these funds are spent wisely.

Fourth and most recently, we have seen the election of school board officials who are determined to force their own political and religious values on the education process, even when it directly conflicts with historical and scientific knowledge that has been widely accepted for decades.

If not an elected school board, then what?

In post-Katrina New Orleans a promising model of school governance is emerging. The new structure respects the concept of local control but also recognizes that the key decisions of schools should be made by the experienced administrators, professional educators and families—not interest groups.

A network of charter schools has emerged in New Orleans since Hurricane Katrina devastated the city and exposed the nation to a school system that many described as the worst in America. This network is governed by nonprofit boards of directors and local citizens who donate their time to ensure fiscal responsibility and student achievement. They are unpaid and don't receive insurance or retirement benefits, as school board members in Florida do, and they are unelected, which means they cannot be influenced by interest groups. This is but one example being considered by leaders nationally to improve school governance.

Increased federal involvement in education together with national concerns about the global competitiveness of America's schools have combined to create the perfect storm for governance reform.

This demand for better schools and better educated children requires a school governance model that is professional, experienced, dedicated and accountable to the public, students and parents. Anything less in our view will stymie public education reform in this country.

## Want a Job? Start Your Search by Helping Your Neighbors.

Bob Graham and Michael Weiser

*Miami Herald*, October 2, 2011

Striking new research suggests that there's an unmistakable connection between the civic health of a community and how well it is able to cope in a recession. In other words, volunteering and working with neighbors to solve problems may actually help predict whether a city or state will be able to weather tough economic times.

According to the new report, released by the National Conference on Citizenship, "Civic Health and Unemployment: Can Engagement Strengthen the Economy?" (ncoc.net/unemployment), states and communities with strong social capital have witnessed smaller increases in unemployment over the past few years. For example, eight of the 11 states with the highest volunteering rates at the outset of the financial crisis—Alaska, Iowa, Nebraska, North Dakota, South Dakota, Kansas, Minnesota and Vermont—experienced among the smallest increases in unemployment in the years afterward. Meanwhile, seven of the 10 states with the lowest volunteering rates—Arizona, California, Alabama, Nevada, Rhode Island, Delaware, and, yes, Florida—experienced among the highest increases.

The report finds that communities with strong civic health foster an environment of trust and a social network that attracts investment. Nearly 60 percent of volunteers believe that community service increases their odds of finding a job. It appears that when citizens spend time with their neighbors they start to contribute to an environment that helps foster the essential networks needed to find and secure employment.

Why does this happen?

Perhaps it's that people who volunteer learn marketable skills and strengthen their professional networks, which in turn helps them find jobs. It could also be that civic engagement encourages people to feel more attached to their communities, and that caring deeply about where you live increases the odds that you will invest, spend, and hire within that community. It could be that communities with high civic health are also seen by prospective investors as more stable, reliable, and as having better and more credible public and private institutions.

These findings, while preliminary, offer a completely new way of discussing what's going on with our economy and create a new sense of urgency for communities to take steps to improve their civic health.

We all know that getting out there and attending a neighborhood meeting, registering to vote, or simply discussing the day's political happenings with your family is a good thing to do. But now, it appears that an active level of civic engagement is also an important social and economic asset. When we get engaged, we help improve the economic prospects of our community.

When we examine our great state of Florida, we can see that we have work to do to improve civic engagement. Our state ranked 49th in volunteering, with just 21.3 percent of respondents in this year's Civic Life in America survey (civic.serve.gov) responding that they volunteered. Here in Miami, we ranked 51st among the 51 metropolitan areas ranked by the Civic Life in America survey, with just 15.2 percent of respondents saying they volunteered during the past year.

Fortunately, Florida has a starting point for identifying ways in which we can turn things around. The Bob Graham Center for Public Service at the University of Florida was established in 2008 to build a community of students, scholars and citizens to stimulate public engagement, and train the next generation of civic leaders. In 2010, the Center in collaboration with the Lou Frey Institute at the University of Central Florida was instrumental in the passage of a sweeping new civics curriculum for middle and high school students, the Sandra Day O'Connor Civics Education Act. The O'Connor Act established some of the highest civic standards for students in the nation.

We call on Florida's thought leaders and concerned citizens to join us—review this new report and this year's Civic Life in America survey (which tracks volunteerism, voter participation and other key measures of participation) and let's take a long, hard look at the state of our state's civic health. Civic participation rates serve as an important indicator of the economic strength of our community. It makes sense: strong communities make for strong economies.

## Virtual Learning Helps, but Classroom Still King

David Colburn and Brian Dassler

*St. Petersburg Times*, October 26, 2011

If you have listened to the radio lately, you've probably heard advertisements touting the Florida Virtual School.

A pioneering effort when it was established in 1997 by Julie Young, it has become a national leader in delivering instruction via technology and currently serves students in all 67 counties in Florida. Nearly 260,000 students enrolled in its online courses in 2010–11, up from fewer than 11,000 in 2001–02.

By contrast, the state of Texas had a virtual enrollment of only 3,600 during the same period.

What accounts for Virtual School's success in Florida? And is it the right thing to do for Florida's future and for its children?

Virtual schools originally emerged to deliver instruction in hard-to-staff subjects or in hard-to-staff places. In 1998, for example, nearly two-thirds of Florida counties did not offer a single Advanced Placement class, which had been mandated by the state to enable talented high school students to pursue college preparatory classes. The Florida Virtual School helped the state address this problem by providing a full menu of AP classes.

After this initial success, policymakers and some educators seized on the opportunity to offer classes online and in real time, competing with schools for students. The virtual school model went from one dedicated to access and equity to one that promised choice and efficiency.

State leaders and school boards also began to see the virtual school as a way around restrictive collective bargaining agreements—essentially as a way to deliver education more cheaply and to supplement classroom subject matter.

With the success of the Florida Virtual School, for-profit companies entered the fray, offering a full array of classes and tutorials. In a remarkably short period, the virtual road went from creating access to saving money to making money.

Learning online is in the vanguard of education reform at the moment. Nearly every state has a Florida-like virtual school. And rarely does a week pass that state and national newspapers don't feature a story about new technologies and online learning. For some policymakers it has become a panacea for addressing perceived teacher shortcomings and balancing state budgets.

We are concerned that in their eagerness to embrace the virtual school model, policymakers and some educational leaders are overstating its success and ignoring the tremendous advantages a classroom environment provides for students.

There is no question that technology can be a great asset to students with learning deficiencies and an excellent supplement to classroom learning for all students. As the technology is refined and expanded, virtual learning may offer more substantial advantages to students and teachers.

For now, however, school districts and state leaders need to be sure they are not buying students and parents a pig in a poke.

The virtual approach may be just that for the vast majority of students. The current evidence makes clear that students learn much better and faster in a traditional classroom setting. And if they are to compete successfully in a global setting, they will need to know how to work constructively in groups. That occurs most effectively in a classroom environment.

While we regard the Florida Virtual School as a serious and substantial effort, we are much less sanguine about the for-profit models. Investing in the education and well-being of young people should not be about making money. Indeed, how does one make money at these ventures? Typically, at the expense of students.

We don't relish the challenge policymakers face in addressing budget shortfalls and the costs of public education. But we urge them not to embrace the virtual world as a cure-all for problems in public education. The end result in our view will be significantly more damaging for the students and for Florida.

## Jobs and Civics Go Hand in Hand

Bob Graham and Sandra Day O'Connor

*USA Today*, November 1, 2011

America's Founding Fathers understood that the success of our republic would depend on our citizens' civic knowledge and participation. Indeed, the original impetus for public schooling was to teach young people about their rights, responsibilities and competencies as citizens. Now comes news that more than our democratic system relies on civic education: Our economy may as well.

According to a recent study by the congressionally chartered National Conference on Citizenship, there is a strong correlation between civic engagement and unemployment. In recent years, unemployment has risen less in states and cities where more people volunteer, register to vote, attend public meetings, and work with neighbors to address community challenges. For every percentage point increase in people who attend public meetings, the study found nearly a quarter percentage point decrease in unemployment. For every percentage point climb in volunteerism, unemployment dipped nearly a fifth of a percentage point.

## Importance of volunteering

Such trends are borne out at the state level. Eight of the 11 states with the highest volunteering rates at the outset of the financial crisis—Alaska, Iowa, Nebraska, North Dakota, South Dakota, Kansas, Minnesota and Vermont—experienced among the smallest rises in unemployment. Seven of the 10 states with the lowest volunteering rates—Arizona, California, Alabama, Florida, Nevada, Rhode Island and Delaware—experienced among the highest increases in unemployment.

These statistics are striking, but not surprising. Sixty percent of volunteers believe that community service increases their odds of finding a job, and they're right. Citizens engaged in their communities have more opportunities to build the networks needed to secure employment. Similarly, communities with higher voter turnout are more likely to elect leaders who pursue policies that reflect local economic needs.

The Census Bureau has wisely expanded its tracking of civic engagement. Last month, the bureau issued a mix of good and bad news.

## Downturn in participation

While nearly 60% of Americans are registered to vote, almost three in four never or rarely discuss politics. While nearly 70% of young people talk with friends and family on the Internet numerous times a week, only about a third talk with their neighbors as frequently. And while most Americans participate in their communities in some form, only one in four volunteer. Even more troubling are reports that nearly three-quarters of Americans have reduced their civic participation in the recent downturn. This bodes a vicious cycle—whereby dwindling civic engagement is exacerbated by, and contributes to, our economic hardships.

For the sake of our democracy and our economy, it is time for America to reinvest in civics. The connection between civic learning and economic success begins early in life, but civics has all but vanished from the public school curriculum. On the last nationwide civics assessment test, two-thirds of students scored below proficiency. Government leaders should work together to improve civics instruction and extracurricular community service activities. Award programs honoring students and schools for contributions to their communities can help put us on the right path.

The secret to America's success is the strength of our civil society. An informed citizenry lays the foundation for not just democracy but also for an innovative, dynamic economy.

---

Sandra Day O'Connor is retired associate justice of the US Supreme Court and founder of iCivics.

## Hold Voucher Schools to Account

David Colburn and Brian Dassler

*Tampa Bay Times*, October 16, 2012

Suppose you were told that a new automobile insurance company in town offered better rates and better service. All other things being equal, would you pursue the matter further?

Of course you would.

Now what if this new insurance company failed to reveal the extent to which you were covered in an accident or natural disaster, or to provide any information on the quality of its service? Would you hesitate before purchasing a policy with this company?

Almost certainly.

While the salesman seeks to convince you that his policy has added value, you are uncertain about what to do. The price seems right and the product sounds good on the surface, but you have serious reservations about his failure to be forthcoming in answering your questions.

This situation mirrors precisely what is happening in Florida, Louisiana and in many other states that are offering school vouchers to parents.

Vouchers have become a fundamental part of the school choice movement. They offer public funds to parents so that students can attend private schools. Often, but not always, student qualification for a voucher requires that the student previously attended a failing or subpar public school. And, on occasion, a student must meet certain family income requirements to qualify.

We have written in support of parental choice in schools previously and continue to believe that charter schools provide healthy competition for public schools and can be a viable option for many parents and students.

But there is something basically wrong when public funds are earmarked for these private schools and the state fails to insist on accountability measures for student achievement outcomes.

How can we be sure that these schools actually deliver on what they promise without such data? How will we know if these private schools are adding educational value when no comparable assessment is provided?

The answer is we cannot.

So why are policymakers reluctant to insist on the same standards for private schools accepting vouchers that they require of public schools?

Those supporting vouchers contend that government should not be monitoring private schools and telling them what to do. Normally that might be true, but when these schools are receiving public funds that would normally go to public schools, the public has every right to know how well those children are doing in comparison with their classmates in public schools.

If we allow a student cohort to continue through private schools on vouchers and then find out 20 years from now that they were much less prepared to enter the private and public sectors, we will have spawned a disaster for these students and our society.

Like the person shopping for a better insurance policy, we cannot afford a system that does worse than the current one. The only way to ensure that this will not happen is to mandate transparency—a system that insists on the same accountability standards for all schools that use public funds.

To do otherwise is to court disaster and face the consequences down the road, when there will be no opportunity to turn back.

## Get Teachers' Input on New Initiatives

David Colburn and Brian Dassler

*Tampa Bay Times*, January 16, 2013

The murder of 20 innocent schoolchildren and their six teachers in Newtown, Conn., last month launched the latest national debate about guns, violence, mental health, and the safety of students and teachers.

At front and center of this discussion is the role of our teachers and the suggestion by some that we ought to arm them.

We currently ask teachers to educate, socialize and serve as substitute parents for our children. Now we propose to have them police their schools and pack weapons to protect the children.

Whether you agree or disagree with this proposal, our society has come to rely on our teachers in extraordinary ways, even while many of us belittle them with the refrain "those that can't teach."

The profession used to command respect from the entire community. But in recent decades this once vaunted profession has lost political favor, and teachers are no longer valued like they once were.

How illogical is this contradiction? Quite absurd from our point of view.

Every day we ask schoolteachers to meet the needs of children in so many different ways that no educational or training program could adequately prepare them for the job. And yet when something goes wrong, it is not the parents or society that we blame. It is the teachers.

As the Florida Legislature begins committee meetings this month, there will invariably be substantive discussions about a batch of new requirements that should be placed on teachers. These legislative mandates originate in the premise that we cannot trust our teachers to do the right thing.

We think it would be wise and appropriate if policymakers started from a different place—one of trusting teachers. In our view, educational policy proposals should result with substantive input from teachers and principals.

Policymakers should start with the assumption that every person in Florida's classrooms is there with the intention of making a difference for the children. They should also understand that when teachers get the support they need and deserve—especially early in their career—they improve dramatically. And, yes, a system of assessment must be place so that, when a teacher doesn't improve after earnest attempts to do so, the teacher should be counseled into another line of work.

Some promising models for teacher engagement in the political process have existed in Florida. Former Gov. Jeb Bush added a teacher-in-residence in his office, for example, as a way to ensure he heard from someone on the front lines. Former Department of Education leaders established an ambassador teacher position to facilitate communication with teachers.

A recent study by the New Teacher Project revealed that two actions would go a long way to improve the retention of excellent teachers. These two proposals are fairly straightforward: one would recognize the accomplishments of top-flight teachers through salary increases and promotions; a second would be to remove ineffective teachers. The best teachers want a rigorous evaluation process, they want the removal of poor teachers, and they want a system that rewards the best of them.

As policy leaders begin to debate how to apply the lessons from Newtown, we need to pause and acknowledge the extraordinary burdens we place on teachers. And we need to value their contribution in the same way we do our first responders.

In the numerous incidents of school violence around this nation, one or more teachers stepped forward to protect the children and were often slain in the process. These examples of their love and devotion to our children cannot be cobbled into public policy. But we can begin to say to our teachers, thank you for all you do for our children, and we are grateful for your contribution to this nation.

## Great Teachers Born, and Also Trained

David Colburn and Brian Dassler

*Tampa Bay Times*, August 20, 2013

One of today's persistent myths about education is that great teaching is innate. In other words, you either have it or you don't. Even some highly talented teachers will tell you that their effectiveness in the classroom resulted from some elusive and unidentifiable set of personal characteristics.

Some teachers do have an advantage over others in the classroom because of their outgoing personality, enthusiasm about life and positive demeanor.

The conclusion, however, that only these people constitute the best teachers is deeply flawed as well as damaging to the profession. It implies that struggling teachers lack some innate talent that they will never be able to attain, no matter how hard they work.

The accumulated evidence, however, suggests that skillful teaching is, in fact, observable, measurable and attainable.

Let's take one specific and very important teaching skill—asking questions. There is nothing innate about knowing how to ask questions in order to elicit student thinking and engagement, but there are few things that take place between teachers and students that are more important.

A skilled teacher learns to pose questions that all students are capable of answering. After asking a question and giving students the time to process it fully, the well-trained teacher does not call on the student who raised the first hand. Nor does the teacher necessarily seek an oral response.

After waiting until more students raise their hands, this teacher might ask the students to turn to their neighbor and discuss their responses with one another. Or the teacher may ask the students to write their answer to the question, after which the teacher might visit the desks of some struggling students to determine if they need additional support or encouragement.

As this single skill illustrates, the work of an effective teacher is nuanced and can often be complex. It takes practice, observation and conversation with one's colleagues and mentor to refine these skills. Very few of us, in other words, will get good on our own.

Earlier this year, the Bill and Melinda Gates Foundation released a final report from the Measuring Effective Teaching project, which sought to identify the particular skills and talents that are essential to great teaching. The project was a multiyear effort involving 3,000 teachers in seven school districts across the country, including Hillsborough County.

The study confirmed two important points. The first concluded that effective teaching can be measured. "The (MET) data show that we can identify groups of teachers who are more effective in helping students learn."

The second point emphasized that "teaching is too complex for any single measure of performance to capture it accurately. . . . The challenge is to combine measures in ways that support effective teaching while avoiding such unintended consequences as too-narrow a focus on one aspect of effective teaching."

Bill Gates elaborated on this point in a Washington Post op-ed in April, cautioning states against rushing to use only one measurement in teacher evaluations. He also criticized the promotion of competitive environments for teachers rather than collaborative ones.

The Gates Foundation study embraced student feedback in assessing effective teaching, observing: "We found that a well-designed student perception survey can provide reliable feedback." Questions such as "My teacher knows when the class understands," and "In this class, we learn to correct our mistakes" are highly correlated with positive student achievement outcomes.

This summer Randi Weingarten, head of the American Federation of Teachers, commented, "If someone can't teach, after they've been prepared and supported, they shouldn't be in our profession."

While we agree in principle with her statement, we believe that the preparation and support of teachers is critical to their success. Without that preparation and support, even the gifted teacher will struggle and most likely fail.

So as the nation begins another school year, we call on district and school administrators to make greater investments in skilled teaching. And we urge teachers to embrace these efforts and the multiple methods to evaluate them, including student perception surveys. Working together in this fashion will advance the quality of education in our schools and enrich the academic environment for students—of that we are certain.

## Federal Push Needed to Improve Colleges

David Colburn and Brian Dassler

*Tampa Bay Times*, September 6, 2013

As the Cold War heated up and the space race took hold of the national imagination, the president and Congress worried about the quality of the public schools and the ability of the nation to compete internationally in science (yes, this is not unique to the 21st century). To facilitate the nation's competitiveness, Congress adopted the Elementary and Secondary Education Act in 1963.

The law provided a substantial infusion of federal funds for K-12 education. Within two years, the education budget more than doubled to $4 billion—a sum that school districts found impossible to ignore.

The new education law, however, went even further when it became linked to the Civil Rights Act of 1964, which barred federal funds from any institution that discriminated on the basis of race. Together, these laws gave the federal government the power to end the costly and ineffective dual, segregated school system in the South.

The ramifications of both laws were historic and dramatic. By 1970, most Southern schools had been integrated as a result, and the quality of Southern schools took a giant leap forward.

Just in the last two weeks, President Barack Obama has proposed a series of reforms that are designed to transform higher education in a similar manner. By most accounts, higher education in America is in crisis and in desperate need of the same kind of dramatic reform introduced in the 1960s.

The collective student loan debt in the United States, for example, is more than $1 trillion, with default rates increasing exponentially. More than two-thirds of bachelor degree recipients borrow money to complete their degree, and they average $27,000 in loans that must be repaid upon graduation. Most students don't graduate from college within six years, and about half of students who start college fail to ever graduate. Well over half of U.S. universities have six-year graduation rates that are under 40 percent.

Meanwhile universities—both public and private—have been steadily raising tuition for the past 35 years. Jeffrey Selingo, editor at large for the

Chronicle of Higher Education and author of an exceptional book about the current state of higher education, reports that annual costs at four-year colleges have risen three times the rate of inflation since the 1970s. At the same time, the relatively new players on the block—for-profit schools—have taken both student and taxpayer dollars with minimal return on investment.

"At the colleges and universities attended by most American students, costs are spiraling out of control and quality is declining just as increasing international competition demands that higher education become more productive and less expensive," Selingo summarizes succinctly.

Obama's plan to bring transparency and accountability to postsecondary education is long overdue and has the potential to change all that. By withholding federal financial aid subsidies from students attending unproductive colleges, the plan offers the chance: (1) to improve those universities in need of and capable of reform; (2) to recognize those that are national leaders; and (3) to result in closing those institutions that should never have existed in the first place.

America's best universities have been the engine of our economic growth, the basis for our international economic leadership, and fundamental to our national security for the past 60 years. They have also attracted the best and brightest to the United States.

They were able to accomplish all this because they were accessible and affordable for young men and women from all walks of life. They gave hope to those who grew up in poor homes or who immigrated to the United States. And they delivered on the hope and promise.

Today, that access and opportunity is in jeopardy unless real reforms are implemented. Like the federal government's role in reforming public education in the 1960s, the ways it uses financial aid to improve the quality of higher education is not just an economic necessity, it is essential to mobility in America and the nation's leadership in the world.

## Path to Improved Teaching Is Clear

David Colburn and Brian Dassler

*Tampa Bay Times*, October 21, 2013

One cannot look at the current state of public education in America, especially in urban and rural areas, and not see a crisis that is worsened by the manner in which new teachers are prepared.

In 2010, a study by the Thomas B. Fordham Institute revealed the extent of the disconnect between teacher preparation and classroom needs. The study of 700 education school professors from around the country found the following:

- Only 24 percent believe it "absolutely essential" to produce "teachers who understand how to work with the state's standards, tests and accountability systems."

- 37 percent say it is "absolutely essential" to focus on developing "teachers who maintain discipline and order in the classroom."

- 39 percent find it "absolutely essential" to "create teachers who are trained to address the challenges of high-needs students in urban districts."

For anyone who is or has been a teacher and anyone who has been a school leader, these skills are nonnegotiable. Having these skills helps ensure that students acquire the knowledge they need to be successful; not having them means they don't.

Training received through alternate routes to teaching, especially Teach for America and the New Teacher Project, emphasize standards-based planning, classroom management and teaching traditionally high-needs above many others. The emphasis provided by these programs, despite some of their well-recognized insufficiencies, underscores why principals rank these teachers so highly and why many studies conclude teachers entering the profession through these routes are more effective in their early years.

A more recent report in 2013 by the National Center for Teacher Quality is even more critical of traditional teacher preparation. In that report of 1,130 colleges and departments of education, the authors write, "Through an exhaustive and unprecedented examination of how these schools operate, the Review finds they have become an industry of mediocrity, churning out first-year teachers with classroom management skills and content knowledge inadequate to thrive in classrooms with ever-increasing ethnic and socioeconomic student diversity."

Among other points highlighted in this study were the low standards for admission to teacher education programs, the lack of academic rigor within the programs, and the absence of coordinated and guided classroom training to become a teacher.

Countries that have surpassed the United States in student achievement train their teachers better, according to Amanda Ripley in her recent book The Smartest Kids in the World. Ripley examined three countries—Poland, Finland and South Korea—to determine why they educate their children so much better than does the United States. Ripley hails Finland, in particular, for its selectivity in admitting candidates to teacher preparation programs.

While Finland admits only the best and brightest to its teacher preparation programs, colleges of education in the United States consistently accept students who, based on the Graduate Record Exam, rank among the lowest applicants for postgraduate study at the nation's universities.

The NCTQ study makes the following recommendations to rectify this situation: increasing the requirements to get into a teacher preparation programs; mandating more subject area knowledge of teachers; and holding teacher preparation programs accountable for the effectiveness of their graduates. Lastly, NCTQ insists that much more substantial student teaching is essential to hone the professional skills of teachers in classroom management and lesson planning. Assessment is also emphasized. Many of these recommendations are embedded in the promising design of a new teacher preparation program being developed at the Relay Graduate School of Education.

Florida is recognized as an early leader in reforming teacher preparation, according to the NCTQ study—an encouraging sign and one worthy of continued and increased support. Just as the state has been willing to close or reconstitute K-12 schools for the persistent underachievement of its students, Florida must be willing to do that with the programs that poorly prepare teachers.

Teacher education finds itself at a historic crossroads: an antiquated model and a disconnect between inputs, outcomes and demands. To continue selecting and preparing teachers in the same way will get the same results. And that is simply not good enough.

## Give America the Old College Try

**Trump should look to higher education to make America great again**

Bob Graham

*US News & World Report*, March 10, 2017

WHETHER YOU LIKE HIM OR not, it should be clear why President Donald Trump's promise to "Make America Great Again" resonates.

The bottom has fallen out of the American middle class. Once the backbone of the world's greatest economy, this forgotten class feels the American dream of continued prosperity and progress is no longer within its reach—ceded to other countries and the richest one percent.

There is a way to reverse this economic freefall and pervasive inequity by taking cues from two of our greatest presidents, Abraham Lincoln and Franklin Delano Roosevelt. Both worked with Congress to fundamentally strengthen the nation by deploying higher education to transform the economy.

Consider 1862, the worst year of the Civil War, when President Lincoln recognized how far the Union was behind Europe in industrialization. The primary reason? America's agriculture was so inefficient that more than 60 percent of America's work force was required to farm and feed the growing population. There were not enough workers left to work in factories and assembly lines or to build the infrastructure for the future. Lincoln accelerated America's industrialization by establishing a state land grant university system. These universities broke from traditional European higher education by using research, development and extension capabilities to bring the best practices of agriculture to the farm and advanced engineering to the factory floor. By 1900, America became the leading industrial economy in the world.

With the end of the Second World War in sight, President Franklin D. Roosevelt in 1944 implemented an extraordinary solution that paid dividends for generations—the GI Bill. When America entered the conflict, 9.3 percent of those over 25 held a college degree. Roosevelt anticipated the need for more highly educated Americans to fulfill the global political, military and economic leadership success in two wars had thrust upon the

United States. The GI Bill provided returning heroes the opportunity to receive training or a college education. Opening the doors to colleges and universities created opportunities for better jobs and a greater capacity to innovate. By the 1960s, the number of adults with some college attainment doubled.

Fast forward to today. 2017 marks another era of uncertainty about America's global position and the strain those uncertainties are placing on many American families. The causes of these uncertainties are primarily our tardiness in adjusting to globalization and technology. Like under Lincoln and Roosevelt, high-quality postsecondary education can be the prescription.

America's current generation of 25–34-year-olds ranks 11th worldwide in the attainment of a high quality post secondary degree or certificate; the previous generation was ranked first. The erosion in the international ranking of Americans with certificates and degrees beyond high school is a primary factor in our nation's losing ground in innovation and wages of middle-income workers. Our challenge, much like for Lincoln and FDR, is that we don't have a sufficient number of people educated to assure international dominance in the 21st century as we did in the 20th century. Innovation and new forms of product development and manufacturing have been moving to countries outside the United States, furthering the nation's decline.

The big idea that can make the nation great again is a new commitment to education beyond high school to dramatically increase the percentage of Americans with postsecondary degrees and certificates. To compete in the 21st century, America must match and eventually exceed countries like Norway, Japan and South Korea, which are leveraging their larger pool of postsecondary graduates into innovation and jobs.

There is a clear solution, and it is based on analysis by the Lumina Foundation-sponsored National Commission on Financing 21st Century Higher Education, which I chaired with former Delaware Gov. and Rep. Mike Castle. The commission composed of private sector CEOs, state elected officials and higher education presidents collectively surfaced a host of ideas for remaking higher education to better serve students and the economy, including:

Enhance innovation, productivity and capacity within public secondary institutions so that 60 percent of Americans 25–64 years of age can achieve a high-quality postsecondary degree or certificate by 2025.

Reduce the economic barriers to postsecondary education by increasing federal and state institutional support by $15 billion annually.

Create incentives for students to graduate on time, such as reducing federal loan repayment for early or on-time graduation.

Like Lincoln and FDR, President Trump can recognize and accelerate the achievement of a 30 percent increase in the single most important long-term driver of American economic growth: well-educated men and women. Putting colleges back in the opportunity-making business can truly make America great again.

# 9

# Environment—Springs, Everglades, Oil Spill

In 1947, Marjory Stoneman Douglas opened her masterful *The Everglades: River of Grass* with these words: "There are no other Everglades in the world." The Everglades are an integral part of a larger set of fragile and irreplaceable environments that comprise the area that we today call Florida. Since the late 19th century, the Sunshine State has been under severe ecological stress from rampant development, large-scale commercial agricultural pursuits, overpumping from the Floridan aquifer, and the threat of sea level rise. David Colburn and Bob Graham recognized these dangers early in their respective careers and have been raising alarms about threats to Florida's environment ever since. Examining a broad range of environmental problems, they both focus on their causes and provide a series of short-term and long-range solutions. They particularly discuss the laws and regulations in place that could provide protection if they were actually enforced. They also talk about the importance of citizen activism in the fight to protect Florida's unique ecology. Focusing on the tension between economic growth and environmental protection, they maintain that these are not mutually exclusive variables. Instead, they assert that environmental protection is necessary for Florida's continued economic growth, as the state's irreplaceable natural beauty is what drives Florida's largest commercial engine—the tourist industry. These pieces examine both human-made and natural disasters, like the 2010 Deepwater Horizon oil spill and the hurricanes that batter the state annually, and conclude that the deleterious effects of these occurrences are exacerbated by poor policy decisions made before and after they occur. While events like these make the headlines, Graham and Colburn stress that daily occurrences, like wetlands removal and continued building on fragile barrier islands, make Florida more vulnerable. Though Colburn and Graham center their particular concerns on areas they know best and to which they have a personal connection, they stress the importance of statewide initiatives that recognize the importance of Florida's relationship to water. As Graham wrote in 2017, "Protecting and conserving Florida's water is an economic as well as environmental issue, not one defined by geography or party lines." To honor Graham for his strong support of these concerns, the Florida Defenders of the Environment presented Graham with its 2020 Marjorie Harris Carr Award for Environmental Advocacy. These pieces represent that advocacy and are a call to action—expressing the hope that environmental protection will once again become a bipartisan issue that all Floridians rally around to protect their beautiful state.

## State-Federal Everglades Marriage on the Rocks

Bob Graham

*Palm Beach Post*, March 19, 2006

The greatest threat to the most challenging environmental restoration in America's history is divorce.

The dream to save the Everglades was first proposed in 1983 but did not become official until 2000 when President Clinton signed the legislation establishing the marriage of the federal government and the state of Florida. Both parties pledged their commitment to provide an equal share of the financing and committed to sharing the decision-making to preserve this international treasure. The newlyweds accepted that it was this marriage which offered the best opportunity for the Everglades to be saved.

Six years later, signs of a cooling romance have become public.

Florida is frustrated by the slowness and unpredictability of federal action. The chapel where the marriage occurred was the 2000 version of the Water Resource Development Act, periodic legislation which authorizes federal water policy and projects. No similar legislation has been passed since then, primarily due to regional and partisan disagreement over a few controversial water projects.

Because of this gridlock, important components of the Everglades restoration have not been completed. The Indian River Lagoon—swamped by discharges of fresh water from the Everglades during rainy and hurricane seasons—sits unattended, despite pleadings of the state to finish the project.

Federal officials are anxious because Florida seems to have lost its ardor for Everglades restoration. This dissatisfaction surfaced earlier this month during a heated meeting of the House committee responsible for Everglades restoration. In dispute was Gov. Bush's alleged efforts to undercut a 1992 federal court order through which the court is overseeing the cleanup of the Everglades. Committee members noted that some of the filter marshes created by the South Florida Water Management District don't meet the state's own pollution standards, and in 2003, the state pushed back the date by which specific pollution limits must be met from 2006 to 2016.

The North Carolina Republican chairman of the committee, Charles Taylor, stated, "Given the state of Florida's track record of noncompliance and unwillingness to respect the concerns of (the Department of Interior) and (the congressional) committee, why would the federal government ever consider joining with the state to urge that the court terminate the consent decree and federal oversight as we now know it?"

There is no undertaking more important to the future of South Florida than the restoration of the Everglades. How can this marriage be saved? Greater respect by both parties. As in any marriage, open and candid communication is critical. No surprises and shared conversation on problems and possible future steps should be the ground rule.

Understand what your partner is saying, not just what you are hearing, and, where possible, adapt. There is no reason that the Everglades restoration should be held hostage to controversial dam projects in the west or dredging on the Mississippi. Environmental restoration projects like the Everglades—there are now over 25 nationwide following the model—should be legislated on their own merits according to a timetable that allows for change but maintains predictability over a multiyear undertaking.

Don't sweat the small stuff. As Florida political leaders scrutinize policies and projects which will affect the Everglades, they cannot let parochial concerns trump the statewide interest in maintaining good relations with our federal partner. The test for any individual issue should be: will this serve the long term interests of both parties?

Florida has a chance to demonstrate its desire to save the marriage by taking a bold initiative—protecting the over 300,000 acres of the Everglades which is now in agricultural use so that those lands will not be converted to subdivisions, industrial sites, or any other uses incompatible with the restoration of the Everglades. This won't be easy, and the conflict could end up being the grounds for divorce 20 years down the road.

It is true that Florida is committed to a $10 billion effort to restore the 1900 sheet flow of fresh water over the heart of the Everglades. However, soil decline, economic and geopolitical factors—particularly the potential for importation of Cuban sugar should the United States normalize relations in a post-Castro environment—could reduce the agricultural competitiveness of the Everglades. Given that the population of south Florida in 2025 is projected to be 2 million to 3 million more than today, the pressure to replace farms with urban development will be enormous.

What can Florida do? During this year's legislative session, start the process of planning and financing the acquisition of development rights or conservation easements in the Everglades Agriculture Area. These would not restrict current agricultural uses but would prevent projects which would defeat the essential purpose of the Everglades salvation. The federal partner should be fully informed and involved in the details of these acquisitions as it would be expected to be an equal partner in this undertaking.

The federal-state marriage—the fundamental relationship necessary for the restoration of the Everglades—is worth saving, but both parties are experiencing problems typical of any marriage. To make it work, they need to ask serious questions of one another and recommit to the relationship, or before we know it, divorce papers will be filed.

## Hurricanes Are an American Problem

Bob Graham

*Miami Herald*, June 18, 2006

The 2006 hurricane season began on June 1. Floridians approached this date with dread. During the last two seasons we have suffered some of the most damaging hurricanes in modern history. In the calm months since then, yet another storm has arisen—the increasing cost and shrinking availability of insurance for wind driven damage for homes and businesses.

The symptoms of this storm are all about us. Some of the largest casualty insurers in the state are refusing to renew policies of existing home customers. Almost all insurance companies are dramatically increasing premiums. For commercial customers, starting with the small businesses upon which most Floridians depend for their jobs, but now threatening the medium and large scale businesses of Florida, the availability of insurance has reached a crisis point, threatening the economic growth of Florida.

It has been a disastrous two years for property insurance companies in Florida. Eight hurricanes have inflicted $30 billion in insured losses. The state's insurer of last resort, Citizens Property Insurance Corp., has been left with a $2 billion deficit which all property insurance policyholders are paying through surcharges on their insurance premiums.

To put it up close and personal, I own a 20-year-old concrete block home in Miami Lakes and a 60-year-old wood frame cottage in Hingham, Mass. They have approximately the same market value. The casualty insurance on the Florida home will be almost 2 ½ times higher than the one in Massachusetts.

If these are the symptoms, what are the underlying causes? Starting with the most obvious, we live in the tropics and are subject to the cycles of hurricanes. Through the decades of the 1970s and 1980s we were spared the frequency of damaging hurricanes we had felt in the previous two decades. Beginning with Hurricane Andrew in 1992, that changed.

We are at the mid-point of a cycle of more numerous hurricanes. Florida has grown by 25 percent since Andrew, with more than four million new residents. There are that many more people, homes, businesses at risk. That many more competing for a limited amount of insurance coverage. The pattern of growth has concentrated on the coastal regions of our state, the areas which represent the greatest vulnerability to hurricane damage.

Insurance companies, meanwhile, are practicing increasingly sophisticated forms of modeling. Through this, risk profiles are identified, categorized and segregated. Those who live in the most threatened communities more likely to have their insurance cancelled or, if insurance coverage is continued, paying substantially the full cost of that risk, rather than the more traditional practice of spreading the risk over a wider range of insurance payers.

You can see this within Florida. Insurance premiums on similar homes in a coastal city like Panama City are more than twice those of an interior city like Tallahassee. This is a partial explanation of the phenomenon that while rates are skyrocketing in Florida, the national insurance companies are profitable, benefiting by tranquil conditions in other parts of America.

The unhappy conclusion is that with the exception of hurricane cycles where relief might come in 10 to 15 years, the other factors are relatively permanent and even likely to increase in their contribution to hurricane damage and the cost to Floridians of insuring against that threat.

The somewhat happy response is that there are practical things that each of us, our communities and American can do to reduce the pain. We must get serious about the impact of global warming and get on with the things that will blunt its effect. The major sources of pollutants that add to the heat of the planet are our cars and trucks. America cannot wait another year to begin the process of moving toward a more energy conservative, less polluting and energy independent nation.

Florida, with more at risk from global warming than any other state, should be in the lead. State and local building codes and code enforcement need to be re-examined, strengthened when they are found to be inadequate, and enforced to withstand the intensity of the hurricanes we will be facing. Most of the homes and buildings we will be using in the next 20 years are already built.

There are things that individuals can do to protect their property—strengthened roof tie downs and storm shutters are two that come to mind. The state and federal governments should assist in the cost of installation, as has been done to encourage energy conservation. Local emergency preparedness agencies should serve as a clearinghouse of information as to best practices and sources of reliable assistance to homeowners and businesses.

The federal government should stop the practice of using taxpayers' money to subsidize the true cost of coastal development. Cheap federal flood insurance has made development in risky coastal areas financially possible. These structures have also contributed to increased wind insurance rates as it is exactly these coastal structures which are the most exposed to wind as well as flood water. As the insurance companies become more compartmentalized in their underwriting, the federal government has a responsibility to assist those regions of America that are more vulnerable to the ravages of hurricanes.

Hurricanes are not a Florida problem; they are an American problem. Earthquakes are not a California problem nor are terrorist attacks solely a New York City problem; they, too, are American problems.

Bill Nelson, our senior U.S. senator and former Florida insurance commissioner, is proposing the creation of an emergency commission to recommend to the president and Congress proposals to establish a national disaster fund. This federal assistance should be supported by state and local commitments to strong building codes and their enforcement.

It's time to stock up with the batteries, bottled water, plywood for this year's hurricane season—it could be another Charlie, Ivan, Dennis or Wilma. But the real challenge is to recognize that the toll of hurricanes on Floridians is not going to subside unless together we are prepared to take even tougher steps for our safety.

## Save the Everglades Marriage

Bob Graham

*Palm Beach Post*, June 30, 2008

Like many Floridians, I followed with great interest the announcement that our state has tentatively agreed to buy U.S. Sugar Corp. for $1.75 billion and use nearly 200,000 acres of company farmland to enhance water flows across America's Everglades. As with any transaction, we should closely scrutinize the fine print. But Florida leaders deserve credit for at least exploring what could be another critical step in the restoration of our unique River of Grass.

Unfortunately, some federal officials seem willing to let Everglades restoration languish in the Washington political swamp. Last November, President Bush vetoed the Water Resource Development Act (WRDA) legislation that would have authorized water projects across the nation, including initiatives to restore America's Everglades. Sen. John McCain has since voiced his support for the President's unfortunate veto.

Traditionally, Congress has passed a WRDA bill each even numbered year. The 2000 WRDA included the historic Everglades Restoration Act, a product of almost 20 years of state and federal action and negotiation. That legislation cemented a marriage between Florida and Washington over the revitalization of America's Everglades, with each partner assuming an equal share of the decision-making and cost. The fruits of the union were to be 60 individual projects' initiatives like removing levees and developing additional water storage capacity that would achieve the goal of restoring natural water flow through the River of Grass. Of the 535 members of the Congress, only one opposed the nuptials.

The 2000 WRDA authorized the first few Everglades projects with the expectation that Congress would authorize additional projects in subsequent WRDA legislation. But then partisan and regional politics intervened over the more controversial waterway, dam, and harbor development measures which typically dominate WRDA. The 2002 WRDA bill stalled over controversy about Missouri River dams. 2006 brought a fight over the aftermath of Hurricane Katrina. As a result, the nation went seven years without a new WRDA.

With each battle and each stalled WRDA, the Everglades were caught in the cross-fire. Congress failed to authorize projccts critical to restoration, which prevented those initiatives from even being considered for federal funding. Meanwhile, Florida exceeded its obligation by paying over $2 billion while it waited. Since one partner doing all the work is no way to sustain a marriage, the state-federal union to restore the Everglades was headed for the rocks.

In 2007, a new Congress brought fresh hopes of reconciliation. With broad, bipartisan support, Congress passed a new WRDA bill containing delayed Everglades projects. When President Bush vetoed the legislation in November 2007, both houses of Congress overwhelmingly overrode his veto. Everglades restoration was back on track.

But this honeymoon period may be short-lived unless Congress changes the way it approves water restoration projects like those in the Everglades. The fate of efforts to restore natural water flows south of Lake Okeechobee or restore wetlands in Wisconsin will always be in jeopardy if they are tied to more controversial canal widening projects in Alabama or dams in South Dakota.

For several reasons, it makes good policy sense to divorce water restoration initiatives from typical WRDA projects. First, because restoration initiatives like America's Everglades are more likely to enjoy bipartisan support, the inevitable delays in WRDA enactment needlessly block legislation that would otherwise become law. Second, Everglades-like water revitalization efforts are often more cost effective than other WRDA projects because the federal government shares the expense with states, localities, or other non-federal partners. Third, where most WRDA development projects need legislative authorization only once, the Everglades and similar restoration ventures are long-term endeavors with interrelated projects that require multiple congressional approvals over time. If one Everglades project is delayed due to a WRDA fight, the entire initiative becomes stalled.

Fortunately, there is a better way which will serve the interests of Everglades revitalization and more than 20 similar water restoration initiatives across America. Students and faculty at the University of Florida's Levin College of Law and Graham Center for Public Service have drafted–tentatively entitled the National Water Restoration Act—that has already won the support of major national environmental and conservation organizations. The concept is simple. If a project is designed to maintain, enhance, or reverse assaults on water quality and natural ecosystems, and the initiative involves collaborative watershed planning between state or local and federal agencies, it would be considered separately from WRDA. Without the burden of WRDA controversy, the water restoration projects could be considered fast enough to ensure that they are implemented on time, financed within budget, and delivered as planned.

Nearly eight years after the wedding, there should be no question about Florida's commitment to the state-federal Everglades marriage. But Washington has yet to fully reciprocate. With the enactment of the National Water Restoration Act, Congress and the President can strengthen the bonds of Everglades restoration.

## Disregard for Safety Led to Deepwater Horizon Spill

Bob Graham

*St. Petersburg Times*, January 10, 2011

The worst man-made environmental disaster in the history of America began on April 20, 2010. The Deepwater Horizon, a modern drilling rig exploring for oil and gas more than 3 miles below the surface of the Gulf of Mexico, exploded and sank two days later.

Eleven men were killed and 16 injured. Almost half a billion barrels of oil spilled into the gulf, causing incalculable damage to sea life and human life. More than $2 billion has already been spent in the effort to contain and mitigate the direct damage of the spill, and economic losses to gulf fishermen and tourism are still being calculated. It could be a decade or more before the long-term effects on the health of coastal residents and sea life can be assessed.

America's confidence in the private sector oil and gas industry was shaken. America's confidence in the capability of government to oversee an inherently risky use of public lands took another hit.

What caused this disaster?

With few exceptions, there has been a culture of complacency around safety issues within the oil and gas industry. This can be traced back to the wildcatter—the man who single-handedly brought in the oil wells of the American Southwest. The casualty in this Wild West culture has been safety.

Government regulation has been woefully underfunded, sometimes incompetent and often characterized by a cozy—literally and figuratively—relationship with the industry it is supposed to regulate. This situation has contributed to a pattern of industrial accidents that are among the highest in the world's oil- and gas-extracting nations.

Multiple failures on the Deepwater Horizon cascaded into the explosion on the rig: At least nine human and mechanical failures, oversights and misinterpretations led to the disaster. This was not an act of nature; it was a completely preventable human tragedy.

The response to the blowout was antiquated, slow and initially ineffective. The first major U.S. oil spill since 1989, when the Exxon Valdez went aground in Alaska, the Horizon disaster dwarfed Exxon Valdez in scale and impact. Stunningly, in those 20 intervening years, no progress had been made in technology or procedures to contain an oil spill or protect the water and land areas affected. It was almost a month after April 20 before an effective response was mounted and another two months before the spill, which spewed upwards of 60,000 barrels of oil a day into the gulf, was contained.

A fundamental question is whether we will learn from the Deepwater Horizon disaster and apply those lessons for a safer future.

Our commission is urging the offshore oil and gas industry to follow in the path of other high-risk industries such as nuclear power and chemical, which have established industry organizations to assure the highest standards of safety and complement effective governmental regulation. Each of these organizations was established in the wake of a disaster—Three Mile Island and Bhopal. It is an open question as to whether the offshore industry leaders will see Deepwater Horizon as a similar mandate and opportunity to act.

As a result of the Deepwater disaster, the Obama administration has committed to improving the offshore safety culture and the relationship between the federal government and industry before allowing further expansion of deepwater exploration and production. It's unclear, however, whether the new Congress—many of them elected on a pledge to reduce the size and influence of the federal government—will support urgently needed safety reforms in the practices and regulation of the offshore industry.

This is a wakeup call to the American people. Why are we drilling in deeper and inherently more risky offshore locations? The United States is consuming about 22 percent of the world's daily extraction of petroleum while it sits on top of less than 1.5 percent of the world's proved reserves. If we "drill baby drill" in an attempt to go totally independent, and if our thirst for petroleum continues at its current level, the United States will drain its remaining proven domestic oil reserves by 2031.

If we stay at our current 48 percent domestic and 52 percent imported oil, that date will only be extended to 2068. Unless we develop and sustain a national energy policy which will fundamentally change our petroleum addiction, the only choice our generation will have is whether to leave to our children or to our grandchildren an America totally dependent on foreign oil producers for its national security, economy and way of life.

I trust we will learn the lessons of Deepwater Horizon better than that.

## Due Diligence for Offshore Drilling

Bob Graham and William K. Reilly

*Politico*, January 26, 2011

In our report on the Deepwater Horizon disaster, we note that over the coming decades much more of America's oil will be found in deep-water regions of the Gulf of Mexico and other offshore areas. Drilling and production will increasingly be in ultra-deep water—5,000 or even 10,000 feet down and then further miles under the ocean floor to reach our largest remaining oil and gas deposits.

These activities, which have been likened to space exploration in their complexity, involve markedly increased risks for our workers, economy and coastal waters.

When we testify Wednesday before Congress, we will urge adoption of specific reforms to greatly improve the safety of this offshore drilling our nation will inevitably undertake. We know that many members of Congress have made commitments to a smaller, less expensive and less intrusive federal government and believe our recommendations are consistent with those objectives.

In the case of the Gulf of Mexico, we must remember that the government is not just a regulator; it is owner of these resources, on behalf of the American people. It should be thought of as a prudent landlord—ensuring that tenants who use the property act in the interests of the Gulf and the nation as a whole.

Our recommendations acknowledge the need for coordination and overlapping responsibility between the government (on behalf of the American people) and industry, as landlord and tenant and as producer and consumer.

For the Deepwater Horizon disaster, as horrific as it has been, was not the worst-case scenario. A combination of weak geologic formations and intense pressures from hydrocarbons could have led to a subsea blowout, which would have been even more difficult to contain and would have resulted in a far larger spill than the already massive 172 million gallons released into the Gulf from the Macondo well.

In addition, we could face a situation in which the responsible party does not have BP's deep pockets or is not inclined to compensate victims in advance of lawsuits. This would leave individuals, businesses and U.S. taxpayers to shoulder tens of billions of dollars of unreimbursed costs.

To minimize the risk of future disasters, Congress should take the following actions:

• Congress should create an independent safety agency within the Interior Department to oversee all aspects of offshore drilling safety, with a director appointed by the president to a five-year term confirmable by the Senate. Building on reforms announced last week by Energy Secretary Ken Salazar, we must wall off safety regulation from the lure of billions of dollars of federal drilling royalties and the surrounding politics. To do otherwise risks a return to a regulatory system captive to industry and political demands.

• Congress should significantly increase the liability cap and financial responsibility requirements for offshore facilities, which date from 1990, taking care to balance the competing concerns of ensuring full compensation for victims and retaining competent smaller, independent operators in the offshore market.

• Congress should dedicate 80 percent of any Clean Water Act penalties from the Deepwater Horizon spill to long-term, regionwide restoration of the Gulf of Mexico, an ecosystem that has been degraded by nearly a century of oil industry activities and government channeling of the Mississippi River.

• To improve government response and containment capability, stagnant since the Exxon Valdez disaster more than 20 years ago, Congress should increase funding for the key regulatory agencies that oversee oil spill response and planning—including the Interior Department, the Coast Guard and the National Oceanic and Atmospheric Administration.

The administration can and should take further actions on its own:

• Interior should use its existing authority to draft leasing provisions that ensure the offshore energy industry pays the costs of its regulatory oversight—as other industries, like telecommunications, do.

• Interior should toughen its baseline safety regulations to address the increased challenges presented by drilling in deeper, riskier waters and less-well-known geologic areas. Interior should supplement those regulations with a risk-based performance approach, similar to the "safety case" used by Britain and Norway in the North Sea. It requires all offshore drilling companies to demonstrate that they have thoroughly evaluated and are prepared to address all risks associated with drilling a particular well.

• The president should create an interagency review process for oil spill response plans and direct the appropriate agencies to develop in-house expertise to oversee containment operations in the immediate aftermath of a well blowout and to accurately estimate flow rates.

Our investigation found that specific BP actions were leading causes of the Deepwater Horizon disaster. However, we concluded that the greater risks inherent in deep-water drilling operations require industrywide action on safety.

This is particularly true because Transocean and Halliburton, whose actions we found also played key roles in the disaster, each perform services for companies across the industry and throughout the U.S. and the world.

In addition, while some companies have exemplary safety records, the United States as a whole does not. U.S. fatality rates are several times higher than those in the North Sea.

• The industry should establish a private Safety Institute, apart from its existing trade association, to develop, adopt and enforce standards of excellence to ensure improvement in safety and operational integrity offshore. Such rigorous standards adopted in the nuclear power industry in the wake of the Three Mile Island accident have helped raise safety in that industry.

Congress, the administration and the industry have it in their power to improve the safety of offshore drilling through these reforms and reverse the culture of complacency regarding safety that existed before the explosion.

The people of the Gulf—and all Americans, as the owners of these resources—deserve no less.

---

William K. Reilly is former administrator of the Environmental Protection Agency and, with Bob Graham, co-chair of the National Commission on the BP Deepwater Horizon Oil Spill and Offshore Drilling.

## Industry Safety the Issue in Gulf Drilling

Bob Graham

*Panama City News-Herald*, February 10, 2011

On the morning of July 10 I was standing on a bluff at St. Andrews State Park. To the south was the crystal clear Gulf. There were noticeably fewer people on the beach than you would have expected on such a beautiful midsummer morning. To the north at the entrance to St. Andrew Bay were men and women hard at work to complete a barrier designed to protect the bay from a tide of oil caused by the Deepwater Horizon disaster. The threat to the Gulf, bay and economy was real. The community was actively preparing for the worst.

Thankfully, the threat has passed. Is it forgotten?

In January, the National Oil Spill Commission submitted its final report on the Gulf oil disaster to President Obama and the Congress. The report examined both the causes of the Macondo well blowout and its implications for future of drilling off America's coasts. The stakes are high, particularly for a downstream state like Florida. As oil exploration moves into deeper and deeper water, the combination of weak geologic formations and intense pressures raises the possibility of a blowout that would dwarf Macondo.

Offshore drilling can be done safely—provided industry and government fully absorb the lessons from Deepwater Horizon. And this needs to happen soon. Our investigation identified troubling weaknesses within the safety culture of U.S. offshore drilling operators and the government regulators who are supposed to look after the public interests in safety and environmental protection.

How can the commission identify an industry-wide systemic failure based on an incident that involved a small group of players? It's a fair question, particularly since there are many companies that take justifiable pride in their commitment to safety and professional operation.

For starters, the management failures that led to the blowout and explosion were not limited to BP. Their contractors, Halliburton and Transocean, are major industry players, employed by many firms all across the globe. It is hard to believe these global subcontractors provided unstable concrete only to BP, or would have missed early warning signs of rising gas only at the Macondo well.

In addition, the aftermath of the disaster revealed a woeful lack of preparedness across the industry for a deepwater blowout, even though such an event should have been anticipated. To take one familiar example, many of the major operators had cut-and-paste response plans referencing walruses in the Gulf of Mexico. We found the industry had not improved its containment and response capabilities since the last major oil spill, the Exxon Valdez spill in Alaska in 1989.

Looking more broadly, the commission identified a truly shocking statistic. The fatality rate for offshore workers in the Gulf is fully five times that of workers in the North Sea between the U.K. and Norway.

Industry assurances that the Deepwater Horizon was an exception to a lengthy and exemplary track record also don't stand up to scrutiny. We have long experience drilling in shallow waters, but not at the depths to which we are heading (Macondo was more than 18,000 feet below the surface). The move to deep water raises risks substantially. Additionally, in the course of our research we documented numerous instances of loss of well control throughout the Gulf in the past several years, involving dozens of companies.

Finally, when the consequences from failure are so high, the industry turned a blind eye to growing risk-taking and unsafe operations by individual companies and subcontractors.

That is why both the industry and the government need to modernize their oversight of deepwater drilling to be more proactive and focused on newly emerging risks. Arguments that state-of-an-oversight will send gasoline prices shooting up are simply not credible. Oil is a global commodity and its price is determined by global supply and demand. The fact that oil is being produced profitably in the North Sea using the safety standards which the commission is recommending supports our confidence the offshore oil and gas sector will continue to thrive even as it pays appropriate attention to risk.

The industry can play its part by creating an independent safety institute, as the high risk nuclear power and chemical industries have already done, to continually push for excellence and hold its members accountable. The institute, along with more diligent oversight, will create a partnership between industry and government that could make U.S. offshore operations the safest in the world.

We cannot run the risk of another Macondo, let alone the kind of cataclysm that a more severe blowout would create. That is why everyone, in government and industry, needs to make safety the priority.

## Land, Water Management Gains Go Up in Smoke

Bob Graham

*Miami Herald*, May 21, 2011

This summer marks the 40th anniversary of the great fires in the Everglades. For weeks flames scorched 500,000 acres of the Everglades. Waves of smoke swelled over South Florida from the Keys to north of Palm Beach. Ten miles from the coast saltwater intruded into Miami's primary water supply. The Washington Post headlined "Drought-Ravaged South Florida Faces an Environmental Disaster."

More than any other event, these fires drove home to Floridians that something was wrong. They were the catalyst for a four-decade effort to protect the Everglades and, more broadly, Florida's land and water.

This anniversary of the fires was celebrated in Tallahassee by legislative and budget decisions that will virtually wipe away those protections and return us to pre-1971 Florida.

Some of the most destructive features are:

• Everglades' restoration: The first steps toward restoring the Everglades to as much like its natural state as possible began in 1972 when the first state land and water management laws were enacted and a major land-acquisition program funded. In 1983 the state launched the Save Our Everglades initiative. It was in 2000 when the federal government joined in a 50/50 marriage with the state that Everglades' restoration took off. Now we fear that marriage is doomed.

Legislation at this session has gutted the laws, which have protected the Everglades since the early 1970s. Other legislation restricts the capability of the South Florida Water Management District to be the state's representative in the marriage by shifting decision-making from independent appointed citizens to the Legislature and cutting the district's budget by 25 percent. The state of Florida's appropriation for Everglades' restoration has dropped from $200 million in 2007–2008 to $30 million in the 2012 budget. If Florida is so indifferent about the Everglades' health, how can we expect a member of Congress from far away to continue spending $200 million a year from a deficit-plagued federal budget? How close are we to the divorce court?

• Concurrency: It has been the means by which projects such as large residential developments and shopping malls—which impose special burdens for roads, drainage, water and sewers, and schools on the region in which they are located—are required to pay a portion of the cost to relieve those burdens. While the local government in which the project is located can require such assessments, the protection that had been afforded to surrounding communities is significantly limited.

Florida is a state where more than 1.5 million homes are now vacant, and there is an unprecedented oversupply of commercial, office and industrial properties. Another enactment of the Legislature will trash the current requirement that developers show a need for the proposed project and that it is financially feasible before the project is permitted.

With regular gas selling for more than $4 in many places in Florida, the Legislature has removed the requirement that new developments be energy efficient.

• Citizens' rights: Citizens, beware! The rights of citizens to participate in the process of land and water management are dramatically reduced. Currently the citizen is on notice that twice a year changes to the local plan can be considered. Under this legislation alterations can be considered at any meeting. Stunningly, the legislation goes further and prohibits local governments from submitting key planning issues to the people through a referendum.

While all state review of large scale proposals is reduced, in the following instances no state planning oversight is allowed: mining, industrial, hotel/motel and movie theaters. That's because they have been taken from the list of potential developments of regional impact. This is a virtual roster of the most influential lobbyists in Tallahassee.

The current land- and water-management system in Florida has provided reasonable state oversight for projects that are of genuine concern to a region of Florida or the entire state. The state role has assisted, not hindered, local governments and applicants in creating projects that serve as good neighbors and contribute positively to Florida's quality. A good example of this:

As Dolphin Stadium was being permitted, a myriad of infrastructure needs that the stadium's construction would generate were identified. Most people in South Florida recognized the importance of the new stadium. Miami-Dade County staff worked with the Dolphins management to ensure that impacts on the drainage, water, sewer and, certainly, transportation were met. This ensured that they could issue a building permit in keeping with county rules and ordinances. However, a significant amount of similar impacts were also affecting residents of the city of Miramar near the stadium. Were it not for requirements in Florida's growth-management laws that impacts occurring outside of the "home" city or county must be addressed before permits could be issued, Miramar's needs might not have been met. Unfortunately, this legislation eliminates the requirement that such extra-jurisdictional needs must be mitigated before permits are issued.

There is a constructive alternative to the debacle awaiting us if this legislation becomes law. All of the major pieces of the current land- and water-management system were the result of thoughtful, citizen-led reviews of the state of Florida's economy and environment. On three occasions, beginning with the response to the 1971 fire in the Everglades, the governor has appointed such a commission and the Legislature adopted its recommendations because they were reasonable, wise and visionary.

Gov. Rick Scott has an opportunity to follow this model. First, he should veto the damaging legislation. Appoint a representative group of Floridians to assess the current state of land and water management, its protection of the environment as well as its effect on Florida's economy and job creation. The recommendations of these Floridians will give the Legislature in 2012 a thoughtful basis on which to make decisions that will be most beneficial to Florida's future, not the after-midnight process which produced the ill-considered legislation at this session.

Floridians don't want to go back to the smoke of 1971 or the smoke-filled rooms of the 2011 Legislature. There is a path to avoid that.

## Everglades Restoration: Can This Marriage Be Saved?

Bob Graham

*Miami Herald*, November 27, 2011

The Everglades is in danger again. This time it is not from a drought, hurricane or other act of nature. It is not from some imminent encroaching development.

It is from the 2011 Florida Legislature and its cascade of damaging legislation which threatens to bring the three-decade-long effort to save the Everglades to a halt.

Everglades restoration is not just a matter of saving one of the Earth's most important and unique environments and protecting the fresh water supply for a third of Florida's residents. Everglades restoration is our state's largest job and economic development program. A 2011 report by Mather Economics to the Everglades Foundation estimated that investing $11.5 billion in Everglades restoration (equally divided between the federal government and the state of Florida) will result in $46.5 billion in gains to Florida's economy and create in excess of 440,000 jobs in the next 50 years.

Among the most important chapters in the salvation of the Everglades occurred in 2000 when the people of America and Florida were betrothed in an engagement to collaborate on the multi-year, multibillion dollar Everglades restoration program.

While progress toward the goal has been delayed due to funding shortfalls-to date primarily by the federal partner, and occasional vacillations in the specific steps necessary to accomplish the objective-many positive things have happened. Highly visible is the commencement of restoration of natural water flow into Everglades National Park through the now underway replacement of a portion of the Tamiami Trail earthen dike with six and a half miles of bridges. More fundamentally, the 2000 America-Florida engagement is the only initiative which has a chance of rescuing this world treasure from destruction before it is too late.

Precisely what did the legislature do last spring?

The South Florida Water Management District (SFWMD) is the agency charged with representing the state's interest in Everglades restoration. It has demonstrated the technical and managerial competence to fulfill its part of the marriage. The SFWMD and its predecessor agency have had strong public and bipartisan political support since their creation in 1948.

In sixty days the last legislature virtually emasculated the sixty-year-old water district.

Funding was cut almost 39.6 percent or over $700 million. Within less than three years, the $400 million fund established primarily +to finance the state's share of Everglades land acquisition and restoration will be exhausted, with no prospects for replenishment.

The professional staff necessary to maintain the confidence of our federal spouse was eviscerated. Almost 600 men and women who had served the SFWMD in its Everglades and other water management functions critical to the southern region of Florida were summarily fired.

For nearly 40 years the state has annually augmented funding of the SFWMD—such as the state's share of the critical northwest corner of the Everglades, the Big Cypress Preserve. Since 2000 state funds were provided through a land acquisition bonding program, Florida Forever. Forever ended this spring. In 2011 Florida Forever funds were totally eliminated.

Since its establishment, the SFWMD and its four sister agencies throughout the state have been managed by citizen boards appointed by the governor. This citizen-led, water basin and science centric system was dramatically altered last spring. For the first time the legislature granted itself the power to micro-manage the budgets of the districts. This injection of partisan politics into water management decision-making will be especially disruptive because Everglades restoration has and will require multi-year plans, funding and commitment. Annual legislative approval will make those impossible. Will this not look to the federal government as a trial separation pending final divorce?

Proposals for the future are more ominous. Ten years ago there was an initiative by an affiliate of the disgraced Enron Corporation to abandon Florida's tradition of recognizing water as a crucial public resource to be managed for all the people of Florida and instead treat it as a commodity owned by private interests. The then leaders of the state were wise and rejected this swindle; however, it is now re-surfacing. Some are suggesting the purpose of the alterations made by the 2011 legislature was to set the table for privatization of Florida's water. You can imagine how well the water-dependent natural system of the Everglades would fare if it had to bid for privately owned water in competition with commercial users.

Into this gloomy picture there has now come a ray of light. Gov. Rick Scott, speaking on Nov. 16 to the Everglades Foundation, said, "My administration is absolutely focused on making sure the right thing happens with the Everglades."

To realize this commitment, the governor must erect an iron curtain of opposition to privatization and any other future degradation in the state's ability to continue the marriage with Washington for Everglades restoration. Beyond that, in the election year of 2012 the legislature should respond to the desire of the great majority of Floridians, who support Everglades restoration, and begin rolling back the mistakes of 2011.

Talking the talk is ingratiating; walking the walk can save the marriage and the Everglades.

## Bad Policies Pose Historic Threats to Fla. Environment

**Bob Graham and Nathaniel Reed**

*Orlando Sentinel*, January 30, 2013

Recent investigative reporting by Kevin Spear in the Orlando Sentinel reveals the dramatic and widespread pollution and flow problems facing so many of Florida's rivers and springs. These reports were echoed by editorials across the state calling on Florida's governor, Department of Environmental Protection and Legislature to take action to protect and restore our impaired waterways.

Yet instead of resolving the serious problems that threaten our state's most precious natural resources, efforts in Tallahassee have focused on rolling back environmental safeguards and growth-management guidelines, cutting funding for conservation and regulation, reducing enforcement against polluters and liquidating public lands.

Severe budget cuts are seriously compromising the ability of Florida's DEP and water management districts to adequately protect our state's natural resources. Funding for many important conservation, restoration, monitoring, research, enforcement and education programs has been drastically reduced or eliminated.

Our state has also lost decades of valuable knowledge and expertise from significant layoffs, resulting in less capable agencies with insufficient resources and demoralized personnel. Although the DEP recently claimed "these reductions have done nothing to erode the agency's role in regulating industry and protecting the environment," it is not hard to find evidence to the contrary.

In 2012 the St. Johns River Water Management District cited "staffing capabilities" when asked why it reduced the number of monitoring stations in the St. Johns' lower basin by nearly two-thirds.

In addition, the recent decision by the Northwest Florida Water Management District to delay setting minimum flows and levels for Wakulla Springs for 11 years raises serious concerns about the ability of Florida's water-management districts to perform their critical missions at current funding and staffing levels. Reduced monitoring and legal protections endanger our environment and public health, while polluters profit.

Efforts are under way now by the DEP to streamline permitting requirements for large water users that will result in longer permits, less oversight and no additional requirements for conservation and efficiency. These changes benefit select industries at the expense of our water resources and the majority of Floridians.

On Gov. Rick Scott's watch, unwise policy decisions, draconian budget cuts and the excessive influence of special interests have put Florida on the brink of losing 40 years of progress on environmental protection, land conservation and growth management. This is bad water-management policy and even worse economic policy for our state.

We now face one of the greatest emergencies in Florida's modern history. Our prized and supposedly well-protected rivers and springs are "sick" from pollution and in need of restoration and protection by our state agencies and a Legislature that shares our citizens' concerns and determination to correct the current abuses of negligence.

The Wekiva River, north of Orlando, is designated as an Outstanding Florida Water and a national Wild and Scenic River, and is protected by two major pieces of state legislation. Tragically, the Wekiva remains sick in terms of both water quality and quantity. The three major springs in the Wekiva River have reported nitrate concentrations 480 percent higher than the maximum levels for healthy waters.

And while the largest of Wekiva's springs, Wekiwa and Rock, have reported flows below established minimum flows and levels for the past two years, the St. Johns district refuses to meet its statutory duty of restoring flows to these natural jewels.

As a result, the Florida Conservation Coalition and our partners are hosting "Speak Up Wekiva" at Wekiwa Springs State Park on Feb. 16. We are organizing this event to celebrate our outstanding water resources, educate and engage the public and policymakers about the challenges facing the river and the springs that feed it and advocate for the protection and restoration of all of Florida's impaired waterways.

It's time for Floridians to speak up for our environment and ensure its protection for generations to come.

---

Nathaniel Reed was former assistant secretary of the interior from 1970 to 1977 and founder of the Everglades Foundation.

## Scott, House Must Join Senate, Protect Florida's Springs

Bob Graham

*Orlando Sentinel*, April 22, 2014

Let's look back in time to the early 1970s, when Florida's population was 7.5 million and growing rapidly. After Florida's lands and waters were polluted and altered for decades to make way for development, our environment was in trouble: Water quality and flow were threatened; and critical natural areas were on the verge of being lost forever.

We were fortunate when Gov. Reubin Askew took office in 1971 to have a governor who prioritized Florida's environment and provided the leadership necessary to move environmental legislation forward. Askew challenged the Legislature to set up a regulatory system and funding to protect Florida's natural resources and guide its growth.

We were equally fortunate to have leaders in both chambers of the Legislature and on both sides of the aisle with the foresight and courage to meet that challenge. In 1972, Florida passed the most comprehensive set of environmental conservation and protection laws in the nation, including legislation to protect Florida's waters, purchase environmentally sensitive lands, protect critical areas and set limits on development. Throughout the heyday of Florida growth and economic prosperity, these laws added an element of environmental protection as Florida's economy boomed as never before or since.

Unfortunately, our government is failing to build upon the foundation laid down in the 1970s and 1980s to protect Florida's environment. To the contrary, in 2011, water-management districts suffered draconian cuts to their budgets and staffs; Florida's state growth-management agency was abolished; land-acquisition funding was cut to only a small fraction of historic levels; and the Florida Springs Initiative was defunded.

Now let's come back to 2014. Florida has a population of more than 19 million, and the dire problems facing our waters from the Panhandle to the Keys have gotten worse. Many of Florida's iconic springs still do not have basic protection; springs are dying from too little flow and too many nutrients; rivers are covered in algal mats; and estuaries and coastal waters are suffering staggering losses of marine life and birds. Now when our waters need strong environmental protections the most, we no longer have them.

But this year we have a bipartisan group of senators who have spent much of the past six months working with stakeholders from every viewpoint to create significant springs legislation that could pass the Legislature this year. The Senate has demonstrated its commitment to this goal by passing Senate Bill 1576 unanimously through its first two committee stops.

Despite its progress in the Senate, the Florida House of Representatives has refused to even allow the bill to be heard in a single committee so far this session. It is clear that House leaders are listening to special-interest lobbyists, telling them to weaken and kill the bill, instead of heeding the citizens of Florida, their Senate colleagues, conservation groups and newspaper editorial boards who have urged the House to take up the Senate version of the bill and pass strong springs legislation this session.

Equally concerning is Gov. Rick Scott's silence on this important legislation that would do so much to protect Florida's springs. If Scott followed the example of previous Florida governors to protect Florida's environment, he would bring House and Senate leaders together to make sure strong springs legislation is signed into law this year.

Although no single law can completely solve the problems facing Florida's waters, the Senate bill, which includes funding, deadlines and common-sense regulations, will significantly enhance the state of our springs.

However, the challenge lies in the House. Time is short. The House must take up the Senate bill, protect it from weakening and from extraneous amendments, and pass it.

The question is: Do this House and governor have the foresight and fortitude to stand up for Florida's springs?

My dear friend and predecessor Gov. Reubin Askew gave the 1972 Legislature the following piece of advice on the opening-day session. His words are truer today than ever.

"Your own elections are pressing down upon you telling you to try and slip through this session as quickly and as quietly and with as little action as possible . . . I ask you to do your best to put aside those thoughts . . . and work instead to come up with real answers to our toughest problems today . . . And it begins with the environment, as indeed it must, if any of our other efforts are to have meaning for tomorrow."

## U.S. Must Ensure Safe Oil Drilling

**Bob Graham and William K. Reilly**

*Miami Herald*, May 4, 2014

After an unsuccessful round of drilling in 2012 and 2013, Cuba's oil and gas industry is poised for further deepwater exploration in the Gulf as soon as 2015. As Cuba explores and eventually drills for oil, Florida and neighboring states have a paramount interest in ensuring that Cuba's drilling operators employ the highest safety standards and the best available technology. From our experience with the BP tragedy, failure to meet these standards would seriously threaten Florida's economy and environment.

A half-century of trade and travel restrictions separates the United States and Cuba. And yet the island's northern boundary floats just 50 miles from southern Florida. For communities in southern Florida whose commerce, especially tourism, depends on a healthy marine system, an oil spill would be disastrous. Coral reefs and mangroves, such as those found in the Everglades, Biscayne National Park and the Florida Keys, serve as protective barriers from hurricanes. They also provide critical nurseries for species that support commercial and recreational fisheries on the east coast.

Earlier this year in Havana, we met with top energy and environmental officials in Cuba to assess the country's preparation to mitigate an oil spill in Cuba's Gulf waters. After successive meetings, we left with a new realization of Cuba's imminent intention to explore for oil. Seismic studies indicate the potential for commercial-scale oil and gas deposits, and the instability of Venezuela, Cuba's main oil provider, is further incentive.

We are confident that Cuba is adopting standards in line with the recommendations developed by President Obama's National Commission on the BP Oil Spill and the Future of Offshore Drilling, which we cochaired. The test will be the capacity to achieve these standards.

Given Cuba's limited human and material resources and lack of substantial experience regulating deepwater oil and gas exploration, the United States should revise embargo-related restrictions to foster the highest standards of safe drilling. It is beyond our intentions to advocate for a total lifting of the embargo; rather, we urge for modifications to specific provisions to achieve maximum protection from a BP-type accident. One such restriction in need of modification is the U.S. sanction that prevents Cuba and its contractors from acquiring advanced technology with more than 10 percent U.S. content. Only one drilling rig in the world qualifies under this criterion.

U.S. travel and export restrictions further limit spill response in the Gulf of Mexico as they prohibit U.S. oil spill mitigation companies from traveling readily to Cuba. This potential danger became a reality during the BP explosion where the delay in capping the surging oil substantially increased the damage. In the aftermath of BP, the U.S. oil and gas industry established two response teams in the Gulf. But under current U.S. embargo restrictions, these response capabilities would not be available in the event of a similar accident in Cuban waters. We therefore urge the president to issue appropriate industry-wide "general" licenses for travel and export so that companies in the oil service and spill response industry can position proper equipment in advance.

The BP oil spill underscored that the Gulf of Mexico waters transcend national boundaries, making all countries sharing the Gulf vulnerable to consequences of a major spill. Within a year of the BP spill, commission representatives and affected U.S. agencies met with Mexican counterparts to coordinate Gulf drilling safety and response. Culminating at the Clean Gulf 2013 conference in Tampa, this dialogue now includes the Bahamas, Jamaica, and Cuba. The result was the establishment of the Multi-Lateral

Technical Operating Procedure (MTOP) to institute safety protocols in the event of a cross-border spill. While this was a substantial start, more needs to be done. Appropriate agencies in the U.S. government should brief oil companies on safety procedures in the agreement. To strengthen their oversight of drilling in the Gulf, these agencies would likewise benefit from creating channels for the exchange of expertise and training between Cuban and U.S. personnel. Given Cuba's serious pursuit of offshore drilling and the potential risk of an oil spill, the slow pace of U.S. preparedness greatly concerns us. To avoid environmental and economic damages reminiscent of the 2010 Deepwater Horizon oil spill, the United States must relax equipment restrictions. It must take comprehensive actions to facilitate cross-border exchange of best practices, mitigation training and response strategies. Until such steps are in place, we cannot be satisfied that every possible measure has been taken to preserve the economic and ecological wellbeing of the Gulf of Mexico.

## Celebrate Florida's Natural Wonders

**Bob Graham and Ryan Smart**

*Florida Times-Union*, September 16, 2016

For more than a century, America's great leaders and scientific minds have promoted and celebrated the conservation of land for nature and people.

On Saturday, Sept. 24, the Florida Conservation Coalition, its partner organizations and Florida Blue invite the residents of Northeast Florida to do the same at Speak Up for Florida Forever, a festival and call-to-action at Camp Milton Historic Preserve in West Jacksonville.

For those of us who call Florida home, our natural areas are not only our heritage but the foremost legacy that we will leave to our children and grandchildren.

Our state's land conservation programs, like Florida Forever, created one of the best state park systems in the nation and resulted in the acquisition of millions of acres of land to shield sensitive natural areas from development, protect waterbodies, buffer farmlands and military bases, and preserve and reconnect wildlife habitat.

## Reduced Funding

Today, however, funding for land conservation has slowed to a trickle at the same time that Florida is losing natural and working lands at an alarming rate.

Florida 2070, a new report by 1000 Friends of Florida, finds that more than 5 million acres of currently undeveloped lands will be developed by 2070 if we do not build more compact communities and conserve natural and working lands.

But that is only half the story.

Florida 2070 also shows that the same projected increase in population can be accommodated, on significantly less land, while permanently protecting nearly half of Florida from development.

What is most clear from Florida 2070 is that growth and conservation are not incompatible and that the choices we make today will determine the Florida of tomorrow.

Nowhere is the impact of land conservation more clear than in the condition of Florida's waters, whose fates are inextricably tied to the land uses surrounding them.

It is not a coincidence that Florida's most pristine major springs are located within the Ocala National Forest where their springsheds have been protected since 1908.

If you share President Theodore Roosevelt's commitment "to leaving this land even a better land for our descendants than it is for us," join us between 10 a.m. and 4 p.m. on Saturday, Sept. 24 for nature exhibits, guided hikes and bike tours, live music, food trucks, Civil War re-enactors and presentations as we Speak Up for Florida Forever.

By joining voices at this event, we can make a collective statement about the importance of preserving Florida's natural heritage and restoring Florida Forever funding. For more information, visit our website: tinyurl.com/zyokk5j.

Camp Milton Historic Preserve abuts the Northeast Florida Timberland and Watershed Reserve Florida Forever project, which stretches from the Etoniah Creek State Forest in Clay County to the Nassau River north of Jacksonville.

Acquisition of the remaining 83,000 acres of this project will preserve habitat for keystone species like the Florida black bear and gopher tortoise, increase urban open space and public recreation opportunities, and protect and restore land, water and wetland ecosystems.

Northeast Florida's legislators should make the protection of these lands a top priority for the 2017 legislative session.

---

Ryan Smart is executive director of the Florida Springs Council.

## Tell Legislators to Honor Amendment 1 and Florida Forever

Bob Graham

*Tampa Bay Times*, April 4, 2017

The Constitutional Revision Commission recently began holding meetings to propose amendments to the Florida Constitution. Based on the Florida Legislature's recent actions, they may as well put an amendment on the 2018 ballot eliminating the first three words of the Florida Constitution, "We the people," because the clear desires of "the people" are being ignored by those elected to represent us in Tallahassee.

Florida voters overwhelmingly support funding to protect Florida's environment because they know what it is that makes our state great. It's our beaches, springs, state parks, rivers, lakes, wildlife and the countless opportunities they provide for Floridians and tourists alike.

A recent poll found that only 4 percent of registered voters support cutting funding to environmental programs. This only adds to the clear message sent by the 75 percent of Florida voters in the 2014 election who supported Amendment 1 to restore funding to Florida's highly successful land conservation program: Florida Forever.

So what does our current state Legislature do? They propose slashing the Department of Environmental Protection's budget by more than 25 percent and completely defunding Florida Forever.

Fortunately, we have past legislatures, who had the foresight to fund land conservation programs like Florida Forever, to thank for wonderful places like San Felasco Hammock Preserve State Park. Located in Gainesville, this preserve protects one of the last remaining mature forests in Florida and provides one of the best hiking experiences anywhere.

Florida voters overwhelmingly support Florida Forever because they know it is the most effective way to protect Florida's environment. It uses an unassailable science-driven process. It embraces free market economics. It promotes good development. And, as Gov. Jeb Bush said when signing the Florida Forever Act into law, it is "the most significant . . . legislation that impacts the citizens of Florida."

Florida Forever is effective because conserved lands perform essential services just by being left alone. They provide habitat for wildlife, recharge our aquifer, filter out pollutants, mitigate the impacts of climate change, improve the quality of life of all Floridians and reduce the need for costly regulations.

Florida Forever is unassailable because it uses a proven process overseen by scientists and conservation and forestry experts to make land acquisition decisions. In 2013, when the Legislature directed the Department of Environmental Protection to sell unneeded conservation lands, the agency ended the program after nine months without selling a single acre due to the thorough evaluation process the lands underwent prior to purchase.

Florida Forever embraces free-market economics by giving land owners who wish to conserve their properties multiple options to do so, including selling the land directly to the state or just selling the development rights, allowing the land to stay in private ownership while protecting it for perpetuity. Both forms of conservation are important and effective.

The former created and enhances Florida's best-in-the-nation state parks and forest system; the latter is incredibly popular with ranchers and farmers looking to preserve not only their land but their way of life for future generations. I am encouraged to see that ranchers representing over a million acres have organized to advocate for increased land conservation funding this year.

Florida Forever promotes good development by protecting areas that need to be preserved and directing development toward more suitable lands. As 1000 Friends of Florida's Florida 2070 project illustrates, more than 5 million acres of natural and agricultural lands will be permanently lost to development over the next 50 years if current growth patterns continue. Restoring Florida Forever funding ensures that we do not lose the best parts of Florida, forever.

Florida Forever impacts the citizens of Florida by protecting special places in their backyards and enhancing the quality of life in their communities. For example, the Lake Santa Fe project, on the Florida Forever priority acquisition list, would preserve the last remaining undeveloped shoreline of Lake Santa Fe from development, protecting water quality, wetlands and wading bird nest sites. Places like this are some of Florida's last stretches of natural paradise; whether they stay that way is up to us.

Don't let your elected representatives ignore you any longer. The Florida Conservation Coalition is calling for a minimum of 25 percent of all Amendment 1 funds to be dedicated to land conservation through Florida Forever and Florida Communities Trust and for increased funding for the Rural and Family Lands Protection Program.

Contact your state representative and senator and tell them to do the will of "we the people" by fully funding Florida Forever. If you need help, contact the Florida Conservation Coalition at wearefcc.org.

## Protect Florida's Legacy—Its Land and Waters

**Bob Graham**

*Orlando Sentinel*, April 7, 2017

When you reach the age of 80, as I recently did, you think about your legacy. My dictionary defines legacy as "something that is the result of events in the past." In other words, the things we create, build or preserve that benefit those we will never know, and may never know of us.

This is a particularly important thought when you have lived "in the arena . . . marred by dust and sweat and blood," as Teddy Roosevelt so forcefully put it. When the people have given you the great honor of spending yourself "in a worthy cause . . ."

When I look back at my nearly 40 years of public service to the people of Florida, my legacy is not the offices to which I was elected, but what I achieved while in those offices. This is something that the current leadership in Tallahassee would be wise to reflect on.

Of all those achievements, there are none more permanent and therefore significant than the land and water we conserved to protect Florida's environment, economy and quality of life. These lands, which define our state, will remain protected from development no matter who is in charge in Tallahassee or Washington D.C.

These lands are my legacy.

We conserved these lands through a series of programs—Save Our Rivers, Save Our Coasts and Save Our Everglades—that spoke directly to the people of Florida. The connection was tangible. Buy this forest, and you will save the Wekiva River. Buy this beach, and you will save Grayton Beach and the Emerald Coast. Buy the development rights on this ranch land, and you will save it for continued productive agriculture. Buy the Big Cypress; it will contribute to the salvation of the Everglades.

These programs conserved hundreds of thousands of acres of lands that Florida visitors and residents continue to enjoy and depend upon to this today. If you have ever swam at Wakulla Springs, cruised up the St. Johns River, enjoyed seafood from Apalachicola, kayaked down the Suwannee, taken a glass-bottom boat ride at Silver Springs, or admired America's Everglades, you have directly benefited from these programs.

These places and experiences are Florida's legacy.

To fund these programs, we used the common-sense approach of allocating a portion of the taxes on-real estate transactions, otherwise known as documentary-stamp taxes, toward purchasing environmentally sensitive lands. The premise could not be simpler: Allow growth to pay for conservation.

These same programs to save our rivers, springs, coasts, habitat, farms and the Everglades exist today under the name Florida Forever. And funding, through doc-stamp taxes, for these programs was enshrined in the Florida Constitution by the 75 percent of Florida voters in the 2014 election who supported Amendment 1.

Unfortunately, what we are missing are legislators who understand the connection between our economy and environment, who are willing to spend their time in the arena on a worthy cause beyond their own election, and who understand the value of building a legacy that stands the test of time.

The Florida Legislature has once again nearly eliminated funding for land-conservation programs, like Florida Forever, in its proposed 2017 budgets. And, once again, we look to our governor to provide leadership.

Throughout our state, there are still lands and waters in need of urgent protection.

A recent report by 1000 Friends of Florida projects that more than 5 million acres of natural and agricultural lands will be permanently lost to development over the next 50 years if current development trends continue. Some of these lands are appropriate for development, while others must be protected.

One example, just outside of Orlando, is the Wekiva-Ocala Greenway project, currently on the Florida Forever priority acquisition list. If conserved it would protect the Wekiva and St. Johns River basins, provide recreational opportunities and natural Florida experiences in the fastest growing region in Florida, and preserve habitat for soaring bald eagles, diving swallow-tailed kites and the largest subpopulation of black bears in Florida. It is believed to have as many as 75 springs within its boundary.

Restoring Florida Forever funding to purchase areas like the Wekiva-Ocala Greenway ensures that we will not lose the best parts of Florida, forever.

The Florida Conservation Coalition, which was founded by concerned Floridians in 2012, is calling for a minimum of 25 percent of the doc-stamp tax funds set aside by Amendment 1 to be dedicated to protecting vital conservation lands for future generations through Florida Forever.

Contact your state representative and senator today and ask them to allocate 25 percent of Amendment 1 dollars to Florida Forever. Tell them their legacy and the best parts of Florida are on the line.

## Trump's Risky Offshore Oil Strategy

**Bob Graham and William K. Reilly**

*New York Times*, July 5, 2017

Seven years ago, a BP oil well blew out off Louisiana, causing the Deepwater Horizon drill rig to explode, killing 11 workers and releasing several million barrels of toxic crude oil into the Gulf of Mexico.

As co-chairmen of the bipartisan National Commission on the BP Deepwater Horizon Oil Spill and Offshore Drilling, we investigated the causes of the disaster and examined the offshore drilling industry to identify ways to reduce the risks it poses to workers, the public and the environment. Although Congress has refused to enact any of the commission's safety recommendations, the Department of the Interior adopted many of them after extensive input from industry, government and the public.

President Trump's April 28 executive order on offshore energy threatens to abolish these safety improvements and, as he put it, start "the process of opening offshore areas" to energy exploration. He took a further step last week to expand oil and gas extraction in the environmentally sensitive outer continental shelf. The commission members are unanimous in their view that the actions proposed in the president's executive order are unwise.

As Americans flock to the nation's beaches this summer, it is important to understand what Mr. Trump's recent moves portend. Specifically, his executive order calls for the reconsideration of a critical safeguard that is the most important action the government has taken to reduce offshore drilling hazards. This safeguard, the well control rule, tightened controls on blowout preventers designed to stop explosions in undersea oil and gas wells. The rule was based in part on lessons the commission learned about the root cause of the BP disaster.

Had this common-sense rule been in place on April 20, 2010, that calamity might well have been averted. Weakening or rescinding this rule would increase the risks of offshore operations, put workers in harm's way and imperil marine waters and coastlines.

Mr. Trump's order also directed the Interior Department to review current rules on offshore drilling. Opening more areas to exploration, as the Trump administration moved to do last week, could threaten the fragile Arctic Ocean off Alaska as well as environmentally sensitive reaches of the Atlantic Ocean and the Gulf of Mexico. A spill in any of those waters could threaten multibillion-dollar regional economies that depend on clean oceans and coastlines.

Nothing has changed to justify these moves since the current five-year offshore leasing plan, which runs through 2022, was finalized after years of public and industry input. Broad public opposition to expanding drilling into frontier areas has not diminished. Nor are the identified potential harms to economies and ecologies any less significant.

In short, drilling in the outer continental shelf remains risky business. Safety and oversight in offshore drilling continues to need improvement, not roll-backs.

President Trump's executive order disregards these facts. It fails to account for the vulnerabilities of the ocean's frontier regions, a lack of adequate federal investment in safety measures for Arctic conditions, or the danger to coastal economies. It will put workers' lives as well as ecologically rich and economically important waters and coastlines at needless additional risk.

## Panhandle at Risk for BP-Style Blowout

**Bob Graham and Frances Beinecke**

*Pensacola News-Journal*, March 11, 2018

The Trump administration is putting Florida's Panhandle at increased risk for the next BP-style blowout by expanding the reach of oil and gas drilling while rolling back common-sense safeguards drawn from the lessons of the Deepwater Horizon disaster. And Congress continues to operate in a state of denial.

That's a dangerous and foolhardy combination. It threatens our waters and coastlines and all of the recreational and economic opportunities they support. The stakes are high for our region and we must demand better from Washington.

The April 2010 BP oil spill killed 11 workers, dumped several million barrels of toxic crude into the Gulf of Mexico and fouling beaches and destroying wetlands from the coast of Texas to Pensacola Bay and beyond.

Along the shores and estuaries of Pensacola and Perdido bays, spilled oil damaged oyster beds, tidal marshes and seagrass meadows that are the nurseries for the shrimp, fish and other marine life. So important to Floridians' tourism-dependent businesses—from commercial and charter boat fishing to real estate rentals and beach weddings—saw revenue plunge 50 percent or more, taking a toll that rocked every comer of the region's economy.

Just weeks after the blowout, President Obama established a bipartisan and independent commission to investigate what caused the tragedy and suggest steps to reduce the risk of a similar catastrophe in the future.

One of our key findings was that inadequate government oversight had helped to set the stage for a series of preventable mistakes, misjudgments and equipment failures that allowed such a disaster to occur.

Federal rules and enforcement capacity had not kept pace with an industry moving into deeper and more dangerous waters to drill. And to make matters worse, the agency entrusted to ensure the safety of these increasingly complex operations was gravely conflicted by a dual mission to promote the very industry it was charged with regulating.

In many ways, the industry was policing itself, a formula for disaster. This was especially true in the case of the Deepwater Horizon, a job that was over budget and behind schedule. Corners were cut. Safety was compromised. Disaster ensued. The commission recommended dozens of reforms, with key roles for Congress, the industry, and the administration.

Nearly eight years after the blowout, Congress has failed to pass a single piece of legislation to implement the Commission's recommendations and reduce the risks associated with offshore drilling in any meaningful way. This is a stunning betrayal of the public trust.

The industry itself has taken some important steps, including establishing the Marine Well Containment Corp., which maintains equipment to respond to a deepwater spill, and the Center for Offshore Safety, aimed at promoting best practices.

The Obama administration restructured offshore energy management in the department of interior by creating a Bureau of Ocean Energy Management to plan and administer lease sales and the Bureau of Safety and Environmental Enforcement to oversee these inherently dangerous industrial operations at sea.

It also instituted rules that enshrine specific lessons learned from the BP blowout. These rules make critical safety practices mandatory. They call for approved auditors to certify the reliability of important safety and environmental equipment. And they require well operators to feed live information to regulators to provide a second set of eyes on critical well operations.

The Trump administration has proposed weakening these rules, allowing companies to self-certify equipment and stifling the ability of regulators to monitor operations when it matters most.

It is beyond foolish to weaken rules designed to minimize the risk of another catastrophic blowout. It is reckless, irresponsible and wrong.

At the same time, Trump has proposed expanding oil and gas drilling and the hazards and harm it brings to roughly 1 billion square miles of U.S. oceans—in Atlantic, Pacific, Arctic and Alaskan waters and parts of the Gulf of Mexico.

In response to intense opposition, Interior Secretary Ryan Zinke's said he would take Florida's waters off the table. The oil industry quickly pushed back, demanding access to all U.S. oceans. And, ten days after Zinke's flip-flop, the acting director of the Bureau of Ocean Energy Management assured a House subcommittee that his boss was wrong.

Congress still has taken no action to protect business owners and communities from the tremendous economic impacts of an offshore oil spill. For example, there has been no attempt to remove the current $75 million cap that has been placed on payouts for damages due to company negligence.

Per the case of BP, a deep-pocket company with an international reputation to uphold, these limits were waived. As of today, BP has paid out more than $61 billion in fines and damages. Had it been a less responsible company, these limits may have been enforced leaving communities like Pensacola holding the bag.

Successful societies learn from their mistakes. Successful nations codify those lessons in rules, reforms and laws.

If there's one thing we've learned from the Deepwater Horizon disaster, it is that we must do more to protect our workers, waters, wildlife and the economy from the hazards of offshore drilling. We owe that much to those who paid the ultimate price for that tragedy, and those who continue to be impacted in its aftermath. We owe that much to our future generations. We are dismayed that Secretary Zinke apparently does not agree.

---

Frances Beinecke is the former president of the Natural Resources Defense Council.

## DeSantis Has a Chance to Manage Florida's Growth Wisely and Protect Its Environment

David Colburn and Cynthia Barnett

*Tampa Bay Times*, November 21, 2018

For months leading up to Florida's chaotic midterm elections, incoming Gov.-elect Ron DeSantis clashed with challengers over race, schools, the economy, toxic algae and "California-style energy policy."

As DeSantis takes office as the state's 46th governor in January, the issue underlying those and so many others is Florida's surging population growth and its spillover effects from pollution to overcrowded schools.

Florida's net growth has reached nearly 1,000 people a day, a rate not seen since the early 2000s. Unlike the last surge of that magnitude, Florida is absorbing newcomers without the growth-management system built in earlier generations—and amid the rising seas of climate change few people thought about back then.

Growth has been Florida's grand paradox for all of the state's modern history, creating prosperity and opportunity as well as ecological injury that threatens the quality of life that drew us here in the first place. And every modern Florida governor has confronted growth-related challenges, with varying degrees of leadership and success.

Gov. DeSantis faces a set of circumstances even more daunting than those that confronted Gov. Bob Graham in the 1980s, when the national press claimed Florida was "going down the tubes." That 1981 Sports Illustrated headline declared "There's Trouble in Paradise." A Time magazine cover that same year called South Florida "Paradise Lost."

From the state's Everglades restoration successes to considerable land acquisitions achieved since then, Florida has a record of "big, hairy, audacious ideas," as Gov. Jeb Bush used to say, to confront its most-serious challenges.

But contrasting earlier eras, today's growth pressures are spread throughout much more of the peninsula, and are already amplified by climate change. Florida stands to lose more homes and more real-estate value to sea rise than any other state in the nation. Hurricane Michael underscored Florida's vulnerability to the weather extremes climate scientists predict will become more frequent with warming. These threats mean Florida's interior counties could see unprecedented growth as more coastal dwellers migrate inland.

The state's largest landowners, such as Plum Creek/Weyerhaeuser in North Florida and Deseret Ranch in Central Florida, are keenly aware of these trends and have planned for the transition of forest and cattle lands to rooftops for decades. Yet just as Florida's growth and interior development take off, the state under Gov. Rick Scott backed off its role in planning major new developments, including requirements for adequate schools, roads, sewage disposal and other resources to balance economic prosperity with quality of life.

Growth has been a litmus test for every modern Florida governor since the mid-1950s, when a nationwide drought crept down the peninsula, revealing the state's vulnerability to water shortages one year and hurricanes the next. By the late 1960s, political leaders inspired by Democratic Gov. Reubin Askew and Republican conservation leader Nathaniel Reed agreed that growth could not continue unplanned, lest it ruin the fragile natural beauty that makes Florida, Florida.

Askew led Floridians to adopt the strongest land, planning and water-use laws in the nation in 1972. As the state grew quickly through the 1970s and '80s, though, it became clear that they were not sufficient to handle the traffic gridlock, the overtaxed sewer systems and the strip-mall sprawl.

Graham's response was a bipartisan coalition charged with "questions of excellence: How can we make growth be of the highest quality, to most contribute to our lives and to the future of our state?" The answer was a statewide system of growth management. Like the land and water laws of an earlier era, it was the vanguard in the nation.

Various overhauls have reflected developers' and local governments' frustration with the state bureaucracy. Upon winning office in 1999, Gov. Jeb Bush kept his promise to target land acquisition as the best strategy to protect the environment, shepherding in the popular Florida Forever program. By purchasing, or negotiating conservation easements on large tracts of environmentally sensitive land statewide, Bush "accomplished more in driving growth to the appropriate places than in any other statewide policy," says his former Secretary of the Department of Community Affairs, Steve Seibert.

As he takes office, DeSantis has an unparalleled opportunity to rally Floridians and the business community to face the state's growth-related challenges. The surprise election of Fort Lauderdale Democrat Nikki Fried as agriculture commissioner gives the pair a rare platform to convene thought leaders from both parties, and from urban and rural Florida, to reach consensus on the audacious ideas needed to clean up Florida's water today while preserving our last wildlands and the heritage crops now falling to rooftops.

Will DeSantis sidestep growth, letting Florida continue to develop haphazardly in ways that put quality of life and natural treasures at risk? Or will he step into the shoes of governors such as Bush, Graham and Askew to bring lawmakers from both parties, science and policy leaders, local governments and citizens together to address the big "questions of excellence" for all Floridians?

We hope he will choose the latter path. But as governor, DeSantis should push beyond the past. He should articulate a bold vision for Florida's future and make it the centerpiece of his first-term agenda. Progress won't be easy or rapid. But with sustained commitment and willingness to listen and learn from all sides, Gov. DeSantis can return Florida to its stature as a national leader in shaping growth that benefits both people and our state's gorgeous, but ailing, environment.

---

Cynthia Barnett is environmental journalist in residence at University of Florida's College of Journalism.

## In Tallahassee, a New Environment for Environmentalism

David Colburn and Cynthia Barnett

*Tampa Bay Times*, January 25, 2019

In his campaign for Florida governor that coincided with plumes of toxic algae and piles of dead fish on the state's signature beaches, Ron DeSantis denounced pollution and declared himself a "Teddy Roosevelt-style Republican," championing conservation as a basic conservative value.

Due in no small part to President Donald Trump's first interior secretary, Ryan Zinke, the TR comparison had lost its sizzle. Zinke channeled

Roosevelt his first day on the job by donning a cowboy hat and riding up to Interior on a horse named Tonto. He then oversaw the single-largest elimination of public conservation lands in American history, dismantling the conservation legacy of Republican and Democratic presidents alike.

Florida's environmental leaders might have been forgiven for worrying that DeSantis, too, a Trump protégé with a poor environmental record in Congress, would be all hat and no cattle.

Instead, two days after his inauguration as Florida's 46th governor, DeSantis signed one of the farthest-reaching environmental orders in state history. As the rest of the nation watches federal inaction, Floridians are seeing action. DeSantis' order called for a record $2.5 billion for Everglades restoration; a harmful-algae task force; a chief science officer; and an office of resilience and coastal protection to fund and coordinate Florida's response to rising seas.

DeSantis did not stop at Executive Order No. 19–12. He has demanded that all eight board members of the powerful South Florida Water Management District step down. As governor-elect in December, DeSantis had asked the board to delay approving a $1 million sugar industry lease that would extend cane farming in an area the Legislature has identified for Everglades restoration. Former Gov. Rick Scott's water managers ignored DeSantis and approved the lease.

"The voters spoke clearly in support of our bold vision for action on the environment," DeSantis wrote in his letter asking for their resignations. "It is time for a clean reset of the leadership of the board to focus the appropriate attention on this bold vision."

DeSantis' decisiveness is classic Theodore Roosevelt. Early in his presidency, TR was determined to rein in the nation's wild-west public lands policy and even demanded the resignation of his own public lands administrator, Binger Hermann.

Of course, there's a difference between making news and making history. In her new book These Truths, historian Jill Lepore unspools a brilliant critique of the rise of story over substance, pinpointing the early 20th century professionalization of public relations and political spin as one turning point when America lost its way, abandoning ideas for photo ops.

The acid test of leadership is not the headline you grab in your opening charge, but the work you do to sustain it over the years. That is the challenge now facing Gov. DeSantis. Just as Theodore Roosevelt worked continually to preserve national lands from the first wildlife refuge at Florida's Pelican Island in 1903 to saving Washington's Mount Olympus on his way out of the White House in 1909, the governors who helped build Florida's environmental legacy dedicated years and hard-won political capital to accomplish it.

Against stiff resistance, Democratic Gov. Reubin Askew methodically championed the progressive land and water laws enacted by the Florida Legislature in the 1970s. During the following decade, Bob Graham sparked the nation's imagination to save the Everglades, then spent his two terms as governor and three as U.S. Senator to ensure their restoration. Republican Gov. Jeb Bush steadily pursued and ultimately amassed a record $1 billion in environmental land purchases over his eight years in office that ended in 2007.

What will count for DeSantis won't be the horse he rode in on, but the one that carries him across the finish line.

## Protect Florida's Waters Statewide

**Bob Graham and Lee Constantine**

*Orlando Sentinel*, March 1, 2019

Protecting and conserving Florida's water is an economic as well as environmental issue, not one defined by geography or party lines. Both of us, a Democrat from Miami Lakes and Republican from Altamonte Springs, have made protecting and restoring Florida's waters a cornerstone of our public service. Today, we redouble our efforts to safeguard Florida's most valuable resource.

Spurred by outbreaks of red tide and blue-green algae leading to another summer of dramatic loss in revenue and decline of water quality and quantity in Florida's springs, rivers, and lakes, the Florida Conservation Coalition (FCC), a coalition of over 80 conservation-minded groups, released "A Water Policy for Florida." This position statement provides an overview of many of the existing threats to our waters and a pathway for their successful conservation, restoration and protection statewide.

The FCC lays out five critical steps that must be undertaken immediately by our policymakers to safeguard our waters.

Prevent pollution at its source. An ounce of prevention really is worth a pound of cure. Preventing pollution at its source is the most environmentally sound and cost-effective way to meet water quality goals. We have proposed common sense solutions to prevent pollution from wastewater, agriculture, biosolids, and stormwater, among other sources, in at-risk watersheds.

Aggressively reduce existing sources of pollution. Since the vast majority of Florida's waters are already impaired by nutrients, it is not enough to just slow the growth of pollution; we must reverse the trend. Adopting a stronger state model fertilizer ordinance, requiring effective best management practices, upgrading wastewater utilities, and replacing or upgrading septic tanks in areas already impaired by excessive nutrient pollution will be an expensive but necessary undertaking if we hope to restore impaired waters.

Protect land to protect water. What happens on Florida's land determines the state of its waters. Florida needs to immediately acquire lands in sensitive areas, minimize urban sprawl and require efficient landscaping in new developments. The Legislature should pass a law that provides significant annual funding to acquire critical natural areas and conserve working farms and ranches.

Secure Florida's Future Water Supply: Public investments in water supply focus on engineering solutions to expand valuable water resources, missing opportunities to reduce demand through conservation efforts. Government programs should prioritize and incentivize water conservation measures as the first means to address Florida's water supply challenges. Additionally, Florida's water management districts must do a better job of accounting for the interests of the environment and public in making water use permitting decisions.

Provide adequate funding for Florida's comprehensive water policy. For decades, efforts to protect and restore Florida's waters have been significantly underfunded. Compared to other important state priorities, like transportation, which receives nearly $11 billion in funding each year, funding for the management and protection of our water resources is sorely lacking. Although a true cost has not yet been determined, estimates suggest funding for Florida's water quality compliance and infrastructure needs to be a minimum of $1–2 billion per year. Traditional funding sources, like water management district ad valorem tax rates, will need to be restored and new funding sources, such as a water withdrawal fee, will need to be identified if we are going to save Florida's waters.

As the 2019 legislative session begins in Tallahassee, we are hopeful that our governor and legislators understand that Florida cannot afford another year, much less decades to come, of the environmental and economic disasters that have become commonplace across Florida. As former state legislators, we know the importance of public input in the legislative process. We encourage you to contact your local state senator and state representative and tell them about the rivers, lakes, springs, beaches and estuaries in your community, and why statewide water protections matter to you.

But first, visit wearefcc.org and read "A Water Policy for Florida" (a ten-page document including a one-page summary) to arm yourself with the facts and information necessary to make a difference.

---

Lee Constantine is a Seminole County commissioner and a former state senator and state representative.

## It's a Perilous Time for Florida Manatees. Yet, Trump Is Destroying the Endangered Species Act.

Bob Graham

*Tampa Bay Times*, August 13, 2019

Would the manatee even have been protected under the new rules?

Floridians love wildlife, especially manatees. The West Indian manatee, of which our Florida manatees are a subspecies, was one of the first species listed as endangered under the Endangered Species Act (ESA) in 1973. In 2017, citing increased numbers, the U.S. Fish & Wildlife Service (FWS) downlisted the manatee's status from endangered to threatened, a less protective designation. The manatees' road to recovery under the Endangered Species Act should be a success story. However, events have caused concern that the population is struggling again. Unprecedented watercraft mortality, Red Tides, severe cold snaps, and relentless algal blooms fueled by nutrient pollution have killed large numbers of manatees and severely damaged essential habitat. We must remain vigilant or the populations may slide irreversibly backwards toward extinction.

In these uncertain times for Florida manatees, what is President Donald Trump's Department of Interior doing? It is destroying the Endangered Species Act.

The Endangered Species Act is the world's preeminent conservation law and our nation's most effective law for protecting wildlife in danger of extinction—99 percent of species that have received protections under the ESA are still with us today. In large measure due to the ESA, iconic species like the bald eagle, American alligator and brown pelican have recovered. And the ESA is incredibly popular—90 percent of American voters support the law.

Yet the Trump Administration has created new rules that will severely weaken the ESA. What would have happened to the Florida manatee if these rules had been in effect when it was originally listed? In fact, they may not have been listed all. Currently, listing determinations are made solely based on science. The changes will now encourage the Fish & Wildlife Service to undertake economic analyses prior to listing any new species. These types of analyses can produce huge ranges in economic costs (from zero to millions of dollars for the same species in the same analysis). And they often only include direct management costs and ignore the tremendous value these species provide. I wonder if the cost of saving manatees would have been deemed too high in the 1970s?

The ESA requires that any agency involved in a federally permitted project must consult with Fish & Wildlife regarding potential impacts if the project affects a listed species or its critical habitat. The new rules significantly weaken these requirements. For example, under current regulations, if a developer wanted to build a federally permitted marina in designated critical manatee habitat, the agency granting those permits would have to consult with FWS. The consultation would examine questions such as whether the marina would shade and kill seagrass that manatees rely on for food, or whether the marina's construction would result in increased boat traffic that would increase risks for collisions. It is often these additional impacts that result in the greatest harm to imperiled species. Under the new rules, however, the federal agency would not be required to consult regarding any activities or effects that are not under its control and responsibility. Instead, it could entirely ignore impacts from such things as increased boat traffic.

These are just a couple of examples of how damaging these rules would have been for manatees when they were first listed and how they may cause irreversible harm to manatees and other imperiled species in the future. And in Florida our wildlife is tied to our economy. According to the Outdoor Industry Association, in 2017 outdoor recreation in Florida created 485,000 jobs, $58.6 billion in consumer spending, generated $17.9 billion in wages and salaries and $3.5 billion in state and local taxes. As our wildlife suffers, so do our real estate and hospitality industries.

This is not the time to weaken protections. Former Interior Secretary Ryan Zinke oversaw the writing of these rules before he left in December, and he is now under federal investigation. Zinke was riddled with conflicts of interest and worked to benefit his industry campaign donors on land deals and oil and gas leasing. David Bernhardt, a former oil and gas lobbyist, the new secretary of interior, is also drowning in conflict of interest. By crafting these rules, he is acting on behalf of industry groups that find the Act a hindrance. The Department of Interior should work on behalf of the American people, not conflicted special interests.

I have dedicated much of my life to protecting Florida's natural environment. I have and will continue to advocate to save our wildlife, especially the manatee. I am calling on Sens. Rick Scott and Marco Rubio and Florida's entire congressional delegation to reject these harmful regulations.

# FOREIGN POLICY

# 10

# International Affairs

We live in an increasingly interconnected world. What happens in Europe or Asia, in Africa or Latin America affects us here in Florida on a daily basis. In this section, Colburn and Graham tackle some of the hot-button international issues seemingly ripped from today's front-page headlines. In 1992, with the conclusion of the Cold War and the demise of statist communism, American political scientist Francis Fukuyama famously proclaimed the end of history and the ascendency of Western democratic ideals and principles. Instead, a newer world order emerged, one maybe even more dangerous than what it replaced, in which religious fundamentalism and right-wing fascist ideology were fueled by new technologies and old grievances. This is the world that the authors examine in this section—a world too often explained with heated rhetoric and simplistic responses. Instead, they use a thoughtful, reasoned approach that relies on an understanding of power dynamics, ideology, and enlightened national interest to both explain the world and offer solutions to international problems. They examine questions surrounding international trade agreements and multilateral and bilateral defense treaties. They look at the need for continuity in American foreign policy, recognizing that different administrations will have different approaches, but also understanding that the basic contours of American foreign policy should not shift dramatically when a new president takes the reins of power. By pointing out the connections between economic concerns and diplomatic ones, they show the connected nature of today's world; that the sale of soybeans to China is as much about foreign policy as it is about financial considerations. David Colburn writes poignantly about the physical and emotional scars of the Vietnam War more than forty years after the war ended for the United States. He ties the war's effect on the nation as a whole to his own Vietnam service, and reminds us that these op-ed pieces are so powerful because they speak to both broad national questions and deeply personal concerns. The pieces in this short section lead to a wider examination of the world in the late 20th and early 21st centuries as they examine the need for a citizenry that is informed, engaged, and willing to consider the hard questions revolving around the place of the United States in the world.

## At Last, a Coherent Guide for U.S. Foreign Policy

David Colburn

*Orlando Sentinel*, August 8, 1996

The nation's foreign policy has been marked by fits and starts since the end of the Cold War. While once most Americans stood united in supporting programs to contain Soviet expansionism, many are now uncertain about the nature and direction of American foreign policy.

Adding to the public's confusion, the president and congressional leaders have disagreed sharply about what constitutes the nation's vital interests and about the deployment of American troops to the nations of Iraq, Somalia, Haiti and Bosnia.

A bipartisan commission made up of 18 men and women, who have been troubled by the nation's lack of foreign-policy direction, just published a report titled America's National Interests. Bob Graham of Florida, one of three U.S. senators on the commission, believes that "America's foreign policy too often gets diverted by domestic affairs" and that the United States has lost opportunities to advance its interests abroad as a consequence.

In contrast to a number of recent studies by scholars and think tanks about America's role in the post-Cold War world, this report is balanced and straightforward. It assumes American military dominance in the world and calls for a series of steps to maintain U.S. leadership abroad.

The authors identify five areas of vital interest to the United States:

To prevent, deter, and reduce the threat of nuclear, biological, and chemical weapons attack on the United States.

To prevent the emergence of a major hostile enemy in Europe or Asia.

To prevent the emergence of a hostile power on U.S. borders or one that controls the seas.

To prevent the collapse of major global systems including trade, finance, energy and the environment.

To ensure the survival of America's allies.

Few would quibble with these priorities, although some will no doubt question the authors' assertion that the United States must be prepared to use its military power to protect and secure these interests.

The report also examines each region of the world. Among its central points are that China's emergence will likely dominate the world stage and international politics for the next quarter century. Graham and his co-authors reject isolating or containing China, calling instead for a multifaceted policy that would tie China to the international system of nations. Human-rights violations should not undermine this effort, they contend, because such violations "do not threaten the survival or freedom of America."

The authors also acknowledge Russia as "the single largest potential challenge to American national interests" because of its nuclear weapons and military capabilities. Although welcoming the collapse of communism in Russia, they note that the transition to democracy and capitalism has been so traumatic that the United States needs to be exceedingly vigilant and realistic in its goals for this relationship.

With the recent crash of TWA Flight 800, the shadow of international terrorism has once again spread over the United States. Writing before the crash, members of the commission warned that the growing tide of terrorism around the world poses a greater threat to the lives and interests of American citizens than at any previous time in history.

One of the great frustrations of Americans is that terrorists seem to go unpunished. Those involved in the bombing of Pan Am Flight 103 in 1988, for example, are still at large. And the concern is that the U.S. government will lack the moral willpower to go after terrorists who hide out in pariah states such as Iran, Iraq, and Libya.

The authors of this report urge that the United States be much more aggressive in pursuing terrorist organizations. Noting the catastrophic possibility that terrorists could acquire biological and nuclear weapons, they call for closer ties with friends and allies to identify and destroy terrorist cells.

The recommendations in America's National Interests are not without controversy, but the report is well-reasoned and offers at last a coherent approach to foreign affairs. Voters and policy-makers owe it to themselves to read this document carefully.

## Bush Must Not Appease Hizbollah

Bob Graham and Tom Diaz

*Financial Times* (London), March 31, 2005

Will the real George W. Bush please stand up? "Our war on terror begins with al-Qaeda, but it does not end there. It will not end until every terrorist group of global reach has been found, stopped and defeated," Mr Bush declared in his September 20 2001 speech to a joint session of Congress.

This call to arms states an unequivocal and honourable policy—the US will not deal with or reward terrorists. It is with some dismay, therefore, that one learns of the president's equivocation regarding Hizbollah, the Lebanese terrorist group that before the al-Qaeda attacks of September 11 2001 was responsible for the death of more Americans than any other group. This is an ominous move toward appeasement.

Condoleezza Rice, the secretary of state, suggested on March 13 that the US would be prepared to accommodate the terrorist group in a Lebanon free of Syrian military and intelligence forces. Two days later, Mr Bush told reporters: "We view Hizbollah as a terrorist organisation and I would hope that Hizbollah would prove that they're not by laying down arms and not threatening peace."

The Bush administration now seems to believe that Hizbollah is an organisation with which it can do business. This sends a dangerous message to what is probably the most violent terrorist organisation in the world—if you act badly enough, and bloody the US enough, it will come to terms. This may win the White House breathing room in Iraq, its apparent purpose, but in the long term it will destroy the world's aspirations for a democratic Middle East.

The thought that Hizbollah will do business with the "Great Satan" of the US and with a president that it compares to Hitler is naive in the extreme. Hizbollah was founded by the ayatollahs of Iran in the aftermath of the fall of the Shah. Since then Hizbollah has been the hit group for Iran and later Syria. It receives tens of millions of dollars annually from Iran and the sanctuary and protection of Syria. Its motto is "Death to the United States."

The signature of Hizbollah has been high-explosive terror bombings with enormous death tolls. In October 1983 a Hizbollah truck bomb killed 241 US Marines in a Beirut barracks. A pending federal indictment for the 1996 bombing of US Air Force barracks at Khobar Towers in Saudi Arabia describes in detail the training and explosives expertise that Lebanese Hizbollah contributed to an operation that took the lives of 19 American servicemen. In all, over 300 Americans have died at the hands of Hizbollah and many more have been maimed and scarred for life. There is little doubt that the fingerprints of Hizbollah were on the vehicle bomb that killed Rafiq Harari, the former Lebanese prime minister, on February 14 this year.

United Nations resolution 1559 demands both that Syria remove all its military and intelligence presence from Lebanon and that Hizbollah be disarmed. It is imperative that those two mandates be pursued concurrently and resolutely. The consequence of separating these two mandates will be a power vacuum in Lebanon, most likely to be filled by Hizbollah's militia. The purpose of Syrian withdrawal, stability based on political legitimacy, will be undermined.

The Bush administration cannot responsibly forget that Hizbollah is a direct threat to the lives of Americans. Hizbollah has maintained an active presence in the US since the late 1980s. This presence has transformed from recruitment and fundraising to preparation for operations. It is generally considered that Hizbollah has the largest number of agents in the US, many more than al-Qaeda. Playing nice with Hizbollah in Lebanon will embolden the organisation's aspirations in the US and put Americans at greater risk.

The president should stay the course of his bold declaration of September 20 2001. He should lay down the law to Hizbollah and insist on full and concurrent implementation of UN resolution 1559. The US should use every available diplomatic, political and economic lever to force Syria to dismantle the terror training camps of Hizbollah and other terrorist groups in Syria and Lebanon. If these efforts fail, we should be prepared to use force. Finally, as the US works with the Europeans to negotiate an end to Iran's dangerous nuclear ambitions, it should also press to end Iran's funding of Hizbollah and other terrorist groups.

The US has committed itself to leading and engaging the world in bringing democracy to the Middle East. Hizbollah is a profound test of its commitment to that goal. It is inconceivable that the appeasement of killers will contribute to a stable Lebanon and Middle East. We have surely learnt that the way to lasting peace does not lie through another Munich.

---

Tom Diaz is co-author of *Lightning out of Lebanon: Hizbollah Terrorists on American Soil.*

## Looking beyond CAFTA

Bob Graham and Mack McLarty

*Washington Times*, July 27, 2005

Central America returns to center stage as Congress debates trade policy, globalization and the relationship with our hemispheric neighbors.

Unfortunately the U.S. free trade agreement with El Salvador, Costa Rica, Honduras, Nicaragua, Guatemala and the Dominican Republic—called DR-CAFTA and which has passed the Senate—continues to be battered by the usual overheated and off-target rhetoric about defending domestic jobs versus growing export revenues and open markets versus protected special interests.

What is missing is a basic understanding of DR-CAFTA and why it is naive to view the pact through the all-too-predictable anti-trade lens.

For starters, DR-CAFTA simply completes a trade circle begun under Presidents Carter and Reagan: The Caribbean Basin Initiative, enacted to accelerate peace and stability in Central America and the Caribbean in 1983, has allowed some 80 percent of DR-CAFTA country exports to enter the United States free of tariffs. What this new agreement does is give U.S. exports to the six partner countries the same free-trade advantages and then slowly expands to cover almost all two-way commerce. End result: a leveling of the hemispheric-trade playing field so that U.S. companies can export to consumers in these emerging Central American economies as easily as DR-CAFTA companies can get products onto U.S. shelves.

Also, this is not an agreement with some go-where-labor-is-cheapest, undeveloped banana republics. DR-CAFTA nations are emerging economies built on the principles of market access, investments in technology and liberal trade policies. U.S. companies already doing business in the DR-CAFTA region include Intel, Cargill, Proctor & Gamble, Hewlett-Packard, UPS and Pfizer. The six nations together comprise the second-largest export market in Latin America after Mexico, with $32 billion in two-way trade supporting about 200,000 American jobs.

Other critical issues involved include U.S. support for democracy, regional leadership and hemispheric cooperation. After all, the DR-CAFTA countries are in positions to either help or hurt U.S. interests—on needs ranging from immigration management to drug interdiction to port and shipping security—and the economic stability and growth catalyzed by expanded trade will help more closely align us with our neighbors.

Both Republicans and Democrats in Congress have been increasingly reluctant to support any free-trade expansions. While traditional concerns like labor rights and environmental standards still play a role in this reticence, the primary opposition is concern over the further job loses [*sic*] through outsourcing and relocations. Even though DR-CAFTA is no significant threat to U.S. workers, and more likely will create and sustain U.S. jobs through expanded exports, it has been battered by the reflex reaction of negativism that attaches to any trade bill.

But DR-CAFTA is really being weighed down by the same failures to articulate why trade is central to U.S. economic vitality and global growth. No nation in history has ever moved itself from poverty to developed-world living standards without trade. Job creation and job loss are the nature of free-market economies, and while the U.S. economy lost 44 million jobs at Sears, Chrysler and AT&T between 1980 and 1998 it also gained 73 million at Microsoft, Dell, Genentech and the like; and while Americans buy $50 and $100 sneakers, auto parts and cell phones from abroad we sell million- and billion-dollar jet aircraft and medical imaging equipment, with the cheaper imports saving U.S. families $2,000 a year from lower consumer costs and high-tech exports supporting high-paying jobs.

Beyond the DR-CAFTA debate, we should not be struggling to protect our economy from the natural competition that comes with open markets and maturing worldwide economies. Instead, U.S. political leaders and policy-makers should be sorting through how this country can always be leading the process by rolling out the technologies, products, R&D and ideas that drive growth, prosperity and job-creation at home and around the world.

This free-trade agreement does have flaws. It was negotiated with the public excluded until presented with a final pact. This only fuels suspicions that multilateral agreements are being crafted by big-money special interests at the expense of the public good. And while resources to address job and industry dislocations have grown—including a $1 billion U.S. trade-adjustment assistance program to help workers and communities in this country, a $1.6 billion Inter-American Development Bank "loan pipeline" to ease trade transition in Central America and a $20 million U.S. fund to help the six trade partners better enforce labor and environmental laws—they give the appearance of buy-offs at the end. If transparency drove the free-trade process from day one, the merits of DR-CAFTA would define today's debate more than amorphous globalization fears.

DR-CAFTA may not be a perfect trade vehicle—if one actually exists—but it is an important policy tool to knit the U.S. together with its closest neighbors in the name of homeland security, friendship and common interest. The gains heavily outweigh the concerns—with economic growth rippling broadly through the U.S. economy and catalyzing positive changes that improve our own security, prosperity and international standing. It is hard to ask for more from any international agreement.

---

Mack McLarty was former chief of staff to President Bill Clinton and former special envoy to the Americas. He is chairman of Kissinger McLarty Associates in Washington, D.C.

## Best, Brightest Shrug Shoulders about Iraq

**Inequality of sacrifice is bad enough, but lack of awareness is tragic**

David Colburn

*Orlando Sentinel*, October 28, 2007

I asked one of my best students the other day why his fellow students are not more engaged in the national debate about Iraq—easily the most important issue facing their generation.

His response was startling in its frankness but also disquieting about what it suggests their role might be as future leaders of this nation. "The war doesn't affect us because there is no draft," he commented. "Without a draft, we feel very few effects from this conflict, and it seldom enters into our conversations."

As we sat talking on a beautiful fall day, he added that he knew no one who was serving or had served in Iraq and thought very few of his fellow students knew anyone serving in the military. His remarks further underscored for me what many have said about this war: It is being fought largely by young men and women from modest backgrounds, many of whom had few other options after high school.

While Americans have become increasingly divided over the war, my student and many of the nation's college students, the best and the brightest of America's youth, are calmly watching all of this from the sidelines.

Like most other college students, my student does not have parents or relatives touched by the war. As a consequence, he and others do not see any sacrifices being made within their extended families. Indeed, sacrifice is seldom spread beyond the soldiers who serve and their families and friends who anxiously await their return.

Without such experience, without direct knowledge of peers losing their lives and limbs, and without the threat of being mobilized for the war on terrorism, my student thought his fellow students were just too far removed from events and that this explained their lack of involvement in the national debate over the war.

One needs to keep in mind that he and his college peers have not ignored public service or the needs of society in general. This particular student has been heavily involved in helping people in New Orleans recover from Hurricane Katrina. His fellow students at the University of Florida, for example, have joined Teach for America and the Peace Corps in record numbers.

But as we talked, I found myself getting increasingly angry over his comments and the failure of his generation to take any responsibility for Iraq. I was less concerned about whether these young people would support or oppose the war than I was about them failing to take part in this national debate.

As a Vietnam veteran, I was also offended that these students should be going about their college life, partying on weekends and celebrating football victories, without recognizing the sacrifices other young men and women were making in Iraq and Afghanistan.

So why are our best and brightest opting to sit this one out when Iraq will affect their lives and those of others for the foreseeable future? Are they simply being selfish?

Not entirely. I believe they are grateful that they don't have to serve, but they are also quite self-centered. Immediate gratification is what makes their world tick. I also think, when they reflect on the war, they feel a tinge of guilt that they and their friends and families are able to live such comfortable lives while others are suffering and dying to guarantee our national security. I think the best of them are reluctant to speak out for fear of appearing hypocritical.

Their lack of engagement and their self-centeredness, however, is not healthy for them or for the nation. We have done them a disservice by sparing them from any sense of responsibility or sacrifice in this war against terrorism. The inequality of sacrifice is bad enough, but their lack of awareness and engagement is tragic.

## Myanmar Needs Our Help

**The United States should work with the United Nations to improve conditions for the Burmese people**

Bob Graham

*St. Petersburg Times*, December 12, 2007

Ask an American what he or she knows about the nation of Myanmar, and you are likely to receive a blank stare in return. Most of us know little about the geographically largest country in Southeast Asia.

But that may soon change, and in dramatic fashion. At a time when neighbors like India, Thailand and Vietnam are joining the global community and realizing increased economic growth and political freedom, Myanmar (formerly known as Burma) has not moved beyond the isolation, extreme poverty and human rights abuses that have gripped it for the last half century. This dangerous mix could easily produce an explosive upheaval not seen in Southeast Asia for decades.

In October, I visited Myanmar for the first time. Nearly 20 years ago, the ruling military junta renamed the nation—a designation that Burmese opposition groups and some foreign governments do not recognize.

The signs of trouble were evident from by first bus ride in the nation's largest city, Yangon (formerly called Rangoon). Our tour guide would not discuss everyday living conditions even though they were clearly demonstrated by the moldy and deteriorating buildings lining the dirt streets of the city.

The guide's reticence was understandable. One month before, Burmese citizens were violently reminded to watch what they say. In September, Buddhist monks led tens of thousands of fellow citizens in protests against the harsh dictatorship. The military response was devastating. According to one account, thousands of protesters were massacred, their bodies dumped in the jungle. A thousand more were sent to Myanmar's infamous prisons, which are known for torture. Soldiers raided monasteries nationwide. I saw few monks during my visit.

Economic conditions mirror the political deterioration. Sixty years ago, Myanmar was the most literate and prosperous country in Southeast Asia. Today, the per capita annual income is $174 compared to its neighbor Thailand's $3,155. Myanmar has a substantial underground economy which primarily benefits the military leaders. Once referred to as the "Harvard of Southeast Asia," the University of Rangoon is now padlocked. Thousands of school-aged children beg on the streets rather than learn in classrooms.

The Bush administration has not made the situation any easier with several missteps. For example, we have clumsily outsourced our diplomatic responsibilities by encouraging Myanmar's neighbor China to push reform. This request ignores that China's main interest—commerce—depends on the military junta's goodwill. Nor will the ranks(?) in prison be reassured to know that we have asked the same Chinese rulers who produced Tiananmen Square and other human rights abuses to advocate for their well-being.

Conversely, though we have recently taken steps to strengthen U.S.-India relations, and India shares a 700-mile border with Myanmar, we have not effectively pushed the Indian government to take a more active role in improving conditions for nearly 50 million people to its west.

Worst of all is the perception that the United States should not even try to succeed diplomatically. Some Burmese reformers have suggested that we use our armed forces to liberate their country just like Iraq. We are seen as a power with no capability other than military might.

The best way for the United States to correct its missteps and change perceptions would be to work with other concerned countries through the United Nations. It was November before U.N. human rights envoy Paulo Sergio Pinheiro was allowed in Myanmar for the first time in four years. He and others are working to establish a genuine national dialogue among ethnic minorities, predominately reformers and the military, and to create space for humanitarian relief to feed the one-third of Burmese children who are malnourished.

The Burmese people are gentle with an ironic sense of humor. When asked why so many have bad teeth, they say it is because they cannot open their mouths. The international community has an obligation to free the Burmese to flex their jaws—and improve their lives.

## I Ran Congress' 9/11 Investigation. The Intelligence Committees Today Can't Handle Russia.

**If they want a real autopsy, they need more resources**

Bob Graham

*Washington Post*, September 1, 2017

Since the Justice Department named a special investigator, Robert Mueller, to handle the government's official inquiry into Russian meddling in the U.S. election, the weight of public expectation has largely fallen on his shoulders. While the two congressional panels, the Senate and House intelligence committees, continue to hold hearings and question witnesses, including Paul Manafort and Jared Kushner, both are led by members of a party that is, with the exception of Charlottesville, skittish about criticizing the president. The greatest hope for an aggressive and impartial inquest seems to lie with Mueller, whose bosses have either recused themselves from the Russia probe (as Attorney General Jeff Sessions did) or volunteered that he would have autonomy to follow the facts wherever they led (as Deputy Attorney General Rod Rosenstein did). The pressure, it seems, is off Congress to act as the primary body holding the president to account.

This is a dangerous sentiment. The two intelligence committees should act as if their investigations will be the final (and possibly the only) ones—because they may be. President Trump has worked hard to undermine Mueller's effort, not only berating it as beholden to a partisan "hoax" but also belittling Sessions on Twitter in a transparent attempt to force the attorney general's resignation. That way, the president could replace him with an appointee who would stymie Mueller's work. A central role for Congress is the only real way to guarantee a full report, with conclusions and recommendations, for the American people.

I oversaw a similarly complex and politically fraught inquiry as co-chairman of the joint congressional inquiry into 9/11, so I know what it takes—as a matter of resources, time, perseverance and, yes, occasional political courage—to run an investigation of this size and importance.

And I know this, too: The congressional intelligence committees, as they are constituted today, are not ready for this burden.

They must tackle three problems.

First, the committees need substantially more capacity. After 9/11, the Senate and House leadership decided to merge the two intelligence committees so they could collaboratively and thoroughly investigate the intelligence issues raised by the attacks. The joint committee had a staff of 24 experience professionals who were dedicated to the inquiry, independent from the regular professional staff of either the House or the Senate intelligence committee. They'd worked at key intelligence and law enforcement agencies and had knowledge of forensic accounting, investigation and intelligence analysis. Staff director Eleanor Hill had previously prosecuted organized crime for the Justice Department and served as staff director and chief counsel for the Senate Permanent Subcommittee on Investigation.

Given the number of highly classified documents under review, the joint inquiry also had its own secure office space, separate from each chamber's committee office. It had its own budget of at least $5 million, dedicated solely to the one-year inquiry. By comparison, the Senate committee had $8.1 million and the House panel $8.1 Million to address regular legislative and oversight responsibilities for the two years of the 107th Congress.

Right now, the Senate has 38 staffers and the House has 31 devoted to the intelligence committees, with budgets for the 115th Congress of $11 million and $12.1 million, respectively. Those personnel and funds are intended to cover all the legislative and oversight work of the intelligence committees, including the Russia investigation. Early in the inquiry, the Senate committee reportedly had only seven staffers working on the probe. It needs many more.

To complete the Russia investigation, the committees need independent staff members who are solely dedicated to this topic: forensic accountants and specialists in international law, financial crimes, counterintelligence investigations, and cybersecurity and coding. Those devoted to Russian meddling should not be regular committee staffers on overtime, unfamiliar with the tasks unique to the Russian inquiry.

After more than six months of separate activity, it is probably too late to merge the current congressional committees. It is not too late, however, to create independent, experienced and substantially larger staffs capable of fulfilling the committees' responsibilities, particularly in a post-Mueller era.

Second, the House and Senate intelligence committees must quickly begin planning for post-Mueller scenarios. Yes, perhaps Sessions will stick around and Rosenstein will continue to guard Mueller's autonomy. But the congressional committees need to devise protocols now that would be activated, if Mueller were fired, to ensure the protection of, and access to, all documents, transcripts, communications and other materials amassed by the Mueller and James Comey probes. The protocols should ensure that these materials are made available to the congressional committees in their original form. If Mueller is dismissed, the congressional inquiry would probably expand, as in the Watergate investigation, to the consideration of impeachment.

Third, Congress must embrace its investigatory role with renewed urgency. The 9/11 inquiry had a deadline of December 2002, the end of the 107th Congress. This investigation has no such finale. But there are serious consequences to procrastination. If Russia has in fact attempted to interfere with democratic elections in Europe, the United States and elsewhere, disclosing that reality and repelling further intrusions are crucial. Preventing future tampering in elections will require the support of an informed American public, which should be told of congress's definitive conclusions as soon as possible. Any delay in publicly sharing clear and convincing evidence will add to the already staggering distrust of many Americans in their government. (Portions of the 9/11 inquiry report remain classified even today, limiting the public's understanding of the tragic event and its ability to influence policy, especially regarding U.S.-Saudi relations.)

The nation's best option is for Mueller to continue his investigation until it ends, wherever it leads. Should Trump find some way to remove him, it would spark a constitutional crisis unlike anything since Watergate; Congress must be ready for this worst-case scenario. In our system of checks and balances, it has the right and duty to exercise full oversight. Now is the time to start preparing for that responsibility.

## Vietnam Documentary Awakens Memories

David Colburn

*Gainesville Sun*, October 1, 2017

Watching Ken Burns' and Lynn Novick's documentary, "The Vietnam War," on PBS has reminded Americans of the horrific nature of the conflict. It has also re-awakened my own memories.

I vividly recall my first day in-country, coming ashore off a troop ship at Vung Tau in Vietnam in September 1966 and planning for an immediate fire-fight. Instead, what my platoon and I found was a remarkably beautiful place that looked nothing like a war zone.

It was so unlike the images that I had seen on the nightly news that I initially had trouble reconciling Vung Tau and its beauty with the brutal television images of jungle warfare.

What would be my reality of this war, I wondered.

As it turned out, the signal corps units to which I was assigned were never in the middle of the jungle conflict that plagued American infantry troops. I soon became aware, however, that this was a war, and a brutal one at that. My first experience was taking supplies to the First Division at Tay Ninh and encountering dead bodies lying alongside the road. Later, I saw the devastation wrought by bombs dropped from B-52s over South Vietnam.

As my year unfolded, I never questioned our government's decision to go to war and halt the spread of communism, but I did begin to wonder why the South Vietnamese I encountered seemed disengaged with the war and the military build-up. If this was a war for their future and the preservation of their democracy, why, I asked myself, weren't they more engaged?

I pushed these observations aside and concentrated on my job, which had me traveling to many of the cities and villages in South Vietnam from Camh Ran Bay to Dalat, Tay Ninh, Vinh Long, Saigon and Bien Hoa. I remained impressed with the beauty of the country and the decency of the Vietnamese people with whom I interacted.

I returned home in August 1967, proud of the men I served with and proud of my service, but troubled by the nature of the war and the death of so many—both U.S. soldiers and Vietnamese. I also learned for the first time about the growing opposition to the war at home. Those of us returning from Vietnam were oblivious to the protests because Stars and Stripes, the military publication we had access to, did not report on the domestic demonstrations.

In September 1967, I started a Ph.D. program in history at the University of North Carolina at Chapel Hill where I soon encountered student protests against the war. I was initially angry at the protestors, but as I read more and more about Vietnam in and out of class, I gradually became convinced that the war was a mistake.

What I could not understand then—and cannot fathom to this day—is why President Lyndon Johnson did not curtail the war. Very early in the conflict, he realized that it was potentially the Achilles heel of his administration, jeopardizing his domestic agenda for which he had fought so hard.

Scholars writing about the Vietnam conflict assert that Johnson felt the Democratic Party was vulnerable to Republican assertions that they were soft on communism and the loss of Vietnam would jeopardize its standing as the nation's majority party.

But in the midst of the Vietnam War, Johnson had taken the incredibly bold step of enacting two civil rights acts in 1964 and 1965, respectively, which ended racial segregation and which guaranteed voting rights for African Americans. Both were every bit as politically contentious as Vietnam. While Johnson was a product of the Cold War, he was also personally shaped by the racism and segregation of his youth.

In the end, whatever his reasons, LBJ embraced civil rights but could not bring himself to abandon the war in Vietnam and the battle against communism.

Fifty-eight thousand American soldiers died as a result of that decision and over 100,000 families lost a child, a brother, a sister or a father. Another 150,000 veterans were permanently wounded or scarred by the war and, for many, their suffering continues to this day.

As the Burns' documentary makes clear, Vietnam was catastrophic. It is a burden that haunts us to this day, as it should.

# 11
# Biological and Nuclear Disasters

We live in a world fraught with dangers large and small. The pieces in this section, all penned by Bob Graham in his role as a former United States senator, deal with issues of world-wide disasters, both natural and human-made. In this time of pandemic, these articles seem increasingly relevant, as Graham sounded the alarm early and often on the dangers of doing nothing to prevent the spread of nuclear materials as well as pathogens and the diseases they cause. In 2009, he warned, "Mother Nature is full of surprises, and preparation matters." That same year, he determined that "the ubiquitous nature of pathogens and the increasing lethality of both natural and synthetic pathogens [have led me] to conclude it's more likely that an attack will come biologically rather than [be] nuclear."[1] He warned of the rather dire consequences of ignoring potential problems associated with biological disasters, developed either by natural causes or as agents of bio-terrorism. "Now, before the next public health emergency," he opined, "is the time to invest in our nation's ability to respond to a public health emergency, so that we will have the tools we need to prevent, contain, and treat disease." As seen in the previous sections, Graham believes that responsibility for responding to these situations lies not just with government, but also with aware, engaged, and civic-minded citizens. The interaction between government and citizen is at the heart of everything that Graham and Colburn write about. In 2011, Graham wrote that "Americans need to prepare, not out of the grim fear of future disaster, but out of the belief that through their own actions, they can be authors of their own survival." Whether preparing for a hurricane or a pandemic, Graham and Colburn stress that knowledge and awareness provide the keys to survival. In December 2008, Graham, as Chairman of the Commission on the Prevention of Weapons of Mass Destruction Proliferation and Terrorism, addressed the Senate Committee on Homeland Security and Governmental Affairs.[2] His words still have resonance today, and tie directly to the message he gave in the op-eds in this section. First he discussed the question of nuclear proliferation. "The United States and Russia are two great powers. . . . Over 95 percent of the nuclear material on the globe is in our control, one of these two countries. We have a responsibility to the world to see that they are properly secure. . . . So our recommendation is that we continue to recognize the primacy of security of nuclear weapons in our relationship and that we do some things that would tell the world that we are serious about this." Then he addressed the issue of biological/medical disasters. "We learned with Severe Acute Respiratory Syndrome (SARS) that a disease that breaks out in one distant part of today's flat world quickly moves across national borders. . . . We need to increase the surveillance capabilities to know that there is something beyond ordinary influenza happening out there so that we can respond quickly, whether it is a benign or a violent attack and confine its consequences and its lethality." These words still ring true today.

### Notes

1. Michael Isikoff, "Q&A: Bob Graham On New WMD Terror Attack Threat," *Newsweek*, December 1, 2008, https://www.newsweek.com/qa-bob-graham-new-wmd-terror-attack-threat-83195.

2. *World at Risk: A Report from the Commission on the Prevention of Weapons of Mass Destruction Proliferation and Terrorism: Hearing Before the Comm. on Homeland Security and Governmental Affairs*, 110 Cong. 45 (2008) (statement of Bob Graham, chairman).

## Finishing the War on Terrorism

Bob Graham

*Boston Globe*, July 3, 2006

THE US SENATE has just completed a contentious and partisan debate on when and under what conditions America should withdraw its troops from Iraq. Within hours of the debate's end, the White House indicated it was developing a plan to draw down troop levels in Iraq, beginning as early as this fall.

Iraq was a distraction from our primary threats. Our country has paid a high price in lives, national honor, and resources for that mistake.

The debate today focuses largely on when and how to leave Iraq. The more important debate is what to do after that. There is a strategy to exit Iraq with honor, contain Iran, and cripple America's real enemies. Each of the rolling rationales for the Iraqi war—destruction of Saddam Hussein's weapons of mass destruction, regime change, creation of a democratically elected government—has been found to be baseless or has been achieved. Mission accomplished.

The conditions on the ground for exit, as the president phrases it, should be the capability of the Iraqi army and law enforcement agencies to assume responsibility for security. America cannot be a permanent police force in Iraq, nor a military guarantor against the spread of civil war. The Iraqis, with US assistance, should have until the end of 2006 to train, equip, and field military forces capable of self defense. The United States and its coalition partners will be able to reduce their military presence as the Iraqi army assumes this responsibility.

The end of 2007 should be the deadline for a police force capable of enforcing the rule of law. This task must be accompanied by reforms, or in some instances original construction of Iraq's rule of law and institutions: the criminal code, courts, the penal system.

A recently retired administration official was asked, "What do you think America should do after we are able to exit Iraq?" His answer was, "There will be no choices; the focus on Iran will suck all the oxygen out of the room."

Iran's aspirations to be a nuclear power are by no means inconsequential. However, it is not necessary that Iran become a more costly diversion than Iraq. Bush should couple his decision to talk with Iran to a strategy that involves a credible threat of military force against Iran's nuclear facilities, an offer to expand trade and investment, the provision of technology from the West for commercial reactors, and, probably most important to Iranians, an American agreement not to attack Iran for the purpose of regime change.

The real war on terror—the war against the murderers of 3,000 Americans on Sept. 11, 2001—has been suspended since at least the beginning of 2002, when specialized personnel and equipment were shipped out of Afghanistan to prepare to invade Iraq. This was directly contrary to what the president said nine days after the attack: "Our war on terror begins with Al Qaeda, but does not end there. It will not end until every terrorist of global reach has been found, stopped, and defeated."

We must recommit to the president's call for victory, one that will be many times more difficult than when the president spoke almost five years ago. Tens of thousands of new volunteers, now trained in the skills of urban terrorism, have been added to the ranks of Al Qaeda, Hezbollah, Hamas, and other international terrorist organizations.

General Tommy Franks said a year before the Iraq invasion that "we need to win the battle against Al Qaeda and the Taliban in Afghanistan and then move on to eradicate their cells elsewhere." When this first mission has been accomplished, America and its allies need to apply the strongest diplomatic, intelligence, surgical, military, and police force action against terrorist organizations. To do so, America must rebuild its alliances with Egypt and other pre-Iraq-invasion friends in the region, in Europe, and with Russia. State sources of anti-Americanism have to be corralled. Saudi Arabia, flush with oil money, continues to be the principal financier of global terrorism. With Iranian petro-dollars, Syria is the umbilical cord for Hezbollah and Hamas and a continuing classroom for training the most sophisticated terrorists.

The president must be honest. Winning the fight against terror will be like no other war. There are no uniformed enemy armies on the battlefield, but instead a guerrilla force emerging from cellars and back alleys. There will be deaths and casualties, and enormous demands on American will.

The president should call on all Americans to be a part of this paramount goal—a safer nation secured through their efforts and sacrifices.

## Nuclear Proliferation Endangers World Stability

Bob Graham and Jim Talent

*Miami Herald*, September 14, 2008

During the first presidential debate in 2004, President Bush and Sen. John Kerry agreed—as stated by the president—that "the single, largest threat to American national security today is nuclear weapons in the hands of a terrorist network." Yet despite that consensus, the subject of weapons of mass destruction proliferation has quickly disappeared from the national agenda.

Few comments or questions on this issue have been posed to the presidential candidates, even though preventing WMD proliferation should be on the short list of priorities for a McCain or Obama White House. And it rarely appears on polls of the most urgent concerns of citizens. So, in 2008, after seven years in which there have been no successful terrorist attacks inside the country, why not relax? Here are the reasons:

• Terrorists have continued to demonstrate the intent to acquire a WMD capability. As Director of National Intelligence Admiral Michael McConnell said in his Sept. 10, 2007, testimony to the Senate Homeland Security and Governmental Affairs Committee, "al Qaeda will continue to try to acquire and employ chemical, biological, radiological, or nuclear material in attacks and would not hesitate to use them if it develops what it deems is sufficient capability."

• The potential human toll of an attack utilizing weapons of mass destruction is appalling. On a normal workday, half a million people crowd the area within a half-mile radius of Times Square. A noon detonation of a nuclear device in Midtown Manhattan would kill them all.

• Another attack—particularly with WMD—would have a devastating impact on the American and the world economies. As former U.N. Secretary General Kofi Annan warned, a nuclear terrorist attack would push "tens of millions of people into dire poverty," creating "a second death toll throughout the developing world."

• The environment for the use of nuclear and biological weapons has changed. Although Russia is doing a better job of securing its stockpiles and therefore is less of a threat, North Korea and Iran have taken its place. North Korea has gone from two bombs worth of plutonium to an estimated ten. Iran has gone from zero centrifuges spinning to more than 3,000.

• In what some have termed a "nuclear renaissance," many nations are now seeking commercial nuclear power capacity that will add to the inventory of nations and scientists who could extend their interest to nuclear weapons.

• With the nuclear surprises we've experienced in Iran, Syria and North Korea, it is clear that current nonproliferation regimes and mechanisms can no longer be certain to prevent more nuclear proliferation or the theft of bomb-usable materials.

• Biologists are creating synthetic DNA chains of diseases which have been considered extinct, such as the 1918 influenza virus that killed over 40 million people. The potential of using these laboratory-developed strains against an unaware and noninoculated population is ominous.

• There is the necessity of engaging the American people. Unlike the Cold War, which was a superpower vs. superpower confrontation, the current asymmetric threat that would be dramatically escalated if the terrorists had access to nuclear or biological weapons. The incorrect claims regarding Saddam Hussein's WMD and his collusion with al Qaeda have contributed to public skepticism. Nonetheless, there was and is a real danger that al Qaeda will get a nuclear bomb and attack an American city.

Faced with the possibility of a mushroom cloud over Manhattan, many people are paralyzed by a combination of denial and fatalism. The president is the best position to rally the resilience and patriotism of Americans to this threat.

We have been asked by Congress to lead a bipartisan commission to assess the current state of our nation's policies to prevent the proliferation of weapons of mass destruction into the hands of rogue states and nonstate terrorists. Our final report will be released in November. Based on our assessment, we will make recommendations to the new Congress and the new president.

We trust that the president and Congress will recognize the primacy of this threat and the consequences should it come to pass. Nuclear terrorism has been described as the ultimate avoidable catastrophe. Whether it—and other WMD catastrophes—will be avoided will depend in large part on where it ranks among the 44th president's priorities.

---

Jim Talent is former US senator and US representative for Missouri and, with Bob Graham, a former vice-chair of the Center for the Study of Weapons of Mass Destruction.

## Preventing a Greater Threat

Bob Graham

*New York Times*, November 18, 2008

IN MAY 2002, I visited Pokrov, a largely abandoned Soviet-era agricultural research center east of Moscow. Originally established to produce vaccines for animals, Pokrov became a laboratory for biological weapons, especially anthrax, in the final years of the Cold War.

We entered the building, which stored samples of all the materials produced at Pokrov. The woven wire and electrified fence that at one time had secured the building was a fallen, rusting heap. The security alarm to the main entrance had been turned off and the door was ajar. Up two flights of steel-grate stairs were the storage rooms, two tennis court-sized rooms filled with commercial refrigerators. Several refrigerators had two common features: note cards listing the materials inside, and flimsy strings encircling them. Our hosts explained that a broken string would indicate that someone had possibly opened the refrigerator and stolen the materials inside.

I left Pokrov without much confidence in the security afforded the most lethal biological materials in the world.

Earlier this month, the Commission on Weapons of Mass Destruction Proliferation and Terrorism, which I chaired, presented its final report, "World At Risk," to President George W. Bush, Vice President-elect Joe Biden, and congressional leaders. The report concluded that "unless the world community acts decisively and with great urgency, it is more likely than not that a weapon of mass destruction will be used in a terrorist attack somewhere in the world by the end of 2013." But the type of catastrophe may be a surprise to some. In fact: "terrorists are more likely to be able to obtain and use a biological weapon than a nuclear weapon."

The closest the United States has come to a bioterrorist attack was in October 2001, when letters contaminated with anthrax bacterial spores were mailed to two senators, a TV anchorman, and an employee of the National Enquirer. Seven letters were mailed, containing less than 15 teaspoons of anthrax. This miniscule quantity resulted in five deaths, placed 30,000 persons at risk, closed government buildings for months, and produced economic damage estimated at $6 billion. It isn't hard to imagine the consequences in death, destruction, panic, and dollars of a large-scale biological attack using anthrax spores manufactured from a vial like those in the refrigerators at Pokrov.

Biological materials are more ubiquitous and less secure than nuclear. Since the fall of the Soviet Union, the United States and its allies have wisely expended tens of billions of dollars to identify, capture, and secure nuclear materials. The same cannot be said for lethal pathogens. The United States has cut back its biological threat reduction programs in Russia, and the Russians have refused greater transparency at their Ministry of Defense controlled biological weapons facilities. There is little reason to believe that the lethal pathogens of Pokrov are secure from falling into terrorist hands.

While the rugged and persistent anthrax spores remain the pathogen of first resort, the last two decades have seen an explosion of biological dangers. Since 9/11, the federal government has poured billions into defensive research on pathogens that might be used for bioterrorism. There are now 14,000 US scientists authorized to work on these materials, increasing the risk of a few bad apples with access. Shockingly, there continues to be no comprehensive regulation within the United States or internationally of the sites where lethal pathogens are produced or of the scientists capable of their production.

Al Qaeda remains intent on securing lethal pathogens for use against the United States. Agents of Osama bin Laden have been intercepted attempting to procure biological capabilities and materials in Europe and Asia. The laboratories we discovered in Kandahar after the October 2001 invasion of Afghanistan have been relocated to the tribal areas of Pakistan. As Richard Danzig, former secretary of the Navy, has observed, "Only a thin wall of terrorists' ignorance and inexperience now protects us."

Nuclear terrorism has been described as the ultimate preventable catastrophe. We hope so, and we also hope and believe our commission report has created a roadmap for significantly reducing the risk that the worst bacteria and viruses will fall into the hands of the worst terrorists and nations.

## Preparing for Pandemics, Natural and Manmade

Bob Graham and Jim Talent

*The Hill*, June 11, 2009

The 2009 H1N1 swine flu epidemic should remind Americans of two important truths: Mother Nature is full of surprises, and preparation matters.

The fact is, the United States is not doing enough to prepare for disease emergencies, either natural or deliberate. We should immediately commit to doing more: by innovating drug and vaccine development; increasing funding for public health and hospital readiness; and improving international cooperation surveillance and response. Over the last several years, the U.S. government has prepared extensively for an avian influenza pandemic by forging partnerships with the private sector to manufacture vaccines and funding university scientists to pursue influenza research. Instead of avian flu, however, this time we were surprised with a different kind of influenza virus. Wasted effort? No, the preparation was well worth it. Americans can rely on the millions of doses of effective antiviral medicines stockpiled whether treating avian or swine flu, and we can now make new flu vaccine in a matter of months. We are becoming more innovative in our ability to respond to future flu outbreaks, as those investments in new technologies and vaccine manufacturing bear fruit.

Unfortunately, we are not nearly as prepared to respond to any infectious disease besides influenza, whether sent from Mother Nature or as part of a deliberate attack. No one doubts that new diseases will emerge and that they could be a health risk to many Americans and even a threat to national security. The scenarios are easy to anticipate: An entirely new virus could take the world by storm, as SARS nearly did in 2003. Treatments for old plagues could become ineffective, as antibiotic resistance makes the drugs we have useless.

Or an epidemic could be the result of a deliberate attack. In our commission report, "World At Risk," we concluded that unless we act urgently and decisively it was more likely than not that terrorists would successfully attack a major city with a weapon of mass destruction by 2013, and we identified bioterrorism as the weapon most likely to be used. One month later, the director of national intelligence publicly agreed with our assessment. In response, the commission was granted an unprecedented one-year extension to turn our recommendations into actions.

One of the best ways to reduce the chance of a bio-attack is to become better prepared to deal with its consequences; terrorists are less likely to use a weapon if its effect is limited.

But what if they do attack? The answer is preparation. Start by adequately funding the office within the Department of Health and Human Services charged with developing the medicines we will need in a public health crisis. The office is the Biomedical Advanced Research and Development Authority (BARDA), created in 2006. Its mission is to make sure that the nation has the right drugs and medical countermeasures not only for flu, but for emerging diseases, as well as chemical, biological, radiological and nuclear public health threats. The team at BARDA has already hired top talent, and is working effectively with the private sector. However, they have received little funding for the rest of their mission. It's time to correct that.

The outgoing Bush administration asked Congress for $900 million in additional funding for BARDA. That funding could and should have been included in the stimulus package but was not. Congress should speedily correct that omission.

This is a national security issue—just as important as the capability to produce world-class military hardware and technology. It's also a no-regret investment.

Improving the infrastructure to respond to a public health crisis is an opportunity for U.S. national security and for global American leadership, technical innovation, and economic stimulus. The United States has an opportunity to lead the world by innovating how vaccines and medicines are made, so that they can be made more rapidly and less expensively. Right now, there is a lot of room for improvement: It requires 10 to 15 years and approximately $800 million from start to finish for one product, and 80 percent of all drug candidates that enter clinical trials fail to get FDA approval. Reducing costs and delay would position the country to make unprecedented contributions to global health.

It goes without saying that the best medicines in the world will do no good if they don't reach the people who need them. Hospitals and public health systems need to be prepared to receive medicines, and have the capacity to deliver life-saving care.

As John F. Kennedy said, "The time to repair the roof is when the sun is shining." Now, before the next public health emergency, is the time to invest in our nation's ability to respond to a public health emergency, so that we will have the tools we need to prevent, contain, and treat disease.

## Lessons Learned from the Anthrax Letters

**Bob Graham and Jim Talent**

*Washington Times*, July 30, 2009

One year ago, Bruce Ivins, the alleged perpetrator of the anthrax mailings of October 2001, died. Ivins was a senior biodefense researcher for the U.S. Army. Assuming the FBI is correct—that Ivins acted alone in the production and distribution of the anthrax that infected 22, killed five and terrorized the nation—this is an appropriate time to review five important lessons from this incident:

1. Bioterrorism is not beyond the reach of nonstate actors such as al-Qaida or lone-wolf domestic or international terrorists. Some have wrongly assumed that Ivins was capable of producing a weaponized version of a common animal disease only because he had access to sophisticated equipment at the Army lab. The equipment he allegedly used can be found in most state-of-the-art laboratories or purchased on various Web sites for considerably less than the cost of a used minivan, and it is available all over the world.

2. Deadly pathogens are widely accessible. Ivins' easy access to a deadly pathogen may have made it easier to obtain the starter culture, but virtually all potential bioterrorism pathogens exist in sick people, animals and in the environment all over the world. Isolating anthrax, plague, tularemia and other deadly pathogens may not be easy for an amateur, but doctors, scientists and lab technicians do this every day as they treat patients or conduct research in human and veterinary medicine.

3. It could have been much worse. If the perpetrator had selected a different method to disseminate the bioweapon—by releasing a small amount of anthrax through the ventilation system in an airport, subway station, or indoor sports arena—there would have been many more casualties. And if he had spent a few weeks or months (not days) producing dry powder, the results would have been far more disastrous. Fortunately, he chose one of the least lethal scenarios—very small amounts of anthrax in a few envelopes.

4. Cleanup is an important part of biodefense. The one overlooked, underresearched and underfunded aspect of biodefense is environmental cleanup. More than $300 million was spent cleaning buildings, from only a fraction of a gram of anthrax spores that seeped out of the letters. Without major improvements in remediation, a subway system would require billions to clean and would likely remain closed for months if not years.

5. Prevention of bioterrorism is far different than preventing nuclear terrorism. Preventing nuclear terrorism is actually quite simple, not easy, but simple. If we do not allow terrorists to obtain plutonium or highly enriched uranium, they will not be able to make a nuclear weapon. It is far beyond the technical and financial capabilities of any terrorist organization to enrich uranium or produce plutonium—they can only buy it or steal it. Therefore, the appropriate strategy is to locate, lock down and eliminate loose nuclear materials with programs such as the Nunn-Lugar Cooperative Threat Reduction Program and the Proliferation Security Initiative. Unfortunately, the same strategy does not work against the biothreat.

The proper biodefense strategy requires three elements. First, it must include continued support and investment in international treaties, such as the Biological Weapons Convention and U.N. Resolution 1540. Then, it requires that U.S. labs are safe and secure and that personnel who work in them are trustworthy. But as a recently released Defense Science Board report asserted, "A determined adversary cannot be prevented from obtaining very dangerous materials for nefarious purposes. . . . The best we can do is to make it more difficult. We need to recognize this reality and be prepared to mitigate the effects of a biological attack. We, as a nation, are not prepared."

Therefore, the third element in biodefense is to prevent an act of bioterrorism from becoming a bio-Katrina. By developing the capability to produce vaccines and therapeutics rapidly and less expensively, we can use technology to remove bioweapons from the category of weapons of mass destruction. That should be America's long-term goal, but we can never reach it if we do not make the proper investments today.

Congress must provide sufficient funding for two of America's most important biodefense initiatives, both in the Department of Health and Human Services: the Biomedical Advanced Research Development Authority or BARDA, which develops an integrated, systematic approach to the development and purchase of the necessary vaccines, drugs, therapies and diagnostic tools for public health medical emergencies; and BioShield, which funds medical countermeasures against biological, chemical, radiological and nuclear agents.

Both programs now face serious funding challenges in Congress.

There are many priorities in the budget battle under way on Capitol Hill. However, congressional leaders must consider the lessons of anthrax as they make difficult choices. Furthermore, they must understand that these biodefense programs are "no-regret investments." Building defenses against man-made bioattacks will also provide protection against the most feared bioterrorist of all, Mother Nature, producer of H1N1, SARS and smallpox.

## Prepare for an Attack

Bob Graham

*Miami Herald*, December 6, 2009

The shortage of H1N1 vaccine underscores the severe lack of U.S. preparedness in responding to pandemics, whether through natural disease or man-made bioterrorism. We rely on a 60-year-old production method, based on chicken eggs, which is a slow process. The United States needs to be able to produce vaccines and other medicines faster and less expensively.

Think about it: There were six months of warning for the H1N1 pandemic. A bioterrorism attack will have none. Advance preparation is not optional; it's an urgent necessity.

The solution is to create an infrastructure of surveillance, communication and dissemination of large quantities of safe vaccines and medicine, produced through modern methods that can be quickly scaled up, on demand, and will shave months off the typical six-to-nine months now needed. This is our best deterrence to a biological attack and the reduction of consequences should it occur.

The Congressional Commission on the Prevention of Weapons of Mass Destruction Proliferation and Terrorism, which I chair, recognized the shortage of the H1N1 vaccine could be a teaching moment. But rather than hold another public hearing, we decided to use social media to engage and educate. We produced a video (fastervaccines.org) and launched discussions on Facebook, Twitter and MySpace.

For me, it has been an important experiment. According to the national Civic Health Index, young people who use social networking sites for civic purposes are more likely to engage in their own communities. The Obama campaign created a phenomenal organizing tool through social media. I wanted to see whether we could engage people on our issue: avoiding the proliferation and use of biological or nuclear weapons of mass destruction.

We launched in late October and have seen a cross-section of opinions—voices of support and some attacks. There is a chaotic town hall quality, but everyone gets a turn.

Common questions have emerged.

Are vaccines safe? A lot of people don't trust vaccines. Or the government. Or pharmaceutical companies. PhilipB's post reflects the confusion, "I simply just want THE TRUTH." The fact is, vaccines save lives around the world, whether developed from chicken eggs or new methods. Safety is critical, and, as "J" noted in a blog, we also need to support the Food and Drug Administration.

Are the alternatives to chicken eggs safe? Yes. A process called "cell culture" is already in place in Europe and China and does not require eggs. Vaccines for polio and the modern smallpox vaccine have been produced for decades using this technology. The United States has invested in cell culture technologies, but none are yet available.

Is the biothreat overblown? No. Just two or three pounds of anthrax scattered over a major city could kill more Americans than the number who died in World War II, according to the National Counter Terrorism Center. Cleanup and other economic costs could exceed $1.8 trillion.

Our bipartisan commission unanimously concluded that unless the world community acts decisively and with great urgency, it is more likely than not that a weapon of mass destruction will be used in a terrorist attack somewhere in the world by the end of 2013—and that a biological attack is more likely than nuclear.

In addition to questions, concerns and criticisms, there is also a desire to take action. Irishgawdess asked, "Are we just a nation of 'wishers and hopers? " And a Facebook visitor wrote: "It's amazing that we can watch Congress spend nearly $1 trillion to stimulate our economy, but we still rely on archaic methods to produce vaccines for serious health problems." Or listen to sposten; "Let's create a government-owned and -run state-of-the-art vaccine production capacity that this country deserves and badly needs. It is time we transcend the old-fashioned chicken egg method of production of vaccines and move this field into the 21st century."

## A New Kind of Deterrence

**Bob Graham and Jim Talent**

*St. Louis Post-Dispatch*, April 14, 2010

As part of the Nuclear Posture Review, national security, intelligence and defense officials are in a heated debate within the Obama administration regarding the purpose of America's nuclear arsenal: whether the sole purpose of our nuclear force is to deter nuclear attack or whether it is the primary purpose. If it is the primary purpose, then the nuclear force would also be a deterrent against a biological attack by a nation-state.

This deterrent is an extension of the Cold War policy of calculated ambiguity. In the early stages of the Cold War, when both the U.S. and Soviet Union arsenals included nuclear, chemical, and biological weapons, deterrence was based on response with like weapons—a chemical response to a chemical attack, a biological response to biological, and nuclear to nuclear.

In 1969, President Nixon unilaterally terminated the U.S. offensive biological weapons program. The policy of calculated ambiguity allowed the U.S. to threaten a nuclear response to a biological attack without actually stating it directly. Most in the national security community, both U.S. and Soviet, were well aware that a Soviet biological attack on U.S. military forces in Europe would result in a harshly worded demarche—but one taped to the warhead of a nuclear-tipped missile and delivered at eight times the speed of sound.

The world has changed dramatically since the height of the Cold War. Russia is no longer an imminent threat. However, nuclear proliferation is expanding the arsenals, particularly in South Asia, and putting nuclear weapons into the hands of lesser, and sometimes more dangerous, powers such as North Korea and maybe Iran. President Obama is right to seek significant reductions in the U.S. and the world's nuclear weapons, but other proliferation trends are equally unsettling.

As the bipartisan Commission on the Prevention of Weapons of Mass Destruction Proliferation and Terrorism noted in our World at Risk report, without urgent and decisive actions, it is more likely than not that a weapon of mass destruction (nuclear or biological) will be used somewhere in the world before the end of 2013, but a biological attack is more likely than nuclear. Biological attacks could come from nation-states (the State Department lists at least six countries with suspected programs), terrorist groups (al-Qaida first built labs to produce anthrax weapons in 1999), or lone-wolf terrorists (according to the FBI, the perpetrator of the October 2001 anthrax attacks was a U.S. government scientist).

While calculated ambiguity from the U.S. nuclear arsenal might continue to effectively deter a biological attack from a nation-state, or a nation-state which is harboring a terrorist organization, the $55 billion we spend annually on our nuclear deterrence force is useless confronting terrorists. If President Obama wants to eliminate our reliance on nuclear weapons to deter biological weapons, he first must take actions to remove bioterrorism from the category of weapons of mass destruction. To do so before would place the nation at unnecessary risk.

There is a critical difference between nutween clear [*sic*] and biological weapons. Both are proven threats. They deliver equal lethality. A recent National Security Council document, signed by President Obama, said that a biological attack "could place at risk hundreds of thousands of people" and "The economic cost could exceed one trillion dollars for each such incident." But while the United States cannot defend its citizens against a nuclear weapons blast, we do have the capability against bioterrorism. Today, we have the option of building a viable biodefense system that could allow a future Nuclear Posture Review to declare that the sole purpose of the U.S. nuclear force is to deter nuclear attack.

Just as President Kennedy gave us the challenge of going to the moon, President Obama can give us the challenge of removing bioterrorism from the category of WMD.

To meet this challenge, America needs to make significant improvements in:

- The rapid detection and diagnosis of disease;
- Development, production and dispensing of new vaccines and therapeutics;
- The capacity for surge medical care delivery; and
- Environmental cleanup after an attack.

Can this be accomplished? Yes. These steps could be taken relatively quickly and at low cost compared to other aspects of national defense. They would go a long way towards defeating bioterrorism as a WMD. They would also address naturally occurring threats such as H1N1, help regain America's lead in the biotechnical revolution (one of the dynamos that will drive the global economy in the decades ahead), and substantially improve the public health and medical care delivery systems. We cannot think of a more urgent priority for the Obama administration.

## Funding Cuts Threaten Vital Defense against Bioterrorism

**Bob Graham and Jim Talent**

*Washington Post*, August 3, 2010

The two of us—at the request of Congress and in the service of two presidents—have for the past 30 months led a bipartisan effort to assess the danger of a WMD attack and recommend steps to reduce it.

In December 2008 the commission we led on the prevention of proliferation of weapons of mass destruction and terrorism unanimously concluded that unless the world community acts decisively and with great urgency, it is more likely than not that a weapon of mass destruction will be used in a terrorist attack by the end of 2013—and that a biological attack is more likely than nuclear. This conclusion was publicly affirmed by then-Director of National Intelligence Mike McConnell.

Information has since come to light about the possibility that one or more nation-states may choose to provide sophisticated biological weapons to terrorist groups. The scenario that would result is not that of more than two dozen people becoming ill and five dying, as happened after the anthrax mailings in October 2001 but a much darker picture, as described in a November 2009 National Security Council document.

The effective dissemination of a lethal biological agent in an unprotected population could place hundreds of thousands of people at risk. The "unmitigated consequences," the NSC paper noted, could overwhelm our public health capabilities, causing untold numbers of deaths. Economic costs could exceed $1 trillion for each such incident.

When our commission issued its report card in January, we gave the government a failing grade for preparedness to respond to a biological attack. Attaining this response capability could help in two ways: Its existence could deter an attack from adversaries seeking a target that would yield the highest death rate; and, if the United States were attacked, an effective response could minimize the death rate.

Our report listed six areas that are key to mitigating the consequences of such an attack: detection and diagnosis, actionable information for leaders and citizens, adequate supplies of medical countermeasures, rapid distribution of those countermeasures, treating the sick and protecting the well, and environmental cleanup. All are important, but the linchpin is having adequate supplies of appropriate medical countermeasures.

Unless we have antibiotics to fight an attack of anthrax or plague, the rest of our preparations won't matter. Tens of thousands of people will die, people who could have been saved had the government taken the common-sense precaution of stockpiling the necessary drugs.

Congress established the BioShield Strategic Reserve Fund in 2004 to ensure that money would be available to purchase critical vaccines and therapeutics required to protect Americans from biological, chemical and radiological weapons. The fund was designed to be an ironclad pledge by the U.S. government to the private sector: If you take the financial risks to research and develop these medical countermeasures, we guarantee the money will be available to purchase them.

There are few incentives for the private sector to invest hundreds of millions of dollars for these important medical countermeasures. The only customer is the U.S. government. If companies spend huge sums on research and development and obtain Food and Drug Administration approval for one vaccine or drug, they need to know that funds will be available for acquisition. That is the only incentive currently provided, but it may soon go away—taking with it the most critical element in our response chain.

The House voted July 7 to raid the BioShield SRF to pay for non-biodefense, non-national security programs. The White House has remained silent on this issue. In a bipartisan vote last week, our former colleagues in the Senate saved the day by refusing to go along with the House version of the bill. But in the past few days, there have been two more attempted raids.

Our nation failed to heed the warning signals that preceded the financial collapse in 2008 and the Gulf of Mexico oil spill. This is one time when our government has the chance to contain and mitigate damage, rather than simply react to yet another disaster. All the officials we have spoken to, Republican and Democratic, are convinced of the danger. The challenge has been how to get our government to follow through on the most elementary steps necessary to guard against the most obvious and calamitous risks.

Congress and the administration must stop treating the Bioshield [*sic*] SRF as an ATM card for pet projects.

## My Word: Take Charge before Disaster Strikes

Bob Graham and Jim Talent

*Orlando Sentinel*, October 3, 2011

When the tornado sirens sounded in Joplin, Mo., Ella Smith and her husband grabbed their two dogs and ran to their basement. There, sheltered from the shrieking wind by sturdy walls, they weathered the storm that flattened their house.

Many people think of big disasters as a government responsibility, but in reality, disasters are a shared responsibility between government and citizens. Government can set regulations, alert citizens to disaster and respond after disaster. But for Ella Smith, it was her own actions that saved her family. In this case, knowing about and being prepared to shelter-in-place turned tragedy into a story of survival and resilience.

Staying inside protective buildings, and going to bathrooms or basements, away from exterior walls, windows and roofs, is usually the best first response to any disaster, except when official warnings prompt you to evacuate, such as for a hurricane. You and your family should prepare before disaster threatens. Sheltering your family can be for a matter of minutes, hours or a few days.

Sheltering-in-place is surprisingly effective even for disasters in which survival seems impossible. In fact, in contrast to Cold War images of wholesale destruction, nuclear terrorism poses a limited range of damage and a high chance of survival, if people just do the right thing.

While serving on the Congressional Commission on the Prevention of Weapons of Mass Destruction Proliferation and Terrorism, we learned about recent work taking place at Lawrence Livermore National Laboratory and the Center for Biosecurity of the University of Pittsburgh Medical Center. We were surprised to learn that hundreds of thousands of lives could be saved if people merely sheltered-in-place.

Americans need to prepare, not out of the grim fear of future disaster, but out of the belief that through their own actions, they can be authors of their own survival.

Simple steps will help prepare you and your family: Build and maintain an emergency kit to help you shelter-in-place for at least three days, make a plan with your family and inform yourself about disasters. Initiative and individual action through simple, inexpensive preparations can save you and your family.

# 12

# National Intelligence, Saudi Arabia, Iraq, and 9/11

As we pass the twentieth anniversary of the September 11, 2001, terrorist attacks, there is much we still do not know about the particulars of that fateful day. In this last section, Bob Graham writes a series of op-eds about the state of the nation regarding national intelligence and foreign policy. Throughout the forty-five years following the end of World War II, American foreign policy was dominated by the struggle between the United States and the communist bloc. In a 2017 oral history interview with WUFT news, David Colburn talked about that battle and how it shaped the way Americans looked at the world. "Those involved in the decision-making process, from President Johnson and President Kennedy to Nixon," Colburn recalled, "all were so caught up in the Cold War and not losing any more territory in Asia to the communists, and the fear that all of Southeast Asia would fall, that they couldn't see an alternative path." With the 1991 breakup of the Soviet Union, it seemed that the United States had not only defeated the communist world and won the Cold War, but was on the verge of ushering in a time of world peace and American economic domination. Within ten years, however, that vision was destroyed by the 9/11 terrorist attacks and the ensuing twenty years of war in the Middle East and central Asia. Bob Graham examines this changing world and the role of the American intelligence community in it through a series of pieces that seek to find out the truth behind the murky origins of the terrorist networks of the early 20th century. As the chairman of the Senate Intelligence Committee when the 9/11 attacks happened, Graham dug deep behind the official stories of rogue extremists acting alone to reveal an alleged sinister network of nation states, particularly Saudi Arabia, financing international terrorism. In a 2002 interview with the *New York Times,* Graham explicitly revealed his reasoning for engaging in such an investigation. Our responsibility, Graham said, is to try to "use the knowledge that we can gather from this tragic event on September the 11th to reform our intelligence capabilities to meet the challenges of the 21st century." Taken more broadly, this statement can be used to describe the rationale for the op-ep pieces written by both Graham and David Colburn that comprise this book. For both Graham and Colburn, the knowledge acquired by civic involvement and public responsibility is the key component to meeting the broader challenges of the 21st century. Hopefully, that rebirth of a common civic discourse will be the lasting legacy of Bob Graham and David Colburn.

## What I Knew before the Invasion

Bob Graham

*Washington Post*, November 20, 2005

In the past week, President Bush has twice attacked Democrats for being hypocrites on the Iraq War. "[M]ore than 100 Democrats in the House and Senate, who had access to the same intelligence, voted to support removing Saddam Hussein from power," he said.

The president's attacks are outrageous. Yes, more than 100 Democrats voted to authorize him to take the nation to war. Most of them, though, like their Republican colleagues, did so in the legitimate belief that the president and his administration were truthful in their statements that Saddam Hussein was a gathering menace—that if Saddam was not disarmed, the smoking gun would become a mushroom cloud.

The president has undermined trust. No longer will the members of Congress be entitled to accept his veracity. Caveat emptor has become the word. Every member of Congress is on his or her own to determine the truth.

As chairman of the Senate Select Committee on Intelligence during the tragedy of Sept. 11, 2001, and the run-up to the Iraq War, I probably had as much access to the intelligence on which the war was predicated as any other member of Congress.

I, too, presumed the president was being truthful—until a series of events undercut that confidence.

In February 2002, after a briefing on the status of the war in Afghanistan, the commanding officer, Gen. Tommy Franks, told me the war was being compromised because specialized personnel and equipment were being shifted from Afghanistan to prepare for the war in Iraq—a war more than a year away. Even at this early date, the White House was signaling that the threat posed by Saddam was of such urgency that it had priority over the crushing of al-Qaida.

In the early fall of 2002, a joint House-Senate intelligence inquiry committee, which I co-chaired, was in the final stages of its investigation of what happened before Sept. 11. As the unclassified final report of the inquiry documented, several failures of intelligence contributed to the tragedy. But as of October 2002, 13 months later, the administration was resisting initiating any substantial action to understand, much less fix, those problems.

At a meeting of the Senate intelligence committee on Sept. 5, 2002, CIA Director George Tenet was asked what the National Intelligence Estimate (NIE) provided as the rationale for a pre-emptive war in Iraq. An NIE is the product of the entire intelligence community, and its most comprehensive assessment. I was stunned when Tenet said that no NIE had been requested by the White House and none had been prepared. Invoking our rarely used senatorial authority, I directed the completion of an NIE.

Tenet objected, saying that his people were too committed to other assignments to analyze Saddam's capabilities and will to use chemical, biological and possibly nuclear weapons. We insisted, and three weeks later, the community produced a classified NIE.

There were troubling aspects to this 90-page document. While slanted toward the conclusion that Saddam possessed weapons of mass destruction stored or produced at 550 sites, it contained vigorous dissents on key parts of the information, especially by the departments of state and energy. Particular skepticism was raised about aluminum tubes that were offered as evidence Iraq was reconstituting its nuclear program. As to Saddam's will to use whatever weapons he might have, the estimate indicated he would not do so unless he was first attacked.

Under questioning, Tenet added that the information in the NIE had not been independently verified by an operative responsible to the United States. In fact, no such person was inside Iraq. Most of the alleged intelligence came from Iraqi exiles or third countries, all of which had an interest in the United States' removing Saddam, by force if necessary.

The American people needed to know these reservations, and I requested that an unclassified, public version of the NIE be prepared. On Oct. 4, Tenet presented a 25-page document titled "Iraq's Weapons of Mass Destruction Programs." It represented an unqualified case that Saddam possessed them, avoided a discussion of whether he had the will to use them and omitted the dissenting opinions contained in the classified version. Its conclusions, such as "If Baghdad acquired sufficient weapons-grade fissile material from abroad, it could make a nuclear weapon within a year," underscored the White House's claim that exactly such material was being provided from Africa to Iraq.

From my advantaged position, I had earlier concluded that a war with Iraq would be a distraction from the successful and expeditious completion of our aims in Afghanistan. Now I had come to question whether the White House was telling the truth—or even had an interest in knowing the truth.

On Oct. 11, I voted no on the resolution to give the president authority to go to war against Iraq. I was able to apply caveat emptor. Most of my colleagues could not.

## The Truth behind the San Diego Two

**Bob Graham**

*Boston Globe*, February 5, 2006

In the State of the Union speech, President Bush defended his warrantless wiretap program by giving one example of where it might have saved American lives: "It is said that prior to the attacks of Sept. 11, our government failed to connect the dots of the conspiracy. We now know that two of the hijackers in the United States placed telephone calls to al-Qaida operatives overseas. But we did not know about their plans until it was too late."

Vice President Dick Cheney made a similar assertion three weeks ago.

Both refer to two of the 19 hijackers who lived in San Diego in 2000: Nawaf al-Hazmi and Khalid al-Midhar. In these sentences the president has committed two sins: He has stretched the truth, and he has distracted the American people from the steps we need to take to truly make us more secure from terrorist attacks.

During the Joint Inquiry of the Congressional Intelligence Committees, which I co-chaired, we determined the following to be some of the major failures involving the San Diego two.

In December 1999, the CIA was alerted that a summit of terrorists would be held at Kuala Lumpur, Malaysia, and that two Saudis, Hazmi and Midhar, would participate.

The Kuala Lumpur CIA station decided to outsource surveillance of the summit to Malaysian intelligence, which was unable to place a listening device in the meeting room. Had it done so, we probably would have heard of al-Qaida's plans to attack a U.S. destroyer, which in October 2000 culminated in the bombing of the USS Cole, and the initial preparations for 9/11.

In January 2000, deaf but not blind, the CIA had secured photographs of all the summit participants and the U.S. visa of Midhar. None of this information was included in the State Department's watch list of suspect persons, and neither immigration and border control agencies nor the FBI were notified. Two weeks after the summit ended, the two future hijackers entered the United States through Los Angeles International Airport undetected.

By March 2000, the CIA also had information indicating that Hazmi had traveled to Los Angeles, but information about the travel of either man was not given to the FBI until late August 2001.

By June 2000, the two Saudis who had been living in San Diego for five months were boarders in the home of Abdussattar Shaikh. Hazmi listed his number in the San Diego telephone directory.

Unknown to them, Shaikh was a paid informant of the FBI, assigned to oversee and report on the activities of young Muslims in San Diego.

Because the FBI did not know of the CIA's information on Midhar and Hazmi, Shaikh was not tasked to keep an eye on the two. Shaikh's handling agent testified that, had he known that the CIA had identified the two as al-Qaida operatives, he would have done a "full court press" in terms of surveillance, informant tasking, and investigation—and believes he could have uncovered the plot and potentially foiled the 9/11 attacks.

According to the San Diego Union Tribune, the director of the FBI office in San Diego stated that the fundamental mistakes were a failure of his agency and the CIA to communicate.

"If we knew what the CIA knew, we'd have been in an ideal situation to locate these people." He made no suggestion that by following the law, securing a search warrant before wiretapping, was a detriment.

It is wrong to suggest that the events of 2000 justify warrantless eavesdropping. Just the opposite. It is by correcting institutional and personal incompetence, rather than sacrificing the rights of Americans, that our safety can be best secured.

Through the Patriot Act, passed in 2001 after the 9/11 attacks, Congress modified or repealed laws that had constrained the sharing of information between law enforcement and intelligence agencies. Other critical changes remain—neither of which was mentioned in the president's speech.

The FBI must install an information technology that will modernize its antiquated internal and external communications, and the intelligence community must recruit and train an adequate staff of culturally sensitive Middle Eastern and Central Asian linguists to serve as agents and analysts.

These are two of the steps that will make us safer. These changes will bring us closer to achieving the president's optimistic conclusion: "We will renew the defining moral commitments of this land. And so we move forward—optimistic about our country, faithful to its cause, and confident of the victories to come."

## Are We Safer?

Bob Graham

*Tampa Tribune*, September 10, 2006

As America reaches the fifth anniversary of the most deadly attack against our homeland in the nation's history, important questions remain:

Have we learned the lessons of 9/11? Have we corrected the mistakes that contributed to 9/11? And, most importantly, are we safer?

The report card is mixed. The answer to the final question is alarming.

The Congressional Joint Inquiry I co-chaired with Congressman Porter Goss and the subsequent 9/11 Commission identified a series of intelligence and security gaps that opened the door to the 9/11 terrorists. The 9/11 Commission issued its final evaluation of the U.S. response to those gaps in December 2005.

Among those conclusions:

The most likely targets for a terrorist attack were not adequately protected. The 9/11 Commission gave two C's, one D and two F's to our homeland security preparedness.

A culture of noncooperation among key governmental agencies—particularly the CIA and the FBI—resulted in many signals of terrorist activity inside the United States being overlooked. On incentives for information-sharing, the 9/11 Commission gave a D.

Within the United States, a terrorist support network provided assistance and helped protect the 19 hijackers from detection. International terrorist organizations have had cells in many U.S. cities, including the Tampa Bay area, some of which have expanded their efforts from fund-raising and recruitment to support for terrorist activity.

According to FBI sources, at least one of the individuals who provided support for the hijackers was seen as a Saudi Arabian intelligence officer who operated in the United States with "seemingly unlimited funding."

Five years later, no individual, group or nation has been held accountable for providing support and assistance within the United States to the 9/11 hijackers.

Twenty years of timidity and distraction abroad contributed to the growing strength of international terrorists. Hezbollah, which has been termed the "A team" of terrorists, has attacked or threatened U.S. interests since the October 1983 suicide bombing that killed 241 Marines, sailors and soldiers in their Beirut barracks. On at least three occasions since then, the United States and its international allies have backed down when offered the opportunity to disarm Hezbollah.

With the cooperation of the Taliban, al-Qaida from the mid-1990s operated training camps in Afghanistan. More than 50,000 recruits were provided with the skills of terrorism. No serious effort was made to close these schools of terrorism.

Hezbollah's capabilities were demonstrated during the August war in Israel and Lebanon. Since 9/11, al-Qaida has orchestrated attacks in Indonesia, Spain and Great Britain.

The White House points to the fact that the United States has not been attacked since 9/11 as proof that we are safer. We are all very gratified that we have not been attacked, and the president deserves a portion of the credit. However, there are other explanations that underscore the need for enhanced vigilance.

Al-Qaida has had a practice of assuring that each attack against U.S. interests is more lethal than its predecessors. It has been reported that the reason the poison gas attack directed at New York City subways was called off by al-Qaida leadership 45 days before execution was the inability of the terrorist operatives to assure that more than 3,000 people would be killed.

So, are we safer?

At home, without question, commercial aviation is safer. But, as the recent failed plot to attack airlines en route from London to America attests, international terrorists still eye commercial airliners as targets. Other domestic targets, such as seaports and cargo containers, have received inadequate attention.

In my opinion, Iraq was a distraction from a smart and robust war against international terrorism, though I recognize the strong feelings on all sides of the decision to go to war.

On Sept. 20, 2001, President Bush in a speech to the nation defined our goal: "Our war on terror begins with al-Qaida, but it does not end there. It will not end until every terrorist group of global reach has been found, stopped and defeated."

Had the United States followed that battle plan, by now we no doubt would have annihilated al-Qaida in Afghanistan and Pakistan, taken down its cells in Somalia and Yemen and been well on the way to demilitarizing Hezbollah.

Instead, the Iraq distraction has allowed al-Qaida to escape and regroup into a more lethal organization with franchises in 60 countries. The war has been a giant recruiting billboard for radical Islamists and a training ground for urban terrorists. I estimate that the number of international terrorists globally has surged, possibly doubling or tripling since 9/11.

James Thompson, former governor of Illinois and a 9/11 Commission member, has written that "every reasonable expert believes the terrorists will strike again." The only questions are when, where, how.

What should we do to reduce this prophesied certainty of attack?

We must accelerate the training of Iraqi soldiers and police. When they are ready to assume the security of their country, the United States should withdraw. It would be helpful if there were a date negotiated between the U.S. and Iraqi governments for completion of this task.

Not all of these troops will come directly home. A sufficient number to complete the task of finding, stopping and destroying every terrorist group of global reach should be assigned to those missions, thus restarting the war on terrorism.

The United States must re-establish relations with NATO allies, Russia and friends in the Middle East. We cannot win the war on terror alone.

At home, we should resist the temptation to look at our future security through the rear-view mirror of how we have been attacked in the past. Vulnerabilities not yet exploited, such as chemical plants, noncommercial aviation transportation systems and municipal water supplies, must be hardened based on the best intelligence and security resources.

This is the beginning of an action plan that will allow us to rest with confidence that we are indeed safer. We owe this to the memory of the Americans whose lives were sacrificed on Sept. 11, 2001.

## Lots of Intelligence Lessons

Bob Graham

*St. Petersburg Times*, May 28, 2007

Breach recently left theaters after a long run on movie screens across the nation. For those who have yet to see it, Breach tells the true story of FBI agent Robert Hanssen, who for 15 years doubled as a Russian spy. His treachery led to the assassination of at least three Russian intelligence agents who provided valuable information to the United States. His treachery and the efforts to detect him cost taxpayers billions of dollars.

It took Hanssen's own arrogance to bring him down after a protracted FBI internal investigation repeatedly failed to snare him. Two scathing reports issued after Hanssen's arrest—one from the Justice Department inspector general, the other from a commission headed by former CIA and FBI director William Webster—found numerous mistakes that contributed to Hanssen avoiding capture for many years.

For example, the FBI failed to utilize recent lessons in spy detection. When CIA double agent Aldrich Ames was caught in 1994, the agency received well-deserved criticism for failing to scrutinize Ames' personal finances. Six years later, the FBI made the same mistake. It knew about but never pursued discrepancies in Robert Hanssen's financial reports, which disclosed suspiciously high levels of spending on a relatively low FBI salary. This included a Mercedes that Hanssen purchased for his longtime mistress and registered in her name at his home address. Yet the FBI did not stumble upon this expensive extramarital affair until after his arrest.

I knew something of the Hanssen case because it was the subject of a Senate Intelligence Committee inquiry. The question was how to put the lessons of the past to the service of the future—how to reduce the chances of another Robert Hanssen. The intelligence community's response was to create a new acronym: CI-21. Counter Intelligence in the 21st Century rested on the theory of prevention through collaboration. It was designed to foster intense cooperation among the intelligence agencies to identify the most valuable American secrets and harden those targets from penetration.

The ink was hardly dry on the agreement when it began to fall apart. The FBI and the CIA could not overcome their habit of withholding information from each other, and few of the agencies were willing to disband their own counterespionage units to provide the experienced personnel necessary for CI-21 to function. The White House, focused on scandal and later preparation for war in Iraq, was unwilling to knock heads to force agreement.

In August 2003, the FBI director verified just how little progress CI-21 had made in the more than two years since Hanssen was arrested. In response to congressional inquiries, he noted that collaboration within the intelligence community meant that "a senior CIA official is detailed to the FBI's counterterrorism division"—essentially the same relationship that existed before Hanssen's arrest. Because CI-21 has stagnated, we are today no more likely to detect a spy or prevent the theft of our national security intelligence than we were when Robert Hanssen was selling information to Russians in a Virginia public park.

The Directorate of National Intelligence created after the Hanssen case was created in part to demand collaboration and accountability from our intelligence agencies. The newly designated director, Adm. Michael McConnell, comes to the job from a career in intelligence and has the perspective to understand just how devastating another Hanssen scandal would be. He deserves support from both Congress and the White House in making CI-21 successful.

While Breach has ended its run on the big screen, Americans will still be able to watch when it is released on DVD on June 12. It should be mandatory viewing for the entire U.S. intelligence community, including Adm. McConnell and the House and Senate Select Committees on Intelligence. If they don't breathe new life into U.S. counterintelligence efforts, it won't be long before the next Robert Hanssen makes an even more horrifying sequel.

## Rushing Past Warning Signs

Bob Graham

*St. Petersburg Times*, June 17, 2007

When the U.S. intelligence community released its October 2002 National Intelligence Estimate (NIE) regarding Iraq and weapons of mass destruction, it had little idea that it would become the political hot potato of the 2008 presidential primaries. In recent Democratic and Republican debates, those candidates who were Senate and House members in 2002 were asked if they had read the NIE before casting their vote to go to war. Though each had access to the NIE before the vote, most had not.

A NIE provides the highest level of analysis from the U.S. intelligence community. The president typically orders an NIE, but the head of national intelligence or the Senate and/or House intelligence committees can also direct its preparation. An NIE represents the collective view of the intelligence community—all 17 agencies gathered around the same table, each contributing everything it knows on the subject. While the NIE states a consensus view, each of the agencies is encouraged to offer reservations from or dissents to the majority opinion.

The October 2002 NIE raised serious questions in my mind about some of the critical assertions supporting a pre-emptive war in Iraq. I became highly dubious about the credibility of the overall case for war. The NIE strongly influenced my vote against giving President Bush war-making authority in Iraq—one of only 23 such votes in the Senate.

In order to understand the significance of the October 2002 NIE, it is first necessary to remember the events that preceded its release. The unprecedented terrorist attack of 9/11 was only a year in the past, and the Senate and House intelligence committees had spent much of those 12 months conducting a joint inquiry into pre-9/11 intelligence failures. While the retaliatory war against al-Qaida and the Taliban started well in October 2001, our effort in Afghanistan had bogged down as the campaign neared its first anniversary. With public concern still focused intensely on 9/11 and its aftermath, President Bush faced a major challenge in shifting that focus to the war he wanted to fight in Iraq. His trump card was a nightmare scenario: Saddam Hussein in possession of chemical, biological and/or nuclear weapons.

As the drumbeats for war in Iraq grew increasingly loud in September 2002, the Senate intelligence committee, which I chaired, held a series of closed-door hearings to assess Saddam Hussein's threat to the United States. Members of our intelligence community provided a grim report. Iraq was producing or storing weapons of mass destruction in 550 sites across the country. The Iraqi military had installed missiles that could deliver a warhead more than 350 miles—enough to strike Israel. Saddam Hussein was developing an unmanned aircraft which could be launched from a ship at sea against a target in the United States. Iraq had the capability to unleash all of these capabilities on 45 minutes' notice. Most distressing, Saddam was reconstituting his nuclear program. With terrorist allies giving him access to enriched uranium, Iraq could produce a nuclear weapon within a year.

With other members of the committee, I asked to see the NIE on three subjects: (1) the Iraqi program for weapons of mass destruction; (2) the likely battlefield scenario during an invasion; and (3) the plan for postwar U.S. occupation until sovereignty could be returned to a legitimate Iraqi government. Since NIEs were routinely prepared on subjects much less consequential than war, we were stunned when then-CIA director George Tenet told us that no NIE had been conducted on those subjects. When the intelligence committee used its legal authority to direct an NIE, Tenet resisted until strong committee pressure forced his hand. Even when Tenet finally agreed to an NIE, he insisted that it be limited to Iraq's weapons of mass destruction.

In early October 2002, our committee received the classified version of the NIE. It was concise, approximately 90 pages in length. It had very high production values—photographs, satellite reconnaissance, graphs, maps and addresses. And it contained a majority consensus of the intelligence community: Saddam Hussein had weapons of mass destruction.

The majority view was tempered by strong dissents. For example, as "proof" that Saddam was accelerating his nuclear program, the NIE cited aluminum tubes intercepted at the Iraq border to show he was assembling centrifuges for producing weapons-grade nuclear material. But the U.S. departments of state and energy—the latter of which oversees our nuclear program—insisted that the tubes were not technically usable for that purpose.

There was unanimity on one issue. Every intelligence agency agreed that if Saddam had weapons of mass destruction, he would use them only if he were first attacked.

When the classified NIE was presented to the Senate intelligence committee, I asked Tenet to identify the primary sources of his information. His answer—Iraqi exiles—sounded loud alarms in my mind. Many of the exiles had not been in Iraq for a decade or more. Since they would not return to Baghdad unless U.S. Army tanks were leading the way, they had selfish reasons to want a U.S. military invasion.

With those doubts, I asked Tenet who in the U.S. intelligence community had verified the exiles' information. His chilling answer was the single most disconcerting moment of this entire sordid affair: nobody. The United States government had not invested even a single man hour to verify that Saddam's weapons of mass destruction program, including the alleged effort to produce nuclear weapons, was real and not a figment of the exiles' self-interested imagination.

Alarmed, I tried to alert the public and instructed the intelligence agencies to produce a declassified version of the NIE. Intelligence officials usually declassify documents by drawing black lines through sensitive matters. In this case, we received a newly minted "declassified" NIE. It was 65 pages shorter. Gone was the debate over the aluminum tubes and any other dissents or reservations. Gone was the unanimous conclusion that Saddam would only use weapons of mass destruction if Iraq were first attacked.

That was the last straw. The Bush administration was clearly scheming to manipulate public opinion in favor of war. I was livid. Five days later, during Senate debate on Iraq, I said that those who gave the president warmaking authority would have "blood on their hands."

The purpose of this article is not to say I told you so or claim redemption for my vote.

Far too many Americans and Iraqis have died to waste time on self-congratulations. But those nations who do not study history are doomed to repeat it. We have much to learn from the history of the October 2002 NIE.

First, the United States must rapidly rebuild our human intelligence capability. While the officials who did not want to see the truth about Iraq were partially responsible for our prewar blindness, we also suffered from a shortfall of hands-on U.S. intelligence resources in Iraq. Unless the president and intelligence community immediately rectify this deficiency, the United States will lack accurate information about Iran, North Korea and other threats to our security.

Second, U.S. intelligence community leaders must restore the tradition of speaking truth to power. In the months before the Iraq war, the Bush administration fostered an intelligence culture that valued subservience to the president's political agenda over the intellectually honest presentation of factual data. Those tactics have no place in a democracy, and our intelligence agencies must be ready to cry foul if another American president tries to make them part of an inaccurate public relations campaign.

In my opinion, those candidates who voted for the Iraq war without first reading the NIE should not be disqualified from serving as president of the United States. For 220 years, Americans have held the office of the presidency and its occupants in high regard. With a few specific exceptions, we have generally presumed that presidents tell the truth in matters of war and peace. Any of the current presidential candidates could have honorably acted on that presumption in voting for the war in October 2002.

But to use a phrase that President Bush once mangled, fool us once, shame on you. Fool us twice, shame on us. As voters closely evaluate potential presidents over the next 17 months, we must determine which candidates believe that the American people should be entrusted with the truth. More lies mean more lives lost around the world.

## Panetta Right One to Repair CIA

Bob Graham

*Atlanta Constitution*, January 27, 2009

Universities selecting new presidents are often advised to choose a leader who reflects where the institution believes itself to be and where it wants to go. President Barack Obama followed that same counsel when he chose Leon Panetta as the new director of the CIA, a battered agency reeling from divisive leadership. The CIA needs a proven leader who can revitalize the agency and restore its credibility.

The CIA's current troubles have three origins. First, the CIA has strayed far from its basic mission. At its best, it is a human intelligence agency, which provides information not otherwise available so decision-makers can make better judgments. In Bush's first term, the administration disregarded that aspiration and demanded politicized intelligence. Whereas the CIA was founded to "speak truth to power," its new mantra became "tell us what you want to hear."

Despite Director Michael Hayden's second-term efforts to stabilize the agency and loosen the White House's iron fist, matters worsened, and the agency became ensnared in the rendition of foreign detainees, torture and use of excessive interrogation techniques. As a result, congressional confidence has plummeted. Panetta will rebuild this essential relationship.

Second, the CIA has lost institutional clout. From 1947 to 2004, the CIA director wore a second hat as director of central intelligence. In this second position, he was ostensibly the first among equals and responsible for the overall direction of the intelligence community. Unfortunately, most directors ignored that responsibility. The massive intelligence failures surrounding the 9/11 attacks and our involvement in Iraq sent a loud signal that somebody needed to take the role seriously.

In 2004, on the recommendation of the Joint Congressional Inquiry into the 9/11 attacks and the 9/11 Commission, Congress created the new position of director of national intelligence. The DNI sits on tip of an intelligence hierarchy that consists of 16 other intelligence agencies. This new arrangement has been difficult for the CIA, which has publicly grumbled about the loss of turf and status. Panetta has the leadership abilities to dramatically improve internal morale and external standing.

Third, the CIA has failed to accomplish its most high-profile, signature mission: the capture or killing of Osama bin Laden. While some would degrade the importance of this goal, bin Laden has murdered more than 3,000 Americans and leads al-Qaida, the terrorist network that most threatens our national interests. The fact that bin Laden remains at large more than seven years after 9/11 is a major embarrassment to the CIA. Panetta is committed to the accomplishment of this vital mission.

Panetta is the right person to lift the CIA out of its current doldrums. He has been a major consumer of intelligence. As President Bill Clinton's chief of staff for three years, he was on the receiving end of massive amounts of intelligence data. In that role, he learned to evaluate intelligence, use it to inform decision-making and task the respective agencies to gather more information.

Additionally, Panetta has the proven managerial skills that a complex agency with tens of thousands of employees desperately requires. When Panetta became White House chief of staff in July 1994, the Clinton administration was weekly seen as apolitically and legislatively adrift. By the end of his tenure in January 1997, Panetta had presided over the passage of welfare reform, a minimum wage increase and President Clinton's successful re-election bid.

At a time when the CIA is perceived as rudderless, Panetta is uniquely prepared to set CIA's priorities and oversee their attainment. His past experience as chairman of the House Budget Committee and director of the Office of Management and Budget is an added bonus in the current fiscal environment.

Finally, Leon Panetta is a politician who understands the importance of relationships both within the intelligence community and with outside stakeholders. As a member of Congress for 16 years and a former White House leader, Panetta will help restore the agency's troubled relations at both ends of Pennsylvania Avenue.

## Eyes Forward on Intelligence

Bob Graham

*Washington Post*, May 21, 2009

Since President Obama released the "torture memos"—the legal analysis of the Bush Justice Department on which the CIA predicated its enhanced interrogation techniques—a familiar pattern regarding U.S. intelligence has recurred: We have become fixated on the rear-view mirror to the exclusion of what is coming toward us. While much discussion has focused on what House Speaker Nancy Pelosi was told seven years ago, the more important issues is the reform urgently needed in the relationship between the intelligence community, the executive branch and Congress.

For more than a year, I have chaired a congressional commission reviewing U.S. vulnerability to a weapon of mass destruction. The unanimous conclusion of our nine members, Republicans and Democrats, was that it is more likely than not that such a weapon will be used in a terrorist attack somewhere before year-end 2013. The commission made 13 recommendations to reduce this probability, many of which rely on intelligence as the first line of defense.

Avoiding a potentially catastrophic attack using weapons of mass destruction starts at the top, with reform of the interaction between the intelligence community and the executive and legislative branches. Congressional intelligence committees were created in the 1970s to ensure accountability. If the committees were fully informed of the intelligence community's anticipated activities, the thinking went, a level of accountability would be provided before specific programs were implemented. Brought in early, the committees would share a sense of responsibility and might be less inclined to point fingers in the event of an intelligence failure. The controversy over "enhanced interrogation techniques" demonstrates that this relationship of mutual respect and sharing of consequences has shattered. Indeed, the CIA's calendar of legislative briefings indicates that even the appearance of congressional notification occurred after waterboarding and other extraordinary methods of interrogation had been in use for weeks.

The president and leaders in Congress should immediately begin the consultations that will build mutual confidence and help take us back to the original ideal. While that is most important, other work must also be done if we are to sustain a relationship of shared responsibility.

The CIA needs to improve its records management system. The imbroglio over dates of interrogation briefings is not the first instance in which CIA assertions of certitude were contravened by my own records. I learned from my gather to keep a detailed daily log of my activities. From my collection of spiral notebooks and my schedule for the dates in question, I confirmed, and the CIA concurred, that three of the four briefings I supposedly attended never occurred. An individual member of Congress should not have better records than the nation's premier intelligence agency. Congress and the CIA might start by establishing a practice similar to that required of publicly traded companies: keeping a transcript or at least detailed minutes of every classified briefing, with the documentation materials contemporaneously circulated among all participants and signed as having been agreed to or specifically dissented from. This would help prevent incidents of conflicting memories of an unrecorded briefing years earlier.

The exception for covert action should be reexamined. Covert actions are activities intended to influence political, economic or military conditions abroad in which the U.S. role will not be apparent or publicly acknowledged. When the president declares an action covert, saying that it affects U.S. vital interests, he may limit notification to the congressional and intelligence committee leadership, known as the "Gang of Eight."

As we learned with warrantless wiretaps and enhanced interrogation, both of which appear to have been treated as covert actions by President Bush, activities subject to the least congressional oversight have the greatest potential to sully our national honor and international reputation. The president should use this authority infrequently and cautiously. I do not believe that gathering intelligence, electronically or from detained human beings, meets the definition of covert action.

When the exemption for covert action is invoked, congressional leaders, who are then the only remaining form of oversight, should have their own version of a bill of rights, holding that:

–No briefing will be held without adequate notice and without the subject matter of the classified briefing being disclosed. (Current practice is notification on an urgent basis with no indication of the topic, denying the opportunity for even minimal preparation.)

–No briefing shall be held without a majority of the Gang of Eight present. (The CIA calendar of briefings on enhanced interrogations indicates that of 18 briefings of members of the Gang of Eight, none included a majority and thus provided the critical mass required for collegial consideration.)

–At the earliest date possible, the full committees should be briefed. This is the law, honored mostly in the breach. (According to the CIA calendar, the first briefing of the full Senate and House intelligence committees took place Sept. 6, 2006, more than four years after enhanced interrogations commenced.)

Balancing the values of an open society with the need to gather, analyze and occasionally act on clandestine information is one of the great challenges a democracy faces. The "who said what, when" public catfight is not the forum to confront such challenges. The United States can and must do better if our intelligence agencies, the president and Congress are to play their crucial roles in slowing the ticking clock of when the worst people are likely to possess and deploy the worst weapons.

## Osama bin Laden Is Dead. Now What?

Bob Graham

*Washington Post*, May 12, 2011

After almost 10 years of the most intensive and expensive manhunt in the history of the world, Osama bin Laden is dead. The inevitable questions: What do we do now? What are al-Qaida's capabilities to do us harm?

For at least the past 15 years, bin Laden sought to acquire a nuclear or biological weapon of mass destruction. Rolf Mowatt-Larssen, a career intelligence officer and former head of the CIA's department on weapons of mass destruction, has observed that "al Qaida is the only group known to be pursuing a long-term, persistent and systematic approach to developing weapons to be used in mass casualty attacks." Bin Laden's quest for a weapon of mass destruction was driven by his dogma that each attack against the United States or its interests abroad should be greater than any previous assault. This became operational in late 2002 or early 2003, Mowatt-Larssen reported, when al-Qaida's central leadership canceled a planned attack using a crude cyanide device on New York subways because it was waiting for "something better."

It is probable that the next leadership of central al-Qaida will not cling to bin Laden's tenet, so if and until the new supreme leader acquires a weapon of mass destruction, Americans are likely to be threatened by significant but smaller attacks.

Meanwhile, the fruits of bin Laden's efforts to acquire non-conventional weapons will be available to the new leader. Advances in technology have reduced the necessity of a significant organizational capacity for such weapons to be secured and utilized. A small group whose organizing principle is hatred of Americans could concoct a lethal brew of pathogens in a basement laboratory and stealthily disperse it through a vaporization machine in the back of a pickup truck, killing tens of thousands in a major American city.

So we must not see this as a time to relax our domestic vigilance. Ironically, the day bin Laden was dispatched was the eighth anniversary of the "Mission Accomplished" ceremony on the USS Abraham Lincoln. After that premature declaration of victory, an attitude took hold that America could quickly close the page on Iraq. That attitude proved dramatically wrong and resulted in an extension of the wars in Iraq and Afghanistan. We must not succumb to the same error again.

We should also be wary of the nebulous slogan "war on terrorism" and should name and target our actual enemies: al-Qaida, its affiliates and other groups such as Hezbollah. At an operational level this means less attention to geography but, rather, a strategy with a laser focus on the specific organizations wherever they are located. For al-Qaida this means not Afghanistan, where fewer than 100 operatives remain, but in Pakistan, Yemen and Somalia, where many are known to operate. Executing this strategy will take the type of close-order combat required to kill bin Laden.

His death will not render al-Qaida impotent. While the symbolic and intellectual force of bin Laden was formidable, al-Qaida has a culture of leadership succession and a recent history of institutional transformation. The West and its Middle Eastern allies have been attacking al-Qaida's leadership structure since before Sept. 11, 2001, killing or capturing hundreds of its top and mid-management. In virtually all these instances, al-Qaida has had a bench that allowed it to quickly and seamlessly replace each dispatched leader. Bin Laden's successor will inherit a daunting challenge, but past experience suggests there is such a person prepared to assume leadership.

Since Sept. 11 al-Qaida has undergone a fundamental transition. Before the attacks, it was a hierarchical structure with bin Laden the dominant figure at the top. Today, al-Qaida is a franchise with 60 or more national or subnational units, with the stronger of these franchisees demonstrating a desire to be more independent of central al-Qaida. Indeed, al-Qaida in the Arabian Peninsula has broken from bin Laden's vision of increasingly larger attacks by launching a series of operations against the United States far smaller than that of Sept. 11, thankfully all unsuccessful. More fundamentally, this decentralization of al-Qaida has provided the organization with enhanced local knowledge and nimbleness and a distributed leadership that reduces the significance of any single individual, even an Osama bin Laden.

What we need to do now is to sustain and intensify the post-bin Laden spirit that America can accomplish whatever it sets out to do. We must be vigilant and assured of full capability to deter, prevent and respond to al-Qaida and other terrorist organizations whenever we discover them and wherever they are.

## Saudi Arabia: Friend or Foe?

**Senator Bob Graham asks why hard questions about Saudi Arabia have gone unanswered since 9/11**

Bob Graham

*Daily Beast*, July 11, 2011

On September 12, 2001, Americans learned that 15 of the 19 commercial-airplane hijackers of the previous day were Saudis. The thought that went through many minds was, What are the Saudis thinking? Were these 15 individual suicidal decisions, or does 9/11 represent a break in our mutually beneficial relationship stretching back to World War II?

From that date until today those questions have largely gone unanswered. Unanswered because the government of the United States has engaged in a sustained and effective campaign to keep the American public from knowing the truth. And we may ask: Why?

These are some of the questions that have preoccupied me since co-chairing the congressional inquiry into 9/11. They arose from the truth that surfaced, which included: The first two hijackers who entered the United States did so through Los Angeles International Airport in mid-January 2000. Within days they were urged by a shadowy man, already described in an FBI report as an "agent" of the Saudi government, to relocate to San Diego with promises of extensive support—promises on which he promptly delivered.

The agent's cover was as a ghost employee of a contractor to an agency of the Saudi government—paid a salary and allowances but never expected to show up and work. His real job was to monitor Saudi youth in San Diego getting an education to ensure they were not also plotting the overthrow of the monarchy.

When the two future hijackers reached San Diego, the agent's allowances were substantially increased. Upon their arrival the agent secured and paid for an apartment. He arranged flight lessons. He introduced them to a tight circle of Muslims, primarily Saudis, who offered additional support.

Yet the support being funneled to the two visitors proved insufficient for their decidedly non-Islamic tastes—alcohol, strip clubs, even a desired, though unfulfilled, marriage to a stripper. The agent then tapped another source of funds: a welfare account maintained for the benefit of Saudis in need by the wife of the kingdom's ambassador to the United States.

That is some of what we do know, and we got a sufficient glimpse to know what we didn't know. Still unanswered after nearly 10 years are the questions of the full extent of the Saudi pre-9/11 involvement: Did any or all of the other 17 receive support from Saudi interests? Why would Saudi Arabia do this? Do the Saudis have the will and capability to aid future attacks against the United States? And most important: Why the cover-up by our government?

I have attempted to address these questions in the final report of the congressional commission and the nonfiction book Intelligence Matters, published in 2004. Each was censored by authorities in the intelligence community, particularly on the role of the Saudis in 9/11. I am now attempting to provide these answers in the form of fact wrapped in fiction in my novel Keys to the Kingdom.

Some have claimed my statements and anxieties are over the top, that there are less incendiary explanations for what the Saudi and U.S. governments have done. But a string of recent occurrences has brought to the surface the suspicion of direct, deep Saudi involvement in 9/11.

Why would the Saudis have given substantial assistance to at least two of the hijackers, and possibly all 19? The answer I have come to is survival—survival of the state and survival of the House of Saud. The Saudi regime in the late 1990s faced the prospect of a repeat of the 1979 Iranian revolution, when young revolutionaries toppled the shah. Osama bin Laden was ascending. He had achieved hero status—in his country of birth, Saudi Arabia, and across much of the Muslim world—for his work with the mujahedin in expelling the Soviets from Afghanistan. He had successfully bombed two U.S. embassies in Africa. He had trained thousands of potential terrorists in his Afghan camps. And he was planning even greater attacks—this time within the United States itself.

But bin Laden recognized a deficiency: Most of those who would be spirited into the United States had never been there before and did not speak English. How could they survive and maintain anonymity while they completed the final planning, practiced and executed an enormously sophisticated attack? The Saudis, who were known to have a global network of agents to monitor their youth against the prospects of another Iran, could provide the support infrastructure to make this possible. The threat of civil unrest against the monarchy, led by al Qaeda, could be the leverage for access to this network.

The Arab Spring has posed a similar threat to the survival of the state and the House of Saud.

There have been at least three responses from the palace.

Beheadings, the traditional means of traumatizing the population into submission, have surged. According to Amnesty International, at least 27 such executions occurred during the first five months of 2011. This was the same number as the total for 2010. Another 100 or more wait on death row.

Religious organizations, many aligned with the austere Wahhabi sect and the religious police, have been allocated an additional $200 million.

The royal treasury, swollen by $214 billion in oil revenues last year, has been opened to essentially buy off the people. Public employees have received an additional two months' salary; $70 billion has been lavished on 500,000 units of low-income housing.

One of the few reformists in the royal palace, Prince Talal bin Abdul

Aziz, brother of King Abdullah, has said, "These people want to preserve their power, their money, and their prestige, so they want to keep the status quo. They are afraid of the word 'change.' This is a problem because they are shortsighted, but the difficulty is I don't know how to change their way of thinking."

An insight into how far the regime might go in defending and perpetuating the status quo occurred in May of this year at the Vienna meeting of the World Health Organization. Advancing its policy of avoiding the proliferation of weapons of mass destruction, nuclear or biological, the United States offered a resolution that would have required all 193 members of the WHO to either declare they were smallpox-free or—as would be the case with the United States—to commit to the destruction of any smallpox pathogens held in laboratories or elsewhere within five years. Throughout history, smallpox has been a scourge of mankind, and the virus remains the only communicable human disease successfully erased from nature, a miracle of organization and determination. There is only one way it can reappear, and that is in a weaponized form from a nation or group bent on mass catastrophe and worldwide havoc. The results of any dissemination would automatically be classified as a crime against humanity. This resolution to destroy all samples was successfully filibustered by Iran. It is not surprising that a country which for more than a decade has sought to develop a nuclear capability would also be seeking a biological weapon. What was surprising was Saudi Arabia, one of Iran's staunchest opponents, declaring that it "strongly disagreed" with the United States' position.

Why would the kingdom abandon its most important ally to support a nation that for the past 30-plus years has been considered its archenemy? Could it be that Saudi Arabia is also developing biological weapons?

The most perplexing unanswered question remains: Why would the United States engage in a cover-up? Many have pointed to the special personal friendship between the royal family and the highest levels of our national government. The fact that the Saudis were allowed to fly a planeload of their elite home from the United States in the days immediately after 9/11, when all other commercial aviation was grounded, is often cited as support for that position. In fact, all that actions such as this do is make America's post-9/11 reaction to the Saudis even more mysterious.

Secrets deemed this critical by both governments are bound to be buried under many layers of official protection and unofficial obfuscation.

The actions since 9/11 are a perverted application of Winston Churchill's truism on the Allies' plans to end World War II: "In wartime, truth is so precious that she should always be attended by a bodyguard of lies."

If one method of disclosing precious truth doesn't work, you try another. I'd always wanted to try my hand at a novel—to place characters of my own invention in challenging and intriguing situations that tested and defined their wits, strength, courage, and moral fiber. Now I had both motivation and material. Having been thwarted in my "real life" efforts to bring out the answers to these questions, which should be among the highest priorities to our citizens, I resorted to fiction, to the imaginative world of "What if?" With the publication of Keys to the Kingdom, I feel I have finally conveyed the reality I've pursued for so long.

## Re-Open the 9/11 Investigation Now

**Bob Graham**

*Huffington Post*, September 11, 2012

The passage of time since September 11, 2001, has not diminished the distrust many of us feel surrounding the official story of how 9/11 happened and, more specifically, who financed and supported it. After eleven years, the time has come for the families of the victims, the survivors and all Americans to get the whole story behind 9/11.

Yet the story of who may have facilitated the 19 hijackers and the infrastructure that supported the attacks—a crucial element of the narrative—has not been told. The pieces we do have underscore how much more remains unknown.

Did the hijackers execute the plot alone, or did they have the support of forces other than the known leaders of al-Qaeda—a network even—that provided funds, assistance, and cover?

It is not merely a question of the need to complete the historical record. It is a matter of national security today.

If a support network was available to the terrorists before 9/11, why should we think it has now disbanded or been rolled up? It may still be in place, capable of supporting al-Qaeda or other extremist groups that hate America—of which there are many.

This is also about justice. Thousands of Americans, who suffered unimaginable loss, have been denied their day in court in part because evidence of support was either never gathered by law enforcement or remains locked away, sealed as "Classified."

From the outset of the Congressional Joint Inquiry into 9/11, it seemed implausible that the hijackers—most of whom spoke no English and had never been to the U.S.—could have executed the heinous plot on their own. The inquiry proved those suspicions justified, and a 28-page chapter in its report centered on sources of foreign support for some of the September 11 hijackers while they were in the United States. That chapter remains censored, denied to the American people.

Sadly, those 28 pages represent only a fraction of the evidence of Saudi complicity that our government continues to shield from the public, under a flawed classification program which appears to be part of a systematic effort to protect Saudi Arabia from any real accountability for its actions. For example, after a nearly eight year delay, the CIA recently responded to Freedom of Information Act (FOIA) requests submitted on behalf of the 9/11 families in 2004, for reports and documents cited in the notes of the 9/11 Commission's Final Report. Unfortunately, when it came to documents such as a 16-page CIA report titled "Saudi Based Financial Support for Terrorist Organizations," our own government redacted every word of substantive text.

Despite the carefully orchestrated campaign to protect our Saudi "friends," ample evidence of Saudi Arabia's intimate ties to al-Qaeda and the 9/11 attacks has come to light. The executive director of the 9/11 Commission, Dr. Philip Zelikow, stated in 2007 that while at that time he did not feel the evidence established "Saudi government agents," were involved "there is persuasive evidence of a possible support network . . ."

The information indicating there were networks, foreign sources of support within the United States other than al-Qaeda, and that those networks had the backing of Saudi Arabia, is today stronger than ever.

Here are some of the pieces of the puzzle.

Much of what we know has been learned through the energy and competence of external investigators, state and local law enforcement officers, reporters and authors, and plaintiffs' attorneys. Concisely:

Often over the FBI's objections, the Congressional Joint Inquiry uncovered a good deal about a support network in San Diego, California.

There, a man named Omar al-Bayoumi, whom the FBI had identified as a Saudi agent even before 9/11, provided direct assistance to future hijackers Nawaf al Hazmi and Khalid al Mihdhar. Those two Saudi citizens, who came to the U.S. only ten days after attending a terrorist summit, were the vanguard of the operation on U.S. territory. Bayoumi, a "ghost employee," was paid by a Saudi company but not expected to report for work. The company's monthly non-salary payments to him increased eight-fold after the two hijackers arrived in San Diego. He and his family left the country seven weeks before 9/11.

The FBI withheld from the Congressional Inquiry, and from the subsequent 9/11 Commission, the fact that it had investigated another potential support pod for the hijackers in Sarasota, Florida. That information became public on the tenth anniversary last year, following persistent work by Anthony Summers, co-author of The Eleventh Day, this year's Pulitzer Prize for History finalist, and his colleague Dan Christensen, an investigative journalist in South Florida with BrowardBulldog.org.

In the Sarasota case, law enforcement officials suspected that several hijackers, including their leader Mohamed Atta, repeatedly visited the home of a Saudi couple in a suburban gated community. Their visits, sources who were involved at the time say, were on record—the license plates of vehicles they used to enter the community had been automatically photographed. The Saudi couple abruptly left their posh home, bound for Saudi Arabia, about two weeks before 9/11. The husband and his father-in-law were apparently on a watch list at the FBI and a U.S. agency involved in tracking terrorist funds was interested in both men even before 9/11.

When the Sarasota case erupted in September of 2011, the FBI issued two public statements, each of which declared there had been a full investigation of the alleged relationship between hijackers and persons in Sarasota; that investigation determined there was no such relationship; and that the Congressional Joint Inquiry and the 9/11 Commission had been informed.

Through personal knowledge, interviews and files which were made available it was found that these public statements were untrue.

In July of this year, the Senate Permanent Subcommittee on Investigations, Committee on Homeland Security, issued a 330-page report faulting banking giant HSBC for ignoring the ties to terrorist financing of

Al Rajhi Bank, Saudi Arabia's largest private bank. The report states that after the 9/11 attacks, "evidence began to emerge that Al Rajhi Bank and some of its owners had links to organizations associated with financing terrorism, including that one of the bank's founders was an early financial benefactor of al Qaeda." This individual was identified in the report as being part of Osama bin-Laden's "Golden Chain" of al-Qaeda financiers.

Other information indicating that there was a Saudi role has come from the determined litigation by survivors of 9/11, the families of the dead and property insurers. A U.S. report, disclosed only after a FOIA lawsuit, hints at deeper institutional links between the Kingdom and al-Qaeda. It states that the Saudi charity, International Islamic Relief Organization's (IIRO), "support for terrorist organizations began in the early 1990s and continued through at least the first half of 2006" and linked a Saudi IIRO official to Khalid Sheikh Mohammed.

The legal efforts that target Saudi Arabia, however, have so far been thwarted. The Saudis have been able to dodge the suits, thanks to what is known as "sovereign immunity" which exempts most foreign states from being sued.

The Saudis claimed, meanwhile, that the 9/11 Commission Report exonerated the Kingdom. As former U.S. senator and 9/11 Commission member Bob Kerrey—and one of the authors of this article Bob Graham, as co-chair of the Congressional Joint Inquiry—emphasized in affidavits filed last March, the Commission and the congressional inquiry did not do that at all.

Our Department of State supported the Saudis' dismissal from the litigation, arguing that delicate matters of U.S.-Saudi relations should be handled not by the judiciary but by the executive branch. An appellate court later found this to be an erroneous interpretation of the law in a case against Afghanistan, but the State Department's intervention on behalf of Saudi Arabia in the 9/11 families' suit had already placed the Kingdom beyond judicial reach.

What should the United States do now?

The investigation of the extent of foreign support for the 9/11 hijackers ought to be reopened by the president, who has the authority to order the FBI to pursue the existing leads seriously, or he should designate another appropriate entity to do so. This investigation should reach all the places where the hijackers spent significant time, such as Paterson, New Jersey, Falls Church and Arlington, Virginia, and Delray Beach, Florida.

The president should also order the declassification of the relevant documents. They have been hidden from the American people too long. That declassification must include the 28-page chapter that has been censored from the report of the Congressional Joint Inquiry, as well as the reports cited in the notes of the 9/11 Commission's Final Report concerning al-Qaeda's financial and logistical support network.

The Congress should amend the sovereign immunity statute. Those who framed it did not intend that it should shield terrorists or their collaborators from claims against them for the murder of Americans on U.S. soil. A bill pending in both the Senate and House called the Justice Against Sponsors of Terrorism Act, which enjoys broad bi-partisan (or more accurately non-partisan) support, would achieve that goal through modest amendments to the sovereign immunity statute, and should be passed immediately.

What the Joint Inquiry learned—and has emerged since—shows where the proverbial finger of suspicion points. It points to Saudi Arabia, and we need to know the full truth.

## Post 9/11: Questions for Obama

**Bob Graham**

*Miami Herald*, July 13, 2013

In the swirl of revelations, contradictions and confusion about the United States data mining program, Mr. President, you have called for a national debate on liberty and security in post 9/11 America.

I welcome this call, but the difficulties with your proposal include: how to have a debate on a subject you don't know exists; and how to have a debate if the facts necessary to engage in an informed discussion are withheld?

As reported over many months in the U.S. and abroad—notably in the Miami Herald and BrowardBulldog.com—a 9/11 series of events that go to the heart of the issue of how to ensure that security is compatible with liberty have arisen from Sarasota.

At the core of this episode is a central, lingering question. Saddled with linguistic and cultural ignorance and limited personal experience, could the 19 hijackers have conducted such a complex operation alone? The co-chair of the 9/11 commission said it was "implausible." Did the terrorists have the support of a network, perhaps directed by elements of a foreign nation state?

The events in Sarasota are directly relevant to those questions. Prior to 9/11, according to law enforcement investigators, neighbors and other witnesses, a prominent Saudi family living in Sarasota had extensive contacts with several of the future hijackers—including key operatives training to be pilots at a nearby flight school. About 10 days before 9/11, apparently in great haste, these Saudis left their Sarasota home and—accompanied by the occupant's father-in-law who had long been an aide to a senior Saudi prince—returned to Saudi Arabia.

When these allegations were disclosed 10 years later, the FBI stated publicly that a thorough investigation in the immediate aftermath of 9/11 revealed no connections between the family and the hijackers. And further, that all of the information derived from the investigation had been made available to the 9/11 commission and the joint congressional inquiry.

Recently released primary source documentation (uncovered through a Freedom of Information request) based on evidence collected by law enforcement agents who participated in the investigation disclosed there had been "many connections between the (name of family redacted) and individuals associated with the terrorist attacks on September 11, 2001." The leadership of the 9/11 commission and the congressional joint inquiry have affirmed they were unaware of the pre-9/11 events or the subsequent investigation.

Neither of the FBI's public assertions appears to be correct. The FBI has declared all the remaining documentation of the Sarasota events and subsequent investigation classified.

How is the public supposed to know or evaluate the truth of the matter?

One way to start would be to open the debate with questions that would illuminate the context of specific actions—such as the recently disclosed National Security Agency's Prism program—but would not necessitate access to classified information.

For example:

• Under what circumstances is it acceptable for the government to withhold information from—even deceive—the public?

In the summer of 1943, after the Tehran conference attended by President Franklin D. Roosevelt, British Prime Minister Winston Churchill and Soviet leader Joseph Stalin, Churchill said, "In wartime, truth is so precious that she should always be attended by a bodyguard of lies." Churchill's statement was justified at that time—decisions on the final battle plans of World War II were made at Tehran.

Some would say we have been in a continuous time of war since 9/11. Let's have a debate as to whether and to what the Churchillian dictum applies today.

• What should be done if it is determined that a governmental agency has deceived the American people and then withheld the evidence of its incompetence or perfidy by the shield of classification? We need a public conversation as to whether it would be salutary to insert provisions in the Freedom of Information Act or elsewhere to sanction an agency which has engaged in this practice.

• Why have the Saudis been treated in a distinctively different manner than other nationalities? This stark difference was highlighted after the Boston marathon bombing in April.

Within hours of the massacre, the FBI was aggressively investigating whether the two Muslim Russian Chechen bombers had acted with the connivance of Muslims from Russia's volatile North Caucasus region. Yet, more than 10 years after 9/11 it appears everything possible is being done to conceal Saudi assistance to the 19 hijackers—15 of whom were Saudi nationals.

• Should the FBI continue to be the domestic intelligence agency for the United States? MI 5 in the United Kingdom and Shin Bet in Israel are stand alone, non-law enforcement related domestic intelligence agencies. One rationale for this separation is difference of mission. Law enforcement agencies are primarily directed to gather sufficient evidence after a crime has been committed to convict the perpetrator beyond a reasonable doubt. Domestic intelligence is structured to gather information to detect a peril and avoid it.

• Has the performance of the FBI been such as to convince Americans we are best protected by an agency that combines these goals?

Mr. President, those are some of the questions that concern Americans. We recall President Dwight D. Eisenhower's call to duty in his 1961 farewell address:

"Only an alert and knowledgeable citizenry can compel the proper meshing of the huge industrial and military machinery of defense with our peaceful methods and goals, so that security and liberty may prosper together." Today the situation is different. But, the challenge to properly mesh security concerns with the protection of our liberties continues.

Let the debate begin.

## Release the Uncensored Truth about 9/11

**Bob Graham**

*Washington Post*, May 11, 2016

Nearly 15 years after the horrific events of 9/11, President Barack Obama must decide whether to release 28 pages of information withheld as classified from the publicly released report of the congressional inquiry into the terrorist attacks that killed thousands of Americans.

On April 10, the CBS program "60 Minutes" aired a story about the missing 28 pages. I was one of several former public officials—including former House Intelligence Committee Chairman and CIA Director Porter Goss, R-Fla.; Medal of Honor recipient and former Sen. Bob Kerrey, D-Neb.; former Navy secretary John Lehman; and former ambassador and Rep. Tim Roemer, D-Ind.—who called on the White House to declassify and release the documents.

Two days after that broadcast, I received a call from a White House staff member who told me that the president would make a decision about the 28 pages no later than June. While that official made no promises as to what Obama would do, I viewed the news as a step in the right direction.

My optimism about the administration's action on this critical issue was short-lived. On May 1, when CIA Director John Brennan appeared on NBC's "Meet the Press," I watched with astonishment as he argued that the 28 pages should not be released because the American people are incapable of accurately evaluating them.

When asked by host Chuck Todd to make the case against releasing the information, Brennan replied, "I think some people may seize upon that uncorroborated, unvetted information that was in there that was basically just a collation of this information that came out of FBI files, and to point to Saudi involvement, which I think would be very, very inaccurate."

With all due respect, that argument is an affront not only to the American public in general but also to all those who lost family members, loved ones and friends on that fateful September day in 2001. Americans are fully capable of reviewing the 28 pages and making up their own minds about their significance.

As co-chairman of the Joint Inquiry Into the Terrorist Attacks of September 11, 2001, I have read the 28 pages. My oath of confidentiality forbids me from discussing the specifics of that material. But while I cannot reveal those details, I strongly believe the American people deserve to know why this issue is so important. All of the references below are from the declassified, public version of the Joint Inquiry's final report.

For the first time in more than 200 years, Congress merged two standing committees from different houses of Congress: the Senate Select Committee on Intelligence and the House Permanent Select Committee on Intelligence. The Joint Inquiry had an impressive staff selected due to its members' experience serving or overseeing key intelligence agencies.

The first order we gave was for the intelligence agencies to preserve any information that might be useful in understanding what happened before, on and after 9/11. While reviewing these files, our experienced staff found documents that raised concerns about the possible involvement of foreign individuals and foreign sources of support for the hijackers. In several instances, agency leadership conceded that they became aware of this evidence through the probing of the Joint Inquiry staff. On Oct. 10, 2002, FBI Director Robert Mueller testified, "I think the staff probed and, as a result of the probing, some facts came to light here and to me, frankly, that had not come to light before, and perhaps would not have come to light had the staff not probed."

The fruit of that probing constitutes the bulk of the material that remains classified. Our final Joint Inquiry Report, released in July 2003 minus the missing 28 pages, reprimanded the agencies for a lack of attention to and action on information in their own files. This data included "information suggesting specific sources of foreign support for some of the September 11 hijackers while they were in the United States." At the time, "neither CIA nor FBI officials were able to address definitively the extent of such support for the hijackers." Given the magnitude of the potential risk to national security, the Joint Inquiry found that gap in intelligence coverage "unacceptable" and referred the information summarized in the 28 pages to the FBI and CIA for investigation "as aggressively and as quickly as possible."

The release of the 28 pages would allow the American people to evaluate important questions, such as:

–Should we believe that the 19 hijackers—most of whom spoke little English, had limited education, and had never before visited the United States—acted alone in perpetrating the sophisticated 9/11 plot?

–Did the hijackers have foreign support? If so, who provided it?

–Brennan stated the 28 pages contain information that is "uncorroborated, unvetted" and "inaccurate." What is the investigatory basis for his conclusion?

–Has the 13-year delay in empowering the American people with the information in the 28 pages affected national security, delayed justice to the families of the nearly 3,000 Americans killed on 9/11, or undermined the confidence of the American people in their federal government?

Former Illinois governor and two-time presidential candidate Adlai Stevenson put it best: "As citizens of this democracy, you are the rulers and the ruled, the law-givers and the law-abiding, the beginning and the end." That unique status gives the American people all the authority and capability needed to review the 28 pages and determine the truth. It is long past time they had the opportunity.

## Release More 9/11 Records

**Bob Graham**

*New York Times*, September 9, 2016

In July, after approval from the Obama administration, Congress released a 28-page chapter of previously classified material from the final report of a joint congressional inquiry into the Sept. 11 attacks. Saudi Arabia's foreign minister, Adel al-Jubeir, said that the document had ruled out any Saudi involvement in the attack. "The matter is now finished," he declared.

But it is not finished. Questions about whether the Saudi government assisted the terrorists remain unanswered. Now, as we approach the 15th anniversary of the most heinous attack on the United States since Pearl

Harbor, it is time for our government to release more documents from other investigations into Sept. 11 that have remained secret all these years.

The recently released 28 pages were written in the fall of 2002 by a committee of which I was a co-chairman. That chapter focused on three of the 19 hijackers who lived for a time in Los Angeles and San Diego. The pages suggested new trails of inquiry worth following, including why a Qaeda operative had the unlisted phone number for the company that managed the Colorado estate of Prince Bandar bin Sultan, then the Saudi ambassador.

Some of those questions might be answered if the government released more of the findings of the Sept. 11 commission, the citizens inquiry that followed our congressional inquest. The commission said that it found no Saudi links to the hijackers. But the government could satisfy lingering doubts by releasing more of the commission's records. Parallel investigations were also conducted by the F.B.I. and C.I.A. How much did they look into whether Prince Bandar or other Saudis aided the hijackers?

The government also knows more today about the 16 hijackers who lived outside California than when the 28 pages were classified in 2003. Much of that information remains secret but should be made public. For example, the F.B.I. for a time claimed that it had found no ties between three of the hijackers, including their leader, Mohamed Atta, and a prominent Saudi family that lived in Sarasota, Fla., before Sept. 11. The family returned to the kingdom about two weeks before the attack. But in 2013, a Freedom of Information Act lawsuit brought by investigative reporters led to the release of about 30 pages from an F.B.I.-led investigation that included an agent's report asserting "many connections" between the hijackers and this family. The F.B.I. said the agent's claim was unfounded, and the family said it had no ties to the hijackers. Still, a federal judge in 2014 ordered the bureau to turn over an additional 80,000 pages from its investigation, and he is reviewing those for possible public release.

There is one more thing our government could do to shed light on the attack. For more than a decade, the families of Sept. 11 victims have been litigating against the kingdom and Saudi interests, asserting that they facilitated the murder of their loved ones. With the support of the Justice Department, the Saudis used a 1976 law providing foreign nations some immunity from American lawsuits to block those efforts to secure justice. Now, both the Senate and House of Representatives have unanimously passed a bill, the Justice Against Sponsors of Terrorism Act, that would allow a thorough judicial examination of the Saudi role.

Some might ask, 15 years later, what difference does all this make?

In fact, a lot. It can mean justice for the families that have suffered so grievously. It can also mean improving our national security, which has been compromised by the extreme form of Islam that has been promoted by Saudi Arabia.

But the most important reason is to avoid the corrosive effect that government secrecy can have on a democracy. The nation that denies its people information about what it is doing in their name is a nation slogging down a dark alley of public suspicion toward decline and mediocrity. As Daniel Patrick Moynihan put it, "Secrecy is for losers."

The government's possible suppression of evidence of Saudi support for the 19 hijackers would go beyond passive cover-up. Is the government releasing false information, while continuing to classify documents containing the truth? As the presidential campaign is proving, appearances of government deception have contributed to wary Americans becoming more and more outraged with their elected officials.

In recognition of another anniversary, 45 years since the publication of the Pentagon Papers, Sanford J. Ungar, who teaches seminars on free speech at Georgetown and Harvard, said: "Nothing is more important to the health and sustainability of a modern democracy than its citizens' awareness of, and confidence in, what their government is doing. Excessive government secrecy—inherent, instinctive, utterly unnecessary and often bureaucratically self-protective—is poison to the well-being of civil society."

I care deeply about our nation's future, its tradition of openness and the necessity of honesty in our international relations. President Obama has less than five months remaining in his term. I commend him for his decision to authorize the release of the 28 pages. He should sign the Justice Against Sponsors of Terrorism Act and use his authority to direct the release of all the chapters of the book of Sept. 11. And then our country must act based on the truths they may reveal.

## JASTA—Congress Should Override This Veto

Bob Graham

*The Hill*, September 27, 2016

After a decade of struggle, the Congress passed by unanimous vote in both chambers the Justice Against Sponsors of Terrorism Act (JASTA) which the president has vetoed. As soon as this week the Congress will determine whether to override.

I am a strong advocate for JASTA. I urge these as some of the facts and context which justified the initial Congressional support of JASTA and compel a vote to override the president's veto.

Diplomacy was always an option available to the federal government to bring justice and closure to those most devastated by the tragedy of 9/11. In similar circumstances, the United States has entered into negotiations with countries for which there was reasonable suspicion they contributed to harm to Americans.

Looking back to our Civil War, England had declared neutrality. After the conflict, the Union secured reparations from England for Americans injured or killed and property destroyed by the Confederate warship Alabama, which in violation of the neutrality pledge had been built in an English shipyard. More recently and akin to the Sept. 11 attacks, a $2.7 billion compensation ($10 million for each victim) was diplomatically and militarily secured from Libya for its role in the explosion of Pan Am 103 over Lockerbie, Scotland. In both these instances our government understood it had an obligation to engage on a state-to-state basis to address American victims' legitimate claims.

Why was there no such initiative after 9/11? The administration of President George W. Bush did not want to antagonize the Kingdom of Saudi Arabia or by opening discussions with the Kingdom on its possible role in 9/11 undercut a rationale for the impending war with Iraq. The Department of State, therefore, did not pursue a diplomatic option. President Obama's diplomats continued that reluctance, refusing to broach the subject even as more and more information trickled out suggesting Saudi entanglements with the terrorists. Is it now the position of the administration that those most grievously affected should have neither a diplomatic nor legal path to justice, but rather must singularly bear the burden? Have they not borne enough?

For more than fifteen years, the U.S. government has withheld much of the information disclosing the truth of 9/11. Our government clings to the belief that the sophisticated attack was planned, practiced, and executed by the 19 hijackers, most of whom could not speak English, had never been in the United States, and had little education, without any external support while they were in the United States. To say that this view strains credulity is an understatement. What is the truth as to whether there was external support and if so by whom?

The 28 page chapter from the final report of the Congressional Joint Inquiry on 9/11 released on July 15 after 13 years of classification provided a sliver of the that truth. If members of congress want more evidence of a Saudi role, demand the release of long withheld information on matters such as the tangle of events in Los Angeles and San Diego. Is it credible that all the activities of Saudis supportive of the hijackers could have been coincidental? Most of the hijackers lived in Florida, Virginia and New Jersey, but the relations between the hijackers and Saudi interests in those locales is largely unknown to the American people.

While the decision to override is primarily a moral and ethical issue, what has 9/11 cost the American taxpayers and what is it likely to cost in the future if the expense is paid exclusively by them, not by those who facilitated 9/11? Billions. As just one example, legislation passed in 2016 provides free life time medical service to responders and survivors. This year the cost will be $330 million. In 2025 it is estimated to be $570 million.

Saudi Arabia and others urging you to sustain the veto of JASTA have claimed that the Kingdom's reforms in the last 15 years have cleansed it of culpability for 9/11. Of course the Kingdom is a valuable partner but what does that have to do with judgments about its actions leading up to Sept. 11, 2001? The very suggestion flies in the face of the principle of responsibility for one's actions.

As we look at events since 9/11, just what has the Kingdom done? Has it abandoned its practice of supporting mosques and madrasas where intolerance and jihad are preached and a new generation of terrorists motivated and trained? Has it removed from its schools the textbooks which teach that all but Wahhabisists are perversions and should be exterminated? Has it stopped funding terrorist organizations outside Saudi Arabia?

The Congress is called to render a final judgment on whether Americans will have their day in court and the opportunity to make the case before a jury of their peers that Saudi Arabia was a facilitator in the murders of 9/11. Let our legal system work. Let the truth be known.

## Saudi Arabia Still Isn't Doing Enough to Fight the Financing of Terrorism

**Bob Graham and Fionnuala Ní Aoláin**

*Washington Post*, February 19, 2019

In 1989, the Group of Seven countries launched the Financial Action Task Force (FATF), an intergovernmental group devoted to fighting money laundering.

Among the challenges facing the FATF since its inception has been the effort to develop measures to prevent the financing of terrorism.

Saudi Arabia is keen to join the task force, because this would ease access to global financial markets.

Recently, the FATF undertook a review of Saudi Arabia's efforts to combat terrorism financing.

The resulting report identified a number of serious deficiencies.

Saudi Arabia is now required to present an action plan outlining how it will address these problems before it can be admitted to the task force.

It is important that the kingdom not be admitted until it has shown demonstrable progress in addressing these concerns.

Terrorism financing originating in Saudi Arabia has been a significant source of funds for international terrorist organizations, including al-Qaida.

As the report noted, however, the Saudi authorities have focused their counterterrorism efforts almost exclusively on threats from within the kingdom, while doing little to tackle those outside the country's borders.

According to the task force, only 10 percent of Saudi counterterrorism cases concern offenses committed outside the kingdom, and these prosecutions focus largely on offenses in the Middle East.

"Given that the support for external terrorist groups is a major . . . risk for the country," the task force noted, "the overall number of cases pertaining to raising funds inside Saudi Arabia and transferring them outside the country is low."

The report also found that "Saudi Arabia has not yet tackled the risk of financing of terrorism by third-party and facilitators, and the financing by individuals for terrorist organizations outside the country."

A 2009 diplomatic cable from then-Secretary of State Hillary Clinton, later published by WikiLeaks, described Saudi Arabia as "the most significant source of funding to Sunni terrorist groups worldwide."

The task force also raised concerns that the kingdom is not sanctioning individuals or requesting legal assistance from other states in a manner that effectively counters the serious threats of terrorist financing in Saudi Arabia.

If Saudi Arabia wishes to appropriately address the risk of terrorist financing, it must prosecute not just the foot soldiers but also the financiers who fuel terrorism around the world.

To do so in an effective manner, the Saudi authorities must amend their counterterrorism decrees.

As the task force notes, the "overly broad definition of terrorism" in these decrees means that the authorities may "divert attention and resources to specious cases from more important cases."

This concern was highlighted in a submission by Ni Aolain, the U.N. special rapporteur on the promotion and protection of human rights and fundamental freedoms while countering terrorism and one of the co-authors of this op-ed.

That report concluded that there is clear evidence that a significant number of individuals who have committed no crime—much less acts of terrorism—have been wrongfully tried under the Saudi kingdom's counterterrorism decrees in its Specialized Criminal Court.

At the same time, there are grounds for concern that a significant number of individuals implicated in supporting internationally recognized terrorist groups have been released only to return to terrorist activity.

Given the risk of radicalization in prison, it is important that Saudi authorities cease prosecuting innocent people for criticizing the kingdom and release those who have been wrongfully convicted.

While Saudi Arabia has made progress in reforming its laws and prosecuting alleged acts of terrorism, the reasons cited above strongly suggest that this progress is, at least in part, illusory.

To admit Saudi Arabia to the task force before it has addressed these shortcomings would send the message that what counts is a high number of prosecutions, regardless of their merits.

The nation should not be admitted to the task force until it has amended its counterterrorism laws to focus on terrorism and demonstrated progress in prosecuting terrorism financing outside the region.

---

Fionnuala Ní Aoláin is Regents Professor at the University of Minnesota and professor of law at The Queen's University of Belfast, Northern Ireland.

## Sarasota 9/11 Connection Remains Cloaked in Government Secrecy, Breeding Suspicion of Saudi Role in Terror Attacks

**Bob Graham**

*South Florida Sun-Sentinel*, May 17, 2019

The facts and the treatment of former Sarasota, Fla., residents Abdulaziz and Anoud al-Hijji are extreme but not unique. Saudi Arabian born, raised in the fringes of palace aristocracy, Abdulaziz al-Hijji and his family had lived for over a decade in a suburban home.

In the hours after 9/11, Sarasota law enforcement was notified by al-Hijji's neighbors that the couple had abruptly moved out of their home two weeks before the terrorist attacks—leaving behind their cars, clothes, furniture and food on the table.

A subsequent investigation of the al-Hijji's home by a state and local law enforcement anti-terrorism task force and the FBI, confirmed that the family appeared to have "fled" their home shortly before the attack with a sense of urgency. When it was ascertained that three of the four 9/11 hijack pilots had trained at an airport near Sarasota, suspicions arose that al-Hijji or members of his family had been a facilitator of the tragedy.

The FBI Tampa field office opened an investigation, which appears to have lasted for about two years. Among other things, agents reportedly obtained evidence that some 9/11 hijackers had visited al-Hijji's home.

But the FBI kept its Sarasota investigation secret for a decade. It didn't inform Congress' Joint Inquiry into the attacks, which I co-chaired. Nor did the FBI tell the subsequent 9/11 Commission about it.

Irish author Anthony Summers stumbled onto the relationship between the pilots and the al-Hijji family while in Sarasota researching a book on 9/11 titled "The Eleventh Day." He joined forces with Dan Christensen, founder of the online Florida Bulldog.

Together, Christensen and Summers confirmed and published news reports revealing that the FBI had conducted an extensive investigation of the Saudi family's flight from Sarasota. The FBI reacted the next day, admitting it had investigated the family but also vehemently claiming it had found "no connection" between the family and the hijackers.

The Bulldog then made numerous attempts to gain access to the FBI's records of its investigation. They all proved fruitless. So, on September 5, 2012, the Bulldog filed a Freedom of Information lawsuit in the United States federal court for the Southern District of Florida.

In response to the suit, the FBI initially claimed it could not find a single record of its Sarasota investigation. As the lawsuit progressed, the FBI changed its story and revealed that it had found a smattering of records, including one memo which stated an FBI agent, in fact, had found "many connections" between the family and the hijackers. The record directly contradicted the FBI's prior public statements.

Judge William Zloch, the federal district judge to whom the case was assigned, was incredulous that the FBI could not find a more complete record of this important investigation. He ordered the FBI to conduct an additional thorough search. He specifically directed the FBI to scour its Tampa Field Office for any records connected to the 9/11 attacks.

The FBI obeyed that judicial directive and then sheepishly reported back that it had located more than 80,000 pages of 9/11 records. It also claimed this entire trove of 9/11 evidence was classified and should never be disclosed to the public.

Judge Zloch ordered the records produced to him promptly so that he could see what the FBI was shielding from public view and decide for himself whether the records should remain sealed.

That was in the spring of 2014. Five years later, the Bulldog is still waiting to hear from Judge Zloch and the nation continues to wonder whether Saudi Arabia aided the 9/11 hijackers.

During this five-year period, the United States has treated the Kingdom of Saudi Arabia as a close ally. The U.S. has provided the capability for the Kingdom to inflict on Yemen what has been described as 2019's world's most heinous human rights disaster and virtually ignore the October 2,

2018, chain saw butcher at the Istanbul Turkey Saudi consulate of Jamal Khashoggi, the Saudi journalist in exile in the United States who reported for the Washington Post.

If in those five years, the secluded Sarasota information had become public and proven that Saudi Arabia was a 9/11 co-conspirator, these and other horrors possibly would not have occurred.

At least America would have had evidence of the character and reliability of the Kingdom.

# Index

STEVEN NOLL is a master lecturer in the department of history at the University of Florida. His research interests include disability history, Florida history, and environmental history. Noll is the co-author of *Ditch of Dreams: The Cross-Florida Barge Canal and the Struggle for Florida's Future.*

DAVID R. COLBURN was a long-time history department faculty member and administrator at the University of Florida. An expert on Florida history and race relations, he served on the Rosewood Commission that helped to uncover the truth behind the 1923 Rosewood Massacre. Reaching out beyond the walls of the university, he worked with the Florida Historical Society and the Florida Humanities Council (now Florida Humanities) to promote civic engagement throughout the state. He died in 2019.

BOB GRAHAM served as the governor of Florida from 1979 to 1987 and senator from Florida from 1987 to 2005. Deeply concerned with public service and civic literacy, he established the Bob Graham Center for Public Service at the University of Florida in 2006. In 2021, he received the latest in a series of awards and commendations when the Florida Defenders of the Environment honored him by presenting him with the Marjorie Harris Carr Award for Environmental Advocacy.

GOVERNMENT AND POLITICS IN THE SOUTH

Edited by Sharon D. Wright Austin and Angela K. Lewis-Maddox

*Writing for the Public Good: Essays from David R. Colburn and Senator Bob Graham*, edited by Steven Noll (2022)